FROM PURSUIT TO PRESENCE

How to slow down and find peace in a chaotic and hectic world

By Tiffany Kay

Copyright

ISBN-13:978-1500630874
ISBN-10:150063087X

For Tim

Thank you. I love you x

CONTENTS

PREFACE

I've dedicated most of my adult life to the field of personal development. I've been on countless workshops and read a library's worth of books on how to better myself and improve my life. But no matter how much I tried to change, there was always a subtle yet constant niggle that I wasn't as happy as I thought I *should* be. There were numerous occasions when I experienced connection, excitement, passion and joy – certainly plenty to fuel the fire that kept me going and convinced me that I was right on track. Yet there were also too many times when I would plunge into the darkness of my own psyche and wonder how I was ever going to reach the place of peace that I envisioned. When the doubts and insecurities arose, I believed that I just needed to refine the vision or dream up a new plan and then ongoing happiness would be mine.

Perhaps you have been committed to your own evolution in a similar way. I'm sure this isn't the first book you have read to inspire the course of your life. But there is a fundamental difference between *From Pursuit to Presence* and most other self-help books. In the following pages you won't find a single word that is intended to improve who you are. That's right – ***this is not a self-improvement book***! Instead it is dedicated to self-acceptance and self-love. I'm inviting you to drop the stick you have been beating yourself with and realise that you are already whole, worthy and complete just the way you are.

Despite all of the effort I had put into my personal growth, I was unable to protect myself from having a breakdown. Burnt out by the endless chase to achieve recognition and results, I became sick and exhausted. Barely able to move, I found myself alone with nowhere left to run. As the berating inner voices punished me for my failings, I had no option but to face the hidden recesses of my personality. Every worry, doubt and thought of unworthiness surfaced – each contained a story of where and how I had gone wrong. I didn't have the energy to fight back. The feelings overwhelmed me. But as I plummeted through the layers of inadequacy, something changed. Slowly and gently a bright light appeared in the darkness. It illuminated the delusion of my fears and revealed an absolute and unquestionable truth: there was nowhere else that I needed to be and nothing I had to prove to anyone. I was enveloped in a blissful feeling of comfort and peace.

I began to question others on their concept of self-worth and I made a surprising discovery. You don't need to scratch the surface very deeply to find underlying thoughts of inadequacy. Everyone measures themselves against perceived societal standards and wonders if they are falling short – *Am I doing enough? Am I earning enough? Am I making a big enough difference? Am I good enough?* Our world is built around protecting ourselves from these thoughts. We are caught up in the endless pursuit of worthiness, not realising that being *enough* is not something to strive for but, rather, an inherent birthright. I assure you that you weren't born doubting your value.

I wanted to write *From Pursuit to Presence* to challenge your opinion of your worth. How would your life be different if you believed in your intrinsic value without the need for comparison or judgment? If you knew you had nothing to prove, would you change your approach to life? I want to assist you in seeing how societal norms hook you into a ceaseless pursuit of happiness. The sustainable contentment that we seek is only possible through releasing our concerns and expectations, and learning to become present to the moment.

The intention of this book is to offer an alternative life philosophy. I present the ideas to expand perceptions and to promote dialogue and discussion. I am not arguing that this path is the correct one or that any other approaches are in some way wrong. My wish is only that you widen your thinking beyond the illusions that are currently accepted as truth.

I invite your questions, feedback and comments. Your opinions are valid and important to me. I have no doubt that these concepts covered in this book will continue to change and evolve.

Be part of the conversation at www.tiffanykay.com.

Tiffany Kay (March 2014)

BONUS:

The Pursuit to Presence Online Workshop

Throughout this book, there are a number of activities designed to deepen your understanding of the themes and topics. Whilst the exercises are explained in each section, some are more complex in nature and may require that you relax and close your eyes.

To make this easier and more comprehensive, I have created an online workshop that offers recordings to lead you through the processes. There is no charge for access to this course and you can register at **www.FromPursuittoPresence.com**.

As you progress through the book, you will notice the exercises contained within boxes. Each lesson that has a corresponding exercise in the online workshop will be marked with the ⓘ symbol.

If you would prefer to simply use the book, you may find it helpful to either have a partner guide you through the exercises or alternatively record your own voice to listen back to. Each of the activities are described fully to ensure that you can get the most from the book.

INTRODUCTION

When you ask people what they really want out of life, you can absolutely guarantee that happiness will rank high on their list. All the other things – career success, wealth, relationships and recognition – mean nothing if you are feeling discontented and miserable. But very few people know how to be happy and, thanks to some cultural norms and misleading expectations, too often we find ourselves locked in the never-ending, fruitless pursuit of happiness. This book is about ditching the constant struggle and finding inner contentment, peace and joy.

As I write this book, my fifteen-year old son is studying towards his first academic qualifications. The familiar messages from school abound – work hard, get good grades and pick a rewarding career. With the best intentions in the world, the teachers advocate this as the path to personal fulfillment. No one talks of contentment. No one mentions inner peace. Joy is irrelevant. The acquisition of roles and rewards is seen as the ultimate destination in life.

I am not knocking academic studies. I am an eternal student that loves nothing more than expanding my horizons. But bizarrely, this passion for knowledge didn't start at school. It began later in life when I had finally found a degree of inner peace. We learn better when we are at ease.

In fact, we do everything better when we are content. Surely the highest priority of education should be to teach children how to be happy?

But it's not just at school that the acquisition of external gains feature highly in recommendations for eternal happiness. Turn on the television or open a glossy magazine and you will be bombarded with images of having it all – the perfect home, the perfect relationship, the perfect family, and the perfect body. If you ask me, it's all a little too… err… perfect! What's wrong with a little imperfection? I'd take a healthy dose of variety over sameness any day.

Material objects seem to promise so much. Advertising thrives on making us believe that with their shiny products, happiness will at last be ours. But I have yet to find anything in mainstream advertising that has the power to cure unhappiness. We may achieve a temporary boost to our mood but it simply doesn't last. If you buy a new car, you might feel good for a few days or weeks but eventually it fades again. Familiarity has that effect on external items.

It seems as though since the 1980's (perhaps even earlier), our culture has demanded us to work harder and faster to achieve more. But what is this *more* we are striving for? After forty plus years around the block, I have discovered a secret worth sharing. This quest for more is totally unappeasable!

When you fight to make your reality match the vision of what you think you want, you find that the vision has a nasty habit of changing and evolving. Breaking news – You will never get *there* – perfection doesn't exist!

You have been conditioned to believe that more is better. Perhaps you don't need anything more in order to be happy? Maybe it is merely a perception that something is missing? Think back to when you were born. Weren't your needs incredibly simple? Sleep, food, nurturing and the occasional nappy change. You weren't thinking about the type of job you were going to do, the big house, the fancy car or how you could get people to like you. You were just being you, being a baby. It gets a bit more complex as we get older and need to support ourselves and perhaps a family. But all of these *mores* - do we really need them for happiness and peace? What if we could return to that basic nature, our True Self, and relish the simple way of being once more.

Too many people are exhausted, stressed and burnt out in their quest for the perfect life. If you are sick and tired of being sick and tired, then you will know what I am talking about. If you are one of the people re-evaluating your priorities, you are not alone. If you are feeling lost, confused or uncertain then you are perfectly placed to make this switch from pursuit to presence. That nagging uneasiness you experience is the call for a different path. You are finally hearing the deeper requests from your soul that chooses connection, contentment and love over anything material you can possess. As a simple rule, if it can be taken away, I can assure you that it isn't something you require for happiness. Divine law makes it so! Knowing this makes letting go of pursuit so much easier.

If the journey to joy isn't working, then maybe it's time for a change. Do we really want to get to sixty, seventy or eighty before we wake up and realise that all the things we thought would bring us happiness turned out to be empty promises? That's why I made a conscious decision to ditch the rat race and now I am content, peaceful and fulfilled most of the time. In this book, I'd like to invite you to do the same – to stop striving and start enjoying the richness and joie de vie found in living right here, right now.

Many of us are finding that we no longer want to be driven by ambition and obligation. We are ready to be more accepting, appreciative and allowing. This involves learning to live from our hearts rather than our heads. If you have spent too much time disconnected from your soul, you will feel that you have been living with a heavy-heart. It's time to let that go. This new consciousness is open hearted, light hearted and whole hearted.

The journey From Pursuit to Presence is not just a theoretical concept – it is an invitation to discover the inherent peace that comes simply from being part of life's beautiful process. If it's more contentment that you are looking for, then you are in the right place. Read on!

My Story

I come from a family of high achievers. My little brother (all 6ft 6" of him) was a key member of the England rugby union team that won the World Cup in 2003 and one of the few players who went on to take part in a second World Cup Final in 2007. My older sister studied at Cambridge University and is now a highly regarded and experienced personal injury lawyer. She was appointed as a Queen's Counsellor (QC) in 2011 and a Deputy High Court Judge in 2013.

My father was also an exceptional barrister who, at 49, was appointed a judge of the Queen's Bench Division of the High Court and knighted. In 2000, he was promoted to the Court of Appeal and sworn of the Privy Council. The Independent newspaper said in his obituary that he had "*all the necessary qualities, which are not always found together - outstanding intellect, common sense, a deep understanding of humanity and its weaknesses and an unfailing instinct for what is fair and just*". Because of his ability, his expertise and knowledge were in high demand, and he was willing to undertake a huge burden of work both in and outside of his professional career.

Growing up, I was especially close to my father. When I was a baby, he was the one who could soothe my tears and tantrums, and I would often turn to him for advice and understanding as I grew up. But my over-riding memory from childhood is that he was always working. It didn't seem to matter what time of the day it was, I would find him in his study. I can still recall the day that I first discovered that Dad actually slept. Up until that point, I thought he had supernatural abilities to survive without rest. One day, when I was about three years old, I crept down in the middle of the night to ask him a question and was mystified when he wasn't at his desk. Not only was I completely baffled but I also terrified my parents who thought I was a burglar!

There is no doubt that my father had a huge influence on me and I wanted to do something with my life that would make both of my parents proud of me. It seemed like the path to happiness and success required the same roles and recognition that my father had achieved. But for a long time, I just didn't seem to be able to get my act together. Attending a highly competitive and driven school, I succumbed to the messages that I wasn't good enough. I was *quite* good at sports and *quite* academic but being '*quite good*' was never going to cut it at one of the most revered schools in the country. I found it difficult to contend with the over-bearing personalities of teachers and classmates and I left school with a sense of inadequacy and inferiority that I carried well into my adult life.

Plagued by feelings of unworthiness, I struggled to make my way in the world. I flitted from job to job and relationship to relationship, lacking any sense of purpose or meaning. I often refer to this period of my life as *flat-lining*. My wake-up call came soon after the birth of my first son, when he was diagnosed with a serious and life-threatening heart condition at his eight-month developmental check-up. Just after his first birthday, he underwent open-heart surgery. Those six hours, spent sitting in a hospital waiting room immersed in my own fears and thoughts, were the turning point of my life. I realised that life was important and I was determined not to waste another day. As my son began his recovery, I resolved to make my life a life that counted.

As I entered this next phase of my life, my motivation and drive to succeed knew no bounds. I committed to a career in personal and professional development and trained as a certified Coach, Master Practitioner and Trainer of Neuro-Linguistic Programming (NLP), Master Practitioner and Trainer of Humanistic Neuro-Linguistic Psychology™ (HNLP), Master Therapist and Trainer of Ericksonian Hypnotherapy as well as taking extensive courses in counselling, psychotherapy and Emotional Freedom Technique (EFT). I wrote my first book, had articles published in magazines and newspapers and was even recognised in the North West

Women in Business, *Most Inspirational Woman* category. But with every success, the desire for more didn't seem to be satisfied – instead it continued to escalate.

By 2003, I had a private coaching practice and a corporate facing Development Consultancy. I was working incredibly long hours, squeezing in as much as I could during the day and after my children had gone to bed. I was prepared to make huge sacrifices and do whatever it took to achieve my dreams, often at the cost of my relationships and wellbeing.

On the 26th June 2004 my father had a cardiac arrest. He was just 60. He was rushed to St Thomas' hospital in London but never regained consciousness. A few days later, we made the horrendously difficult decision to turn off his life support machine. The last time I had seen my father was on the weekend of my birthday and Father's Day. At that time, there was talk about him achieving the highest honours. I still remember our final conversation. Sitting outside in the sunshine at a BBQ, I asked him what his future plans were. He told me that he felt ready to retire. There were so many things that he wanted to see and do, and there just wasn't the time or space with his professional commitments. Tragically, he never got to enjoy the experiences that he worked so hard to create.

Looking back I wish that I had learnt from my father's path. Instead, I channelled my grief and pain into my work.

By now, I was a single mother of two young boys whilst running two businesses – my own coaching practice/consultancy and Co-Director of a training company offering qualifications in Coaching, NLP and Hypnotherapy. I hid my thoughts of unworthiness behind the desire to provide for my family and the need to achieve. I was praised and acknowledged for my skills and resourcefulness. But no amount of success could fill the gaps in my life. It felt as though the happiness I sought was always "*just around the corner*". I thought that I would be happy when I had *made it* – which in my case was achieving *International Author and Speaker* status. Secretly, I think I just wanted to have a large following of fans that would somehow prove that I wasn't as inferior or inadequate as I believed myself to be.

I came across an online marketing programme that seemed to offer the missing piece of the jigsaw. I saw it as my path to the fame and rewards that I craved. Over the following year, I worked harder than ever to *make it*. Even when I was resting or taking a break, my mind was busy plotting the next key step in the plan. The ideas and inspiration came thick and fast and I struggled to keep up with my own thinking. I invested everything I had into an online campaign and when it flopped, I was left reeling and totally devastated. By this point my health had deteriorated and I had manifested liver damage. Without the surges of adrenaline-fueled motivation to keep me going, I crashed and burnt out. For the next six months, I was barely able to do a thing. Even the simplest of tasks left me feeling exhausted and drained. I had no option but to surrender to the experience. I simply didn't have the energy to do anything else.

The first few weeks weren't easy but gradually, day-by-day, my state of being began to shift. I re-evaluated my priorities and I began to realise that I had been searching for happiness in all the wrong places. I let go of all the dreams and desires that had dominated my thinking for so long. I stopped arguing that what I had was wrong or lacking, and instead began to appreciate every small gift or experience that came my way. I faced the thoughts of unworthiness that had been my constant companion. When I realised that there was nothing to do and nothing to prove, I was finally free. That liberation brought with it unparalleled levels of inner joy, peace and contentment.

My own journey *From Pursuit to Presence* was intense and dramatic and was an experience that changed my whole outlook on life. I have learnt that there is nothing more important than learning to live fully in the moment. When you are in the present – not reviewing the past or trying to predict the future – life is simple and wonderfully rewarding. At times, I still slip up and find myself becoming consumed by unhelpful thoughts or self-created demands.

And every time I suffer and struggle, I can directly trace the problem back to my own separation from the moment. So I acknowledge the insight and gently re-orientate myself back into living in the now. You never have to justify or explain your path to anyone. All that matters is that you are consciously aware, rather than blindly following the masses. And for that, you need presence.

"I continue to evolve and expand and change
Every day and in every way
Sometimes I delight and astound myself
Sometimes I am left bemused and bewildered by choices I make in the moment
when I am not in full alignment with all that I am
And even then, I shall look inside, take a breath
And remember
I am whole and complete and perfect just as I am
Because this is me
This is who I am...I AM"

Why is the lure of the rat race so compelling?

For so many of us, our lives follow a stereotypical pattern. We work five days a week for forty-eight weeks of the year to create the funds for our chosen lifestyle. This may include a nice house or car, a family, holidays and all of the other things that keep us entertained. There is absolutely nothing wrong with living this way. We may feel inspired by our work and have a life full of adventure that ticks all of the pleasure boxes. If you are experiencing a constant stream of joy and fulfillment, then keep doing what you are doing. An inspired life can take many different forms.

But if you are finding that enduring satisfaction and contentment are eluding you, maybe you are caught up in the metaphorical *rat race*. According to Wikipedia, the rat race is *"an endless, self-defeating, or pointless pursuit."* It originates from the practice of lab rats stuck in unsolvable mazes with no way to escape. The analogy can be mapped across to our professional and personal lives – how many times do we find ourselves at a dead end with nowhere to turn?

Being busy has become a badge of honour. There was a time when *fine* was the standard answer to "*how are you?*" Now we are much more likely to hear *busy* as a response. I was never a fan of fine (what does *fine* actually feel like?)

but I am even less keen on busy, especially when we say it like it is a good thing. Busyness isn't a state of being; it is a condition that prevents you from finding the stillness to listen to the quiet voice within. If you are constantly busy, now is the time to take stock.

When you are immersed in the rat race, you may well have a sense of purpose or passion for what you do. Pursuit is highly motivating. But over time, it is easy to lose sight of your personal freedom. We usually think of freedom as being liberated from the constraints of our external circumstances. That's why we strive to create the perfect lifestyle that, in our minds, epitomizes the independence we crave. But true freedom has nothing to do with our outer world. It comes from no longer being driven by misplaced desire or all-consuming states.

An all-consuming state might be fear – the fear that our job might be taken away, the fear that we might run out of money, the fear that we aren't good enough and if we stop and rest for a moment, the fear that we might just get found out. Misplaced desire is the wanting that comes from examining our personal circumstances and finding them falling short. On some level, we still believe that there is something or someone that can bring us the personal fulfillment we are seeking. So we search for the soul mate, the promotion or the abundance that we believe will complete the jigsaw puzzle. Yet it rarely does. Usually we just find it was the wrong piece or even the wrong jigsaw entirely.

Our striving is intrinsically linked to the way in which we measure our value. Deep down, we need to know that we matter and so we want to prove our significance. We are looking for the external world to validate our own measures of self-worth. When life meets our expectations and acknowledges our value appropriately, we feel satisfied. But if we think we are getting a poor deal, we will do whatever we can to close the gap. We set goals and work at achieving them in an attempt to reconcile the difference. Some attempts succeed and we will temporarily feel a sense of fulfillment. Many will fail and so we set even more ambitious goals to overcome our disappointment.

It is easy to see how this rat race locks us in. We are in a never-ending satisfaction hunt. But nothing we really want will be found on a to-do list. The dreams just have to keep getting bigger and more compelling. We never get to reach a place of peace – the lust for satisfaction keeps pulling us back.

We may talk about getting out of the rat race. Only a few successfully make it. Most do nothing to change their circumstances or, worse still, repeat the same patterns over and over again. Like the seeker who escapes the confines of employment, only to recreate the exact same experience in their own business. You may not be ready to totally ditch the rat race (yet). But if you are now recognising that the desire for satisfaction can never be fulfilled externally, you'll be looking for a way to break the cycle. So what's the alternative?

Welcome to presence!

If we want to bask in the delicious richness and depth that life has to offer, we have to be present to our experiences. You just can't feel anything good unless you are emotionally connected to what is happening. Our frantic minds will convince us that we are living fulfilling lives as we attempt to squeeze yet another appointment into an already packed schedule. But we find that without any space, our minds are constantly moving onto the next thing to be done rather than being consciously present to what is occurring in this moment.

Let's be clear: frantically rushing around interspersed with temporary moments of calmness can never bring long-lasting contentment. Whenever you are rushing, then you can't be present. The two are mutually exclusive. You can only find peace in stillness. When we deliberately slow down, we create space to fully embrace the experience. Instead of being locked into the drive to get things done, we start to notice the pure and simple things that give each moment a magical quality. It may be as you watch a leaf dancing in the wind, the way that clouds shape-shift or the sparkle of delight in a child's eye when they take a lick of ice-cream. These are the joyful by- products of conscious and aware living. None of these things can be fully encountered by the busy mind.

Many of us are asleep to life's joy. When was the last time that you *really* felt the rain on your face or tasted your favourite hot drink or smelt the freshly cut grass? Sure, we may notice them but do we deeply experience them? Not if we are too busy rushing on by. Being present means bringing your awareness to each aspect of every moment. You witness everything in full glory allowing the magic to permeate your heart and soul. The simplest of tasks, like drinking a glass of ice-cold water, becomes a wonderful banquet of joy radiating on your senses.

In principle, this concept of slowing down seems easy – simply stop and be still, and the bliss of the moment will reveal itself to you. But if we have been fuelling our lives with adrenalin, we won't be able to make the transition from stressed to still in one fell swoop. Many of us have tried to compensate living in overdrive with practices such as meditation or a massage. These temporary fixes can't create the stillness we really need. How often do we find ourselves spending the first fifteen minutes trying to quieten our mind and the next fifteen asleep?

As you begin to slow down, the fear gremlins might

question your approach. Doubts and insecurities may creep in if you aren't crossing items off your to-do list. Your mind will try to convince you that space is a luxury rather than a necessity. People around you may attempt to cajole you back into a life of pursuit. You may get strange looks when someone asks you how you are and you respond with '*happy*'. But I promise you that if you see it through, you will find a new level of joy and tranquility and you won't ever want to look back.

ⓘ **Lesson 1** - *Getting Still and Meeting Yourself:*

Before we go any further, I want to invite you to take some time out to get still and present. If you have been rushing and striving, this exercise will be the starting point for your commitment to a life of presence. Even if you are relaxed, this exercise will connect you more deeply to a state of inner peace. Sitting still means getting to know your self. When the meaningless distractions are taken away, it is just you and YOU. And if we haven't been giving ourselves enough quality me-time, we will stand in front of our True self like an apologetic and inattentive partner. How will you explain your reasons for being absent for so long?

So here is your challenge, take five minutes to just sit and be with yourself. You can use the exercise in the online workshop (see the bonus section) or I'd suggest using a timer or alarm so that you can fully relax into the moment without needing to watch the clock. There is no objective of this exercise other than to meet your self exactly where you are. You may want to make yourself comfortable and close your eyes. Become the quiet observer noticing your thoughts and feelings as they occur. Let go of any judgments and simply allow whatever wants to be, even the inner chatter. Just watch yourself and your mind with interest.

What did you find? Perhaps you were able to immediately experience that space of connection and peace. But maybe you noticed something different. Quite often, our re-encounters with our True Self can bring uncomfortable emotions – anxiety, loneliness, frustration, impatience or sadness and so on. We aren't taught to enjoy such feelings and so our natural tendency is to turn away or avoid. But when we make them welcome just as they are, without the need to change or fix the experience, we are able to drop through the discomfort. Beneath all of those ego-fueled emotions, we discover the real truth that was there all along – inner peace was never hiding from us, we were just searching in the wrong place.

Any time we want to feel the full, spacious nature of our inner being, we simply need to stop, let what will be just be and allow the doorway to the peace we seek simply to open through our hearts. Throughout this book, more of these exercises will deepen your connection to your natural joy.

How to use this book

My intention with this book is to offer a different way of being in the world. Some of the concepts may not seem to make intellectual sense and you might be tempted to dismiss such ideas. But remember part of the problem of being in the rat race is that you have been conditioned to live from your mind. Our minds like to feel in control and have a clever way of deflecting anything that seems to threaten their hold on your life. Reasoning and rationalising can be strategies of defence and avoidance.

I will never suggest that you take my word on anything. Rather, I will present theories and share exercises that will give you a direct experience of presence. All I ask is that you give each aspect your full and undivided attention before you embrace or reject it. What appears to be illogical or irrational may be very different in the experience of it. You just won't know until you try!

Unlike pursuit, which often involves the setting and achievement of goals, presence lacks definition. There isn't a fixed point in time when you can check presence off your to-do list. Instead, it is a continually evolving and expansive process with no beginning and no end. I count myself as a beginner, for as much as I have learnt, there is so much more I can learn about presence, about myself and about this moment. That is what makes it so magical. You aren't trying to achieve a specific result, rather learning to move and flex with the flow of life.

The book is laid out in sections that explore different aspects of presence. You may enjoy reading through the book in its entirety to understand the journey but do come back to each chapter and spend time completing each of the exercises. Some of the activities may ask you to fully relax and you may find it easier to close your eyes. To help you with this, I have created a complimentary online workshop. To sign up for free access, simply visit www.FromPursuittoPresence.com. Alternatively, you can have a friend guide you through the process or pre record your own voice. You'll find each exercise is described in full so that this book works just as well on its own.

Throughout the book, I will explain different ideas using models and theories. All models (including what we call factual science) are nothing more than a metaphor – a useful way of intellectually understanding a concept. Every theory is radically limited because we are synthesising, filtering and generalising complex and detailed information in order to make sense of it. As you apply the model, you shift from intellectual comprehension to whole body knowing. This integration is what we feel when we have an a-ha moment and the penny drops. Sometimes the a-ha moment happens in the revelation of a new idea but more often it comes as life provides the perfect illustration. I don't want you to take any concept as the right answer but rather to find your truth through your own life examples. This journey from pursuit to presence is about bringing you home to yourself and honouring your inherent wisdom.

Why do fresh starts often fail?

From Pursuit to Presence will take you on a journey to connect with your soul and raise your consciousness. We will discover that our external world never had the capacity to bring us what we most wanted. We will come to see that contentment arises from our inner world. How many times have you attempted to reinvent your life in some way, only to create the same conditions all over again? Even if we successfully implement changes to our lifestyle, how we feel about our self and our life often changes very little. Why is this so?

No matter how committed we are to our evolution, there is one factor that inhibits our personal growth more than any other – our ability to be present to our lives. When our consciousness is offline, the old habitual patterns and beliefs will pull us back along the well-worn track of familiarity. After the initial surge of enthusiasm for something new, we fall back asleep. Now is the time to ask yourself if you want it to be the same all over again?

So as well as reading the concepts in this book, I am going to ask you to practice presence for as long and as often as you remember. You will fall asleep again. We always do. But keep persisting with bringing your attention into the moment and like a toned muscle, you will develop strength of focus to be awake more of the time. This will switch you from being unconsciously driven to consciously choosing the best options in the moment. This is the only way that life can significantly change.

As you integrate the ideas in this book, you may find that your life seems to stall for a while. This is part of the transition. In all likelihood you have been running at full steam for a long time and in order for things to change, stillness is required. I will talk about letting life come to you rather than chasing it down. As you let go, it may appear like nothing is happening. Allow the path to unfold in its own way and at its own pace. As the natural balance is restored, life will bring gifts to you but it won't speed the process up if you keep opening the door to check for a delivery. Trust me, I tried that to no avail!

If your life begins to feel boring or empty or lacking

purpose, I can guarantee you that this is not real. The equilibrium is being restored and it will take time to acclimatise to the new way of being. Practice patience and very soon you will be discovering the simple pleasures contained in every moment.

I already know how magnificent you are and the breath-taking relationship with life that is available to you. Will you get everything that you want and desire? Highly unlikely! Will you discover that you really don't need everything that you think you want? Of that I am sure. When you make the journey from pursuit to presence, you find a safe and welcoming sanctuary hidden inside your soul that cannot be disrupted or corrupted by anything outside of you. If that sounds appealing, let us begin.

CHAPTER 1

Levels of Consciousness

By reading this book, one of my heartfelt wishes is that you learn to live from a different level of consciousness. Consciousness is one of those words that is frequently bandied around in spiritual circles and it may seem as though raising our awareness should be the main focus of our lives. This can cause a problem because we simply swap the pursuit of material or external gains for the *pursuit* of a higher level of consciousness. Rather than liberating us, it simply locks us into a new pattern of inadequacy and leaves us feeling unfulfilled.

So I am not asking you to *pursue* a different level of consciousness. Rather to become the witness to the way in which you are currently operating. There is nothing you need to fix. Just bring your awareness to what is already occurring and the natural process of realignment and readjustment will begin. Become the intrigued and curious observer to your own patterns and simply allow the wisdom to be revealed to you.

Before we go on, let's just define consciousness. In Beyond the Personality[1], consciousness is described as "*one's level of awareness at any given time and place and to the context within which this awareness operates at that time*".

The first part – *'one's level **of awareness** at any given **time and place**'* – indicates that our point of attention is fluctuating in both time and space. Again, this is important because we aren't seeking some kind of static end goal. Awareness is a process and it will be in a continual state of movement and change.

We can think of our attention as being rather like a spotlight. It will hone in on one particular aspect of our experience. Throughout our lives, we have learnt where to shine our spotlight at a given place or time. We call these habitual patterns of focusing *'conditioning'*. These conditioned habits are designed to streamline our responses so that there are certain processes we can do without much conscious intervention. Achieving a level of unconscious competence (where there is little need for us to be thinking about our actions) can be really useful if we are talking about walking. Imagine if taking a few steps remained as challenging to you now as it was when you were a toddler. The problem is that we are now operating without awareness in the majority of our life experiences. It is time to question if being unconsciously competent at feeling upset in the face of criticism or getting angry when someone won't do as you ask is all that helpful to you.

The second part of the definition *'**the context** within which this awareness operates **at that time**'* is also illuminating. Our consciousness is defined by the context, or in other words the situation, within which the experience is taking place. Why is this important to know? Because our awareness is context or situation dependent. There may be times when we find it really easy to stay awake but other times where we seem to fall back into unconsciousness. I have noticed this in meditation when I can be aware of almost everything including my heartbeat, my breathing pattern and the way the back of the chair feels against my body. But less than an hour later, when the phone is ringing, the children are asking for help and I am trying to finish the housework, my consciousness is diminished once more. The spotlight has moved to external demands and my awareness is offline again.

Unfortunately, as tempting as it may often seem, we cannot spend our lives meditating in solitude. We are meant to interact with and be part of life. If we are rushing and pushing, it is less easy to stay conscious – our awareness will be pulled back into those automatic conditioned patterns. Perhaps you have had the experience of attending a workshop or retreat and being able to easily spot your limiting behaviour. You may have been absolutely convinced that your life had changed as a result of this insight. You return back to normal life and within days are hooked back into the old ways of being. That is how powerful our conditioning is at sending us to sleep. It is why simplifying and creating space is so important so that we can be more awake more of the time. We will explore this in depth later in the book.

Before that, I want to describe some generalised patterns of consciousness that may resonate with your own experiences:

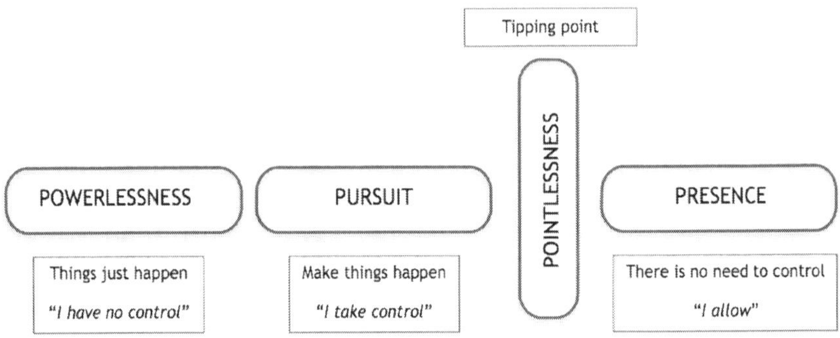

Powerlessness

When we first emerge into the world, we have no capacity to take care of ourselves. Without food, water or shelter provided for us, we would die. We are born totally dependent on others for our survival. Through our formative childhood years, with the right support and guidance, we will be taught how to fend for ourselves. By the age of two, we can move towards something that we want. By the age of three, we have enough dexterity to direct a spoon to our own mouths and eat. Fast forward to our teenage years and we can visit a shop, purchase food and prepare a meal that will sustain us (even if that meal is just baked beans on toast!) Sadly, the capacity of teenagers to fend for themselves is only too evident by the large numbers that live and survive on the streets.

But as well as our *physical* development in these early years, there is also an accompanying *psychological* journey – the conclusions we make about our level of personal power. Given the right set of conditions, a young child will develop a healthy understanding of their ability to lead and influence their own life. They will learn to make choices, take action that leads to specific results and to understand the consequences of decisions that they have made. By the time they fly the nest, they should be ready to fully engage with life on their own terms.

For some people, that concept was not their reality. Rather than believing in a loving universe that will support their dreams, they were conditioned to believe that life is working against them. If they perceive that they are overpowered by the world, they fall into victimhood. There are a number of factors that contribute to the victim mentality, for example, over-bearing authority figures who seek to control a child's life (the *'I know best for you'* attitude); bullying by siblings or school friends; an early trauma or emotionally negative and intense experience; even a deeply caring parent who wants to protect a child from hurt or making mistakes can inadvertently teach a child that they aren't powerful enough to take care of themselves in the world.

If we don't learn to be empowered in our childhood years, we feel powerless. We don't believe that we have the ability to shape our destiny or direct our life. Rather like a ship without an anchor, we will simply be blown by the biggest gust of wind – usually the person who is shouting loudest or demanding the most from us.

We probably all know someone who is stuck in powerlessness consciousness. Sadly, a few will live their whole lives believing that they are victims of life and never do anything to break free from this mindset. Most eventually tire of being at the receiving end of a demanding and relentless world and decide to take back the reigns. They enter a new level of consciousness, that of pursuit.

Pursuit

Perhaps you were fortunate and your parents or teachers taught you from an early age to go out and get what you want. Or maybe you made the break from powerlessness after years of suppressing your own wishes and desires. But my guess is that if you are caught up in the unfulfilling rat race, then you are living from pursuit consciousness.

In fact, this is where most of the Western world is right now. Many of us are hooked into the quest for more. Pursuit consciousness is trying to fulfil our life through controlling our destiny. On the surface there are many advantages to taking this life position. We are no longer subject to agreeing to the demands of others. We can set goals and achieve them. We can have a sense of moving towards something and if things don't go to plan, we can decide on a different course of action.

The problem is that we aren't really clear what we are pursuing. It may seem like we are seeking freedom or happiness but the end result is often very far from our objectives. Just ask those who seem to have it all – the big house, the executive job, the high-achieving family – rather than delivering the peace they wanted, it more often feels like they are trapped on a treadmill. Freedom and happiness are intrinsically linked. If you have created a jam-packed schedule that prevents you from living in the moment, in all likelihood you will end up feeling caged in by your own choices, and contentment will continue to elude you.

There is a cultural myth that is the basis of pursuit consciousness – that hard work equals success. Very few ever question this idea but it is worth examining our beliefs. First of all, we need to define success. Your version of success will be unique so take a moment just to explore what it would look and/or feel like. Write down the key words that come up for you.

Review your list. How many of those things are external gains (such as money, a house, a car, a job or a relationship) and how many are internal states of being or emotions (like peace, confidence or joy)? If you notice that you have any external gains then I'd like you to think about what you think that would give you. For example, if having a relationship is on your list, it might be because you think it would give you love, connection or security.

We only ever want something external for the states of being it creates in us, so when we talk about success, we are connecting to the emotional benefits and that is what makes it so appealing. But do we have to have the external gains to feel the emotions we want? In the relationship example, does it have to be a partner to experience love or connection? Of course not. You can have that with friends, other family members or even a pet. You might want to argue that it is a different type of love that we experience in an intimate relationship – and to an extent that may be true – but it also depends on your beliefs and your conditioned thinking.

In my experience, the most intimate and deeply rewarding type of relationship is the one within – between the you that is reading this and the you that exists beyond physical boundaries – you may call this your spirit, your soul or your higher self. I'm not asking you to take my word for it, I am just inviting you to expand your perceptions and realise that the thing you think you want might not be the only answer. There might be something even better.

So let's rewrite the belief *hard work equals success* as *hard work will bring me the emotional states I desire*. Is that true? Can you honestly know from this vantage point that the goal you have set is ultimately going to make you happy, peaceful, secure or any other emotion on your list? Based on all the information we have available to us when we set the goal, we probably think it will but we can't know for sure until we get there. Have you ever set a goal and found it to be very different when you actually achieved it?

A few years ago I was working with a client who was absolutely devastated at being passed over for a promotion. She had worked for the company for a number of years and steadily climbed the career ladder. When her immediate boss had resigned, she was certain that the position would be given to her. But the role was assigned to someone else in her department and she was left reeling. She was determined to cause as much disruption as possible. The company asked me to help re-engage her with the team.

What was fascinating was that as we unpacked the purpose of her original goal (i.e. promotion), it was clear to see how little it aligned with her core values. As she defined her version of success, she talked about being there for her family when they needed her and feeling fulfilled as a mother, yet this role would have involved travelling for significant amounts of time.

This is one of the issues with pursuit. We lose sight of

what is really important to us. She was so fixated on having the role that she had missed the impact it would have on her and her family. She might have experienced a temporary sense of achievement in being promoted but this would soon have been surpassed by feelings of angst and unhappiness at not having what she really wanted – time with her family.

I see this pattern often with clients. I call it *ladder against the wrong wall syndrome*. At some point in our life we decide that there is some*thing* that will make us happy and are so busy pursuing it that we don't notice that things are changing. Something you want when you are eighteen or twenty-one won't necessarily be what you want when you are thirty or forty. This doesn't just apply to careers. It is true of any goal. You will change over time and it is crazy to think that what you want will stay static. It doesn't matter how hard you work if you spend decades climbing a ladder only to find when you get to the top that it was against the wrong wall. No amount of hard work in the wrong direction will bring you the feelings you seek if you have lost sight of your values. That's why it is so important to stay connected to the present moment and your emotional state. This is the only place that you will find relevant and reliable information.

But let's just assume that your ladder is against the right wall and the goals that you have set for yourself will bring you the success you have defined. Pursuit is about closing the gap between where you are and where you want to be – the place that you think will bring those emotional rewards. If I think that earning £20,000 more a year will bring me peace or security then I'll come up with a well thought out plan for how I will achieve that result. I will probably break it down into manageable milestones. I may even map out the tactics that I can deploy to make it happen. It all looks good on paper.

I have everything in place. I have a plan. I am willing to put all my energy into making it happen. I am highly motivated and willing to do what it takes. So is it a sure fire thing that I will achieve my goal? Have you ever set a goal and not achieved it? If so, was a lack of hard work the reason you weren't successful? I know enough people who have slaved over a project and still had it fail. That belief that hard work equals success is starting to look a bit shaky isn't it? Conversely, you may know people who seem to do very little and yet achieve a great deal. They just always seem to be in the right place at the right time and cruise to success. It may be that we just don't see all the effort they are putting in behind the scenes but perhaps it is because they know that success is not necessarily dependent on how hard they work. If some people are working hard and not getting results and others are doing very little but achieving a lot, then the belief that hard work equals success cannot be proven. In simple cause and effect terms, success cannot be the direct effect of hard work. There have to be other criteria that play a part. If you are one of the people that have experienced the failure of a project despite your efforts, maybe you have already begun to question this belief. You may well have established a list of other criteria to add to your success philosophy. Maybe you have attributed your lack of success to not knowing enough, not being aligned enough, external obstacles, inner fear, limiting beliefs or the gods not shining favourably on you.

If your goal is important enough to you, my guess is that you are willing to pursue it from multiple angles. You will change the plan. You will seek out help and guidance from a coach, a mentor or self-help books. You might connect to divine guidance, angels or a psychic. Pursuit consciousness can be relentless in its strategies for success. But what happens when you have exhausted all the options. You are tired, stressed or burnt out. The thought of one more plan or the next well-meaning piece of advice tips you over the edge. Your heart and soul are screaming for a break. Enough is enough. You are tired of being pushed around by something or someone. What do you do? This is the pointlessness phase!

Pointlessness

Pointlessness is a temporary state of consciousness that represents the tipping point. It comes when we have been trying too hard for too long to get something we want. The endless pursuit takes its toll on our psychological well-being and triggers a point of collapse. This collapse may take different forms but will incorporate some kind of breakdown in our usual way of functioning. In my experience, it was an emotional breakdown that gradually crept up on me. One day I woke without the energy to even lift my head off the pillow. Suddenly nothing really mattered any more. I didn't care if I didn't get dressed. I didn't care if I couldn't pay the bills. I didn't care what anyone said or thought. It was a state of total demoralisation. Mine was a dramatic and intense period that definitely served to capture my attention! I've since heard others describe their own *dark night of the soul* episodes in a similar way so I know that I am not alone in my experience.

Others I have worked with have been through an external event like a divorce, an illness, bereavement, a redundancy or even an accident that plunges their previously secure world into chaos and uncertainty. I also know people have had a more gentle transition and gradually woken up to the realisation that their current way of living won't ultimately bring them the states of being that they want.

However it manifests, this pointlessness phase represents a period of letting go of the life that has been before (i.e. the life of pursuit). I call it pointlessness because what the experiences share is a period of doubt, confusion and uncertainty.

Human beings are generally adverse to any lack of clarity. We like to know what is going to happen next. This is part of the pursuit trap and the illusion of being in control of our lives. So suddenly moving from knowing what (we think) we want to feeling doubtful is disconcerting. We may resist this phase by refusing to give up on a plan of action or by setting different goals. A sense of direction – no matter how misguided it might be – feels much better than pointlessness.

But what is pointlessness really? A quick look in the English Dictionary brings up this definition, "*Something that is pointless has no purpose and it is a waste of time doing it.*" No wonder we seek to avoid these experiences! But let's take a more literal description. A pointless experience is one that lacks a *point*. If we broaden our perspective, could there be a time when living without a specific focal point in time or space could be useful? Isn't that really what we are seeking to achieve in states like meditation? What happens when we take away *the point*? Having no focal point removes the boundaries between our experiences and us. Separation is dissolved and we are brought into a place of oneness and connection with everything else in the Universe.

The pointlessness consciousness therefore has the capacity to take us beyond the constraints of our ego-based personality. Rather than being something to fear or to dread, the emotional and psychological crisis creates the opportunity and possibility of an awakening. It can feel so terrible because we resist it. But when we allow it, pointlessness takes us out of the vicious cycle of doing and into a state of pure being. As we embrace this phase, an unquestionable inner peace begins to permeate our soul and our consciousness shifts once more.

During the pointlessness phase, there is a realisation that nothing outside of yourself can bring you what you seek. It is a bitter-sweet pill to swallow. You now see the cultural myth that only served to keep you from your own happiness. You may feel sadness and empathy for the old version of you that has been struggling for so long. But this pivotal moment also brings the gift of a new awareness. The uncertainty and confusion of the pointlessness phase suspends your ego's need to control events long enough for a new door to appear before you. Beyond this doorway is presence and the life you have been seeking all along.

Presence

In pursuit consciousness we are driven to do things

that we think will help us to feel complete. Presence consciousness is the realisation that we already are. We come to understand that there is nowhere we need to be other than here, in this moment. We surrender our expectations. We release the need to control. We accept the cards that life deals us. We are willing to look beneath the surface and see that every event and experience is serving us in some way. We stop fighting for what we want and we end the conflict within. With that comes inner peace and a pervading sense of contentment that cannot be disrupted or destroyed by anything in our external world.

According to the Tao de Ching[2], the essential mission of our lives is to go back and to get to know our *originating source* before our death. Our originating source is the essence from which we were born. It provides us with a deep sense of connection, well-being and purpose beyond anything our limited minds can conceive. Just as every wave is a part of the ocean, we are part of this source energy and it lives within us. The only reason we don't experience it on a regular basis is because we have been so caught up in the demands of our ego that we have lost touch with this core of who we really are – our True Self.

Any feelings of loneliness, separation or confusion are the emotional manifestations of our disconnection from the divine source. And life is compassionate enough to show you where you are going wrong. This is your wake up call.

Reaching this point in our consciousness is an understanding that our job is not to make life happen but rather, as Michael Bernard Beckwith[3] so beautifully puts it, "*to make life welcome*". We learn to let go of the elaborate plans we have been attached to and embrace the experiences laid before us as they are. There is a beautiful and magical quality to living in sync with life's flow rather than trying to force it in the direction of our choosing.

Being *in the flow* is a catchphrase of our generation often used to describe a period when life's events are going in our favour. If we find ourselves facing challenges or difficulties, we may scramble to regain our flow as quickly as possible. Let's be clear, a life of presence doesn't mean that everything is going according to your plan, it means that you are willing to stay present to every event that life brings to your door – the good, the bad and the ugly. Being in the flow means letting go of your resistance to the unwanted aspects of life. You can be in the middle of an unwanted experience and still be present. I once had the great privilege of coaching a lady who stayed connected despite the death of her partner in a car crash. Yes, she was grieving and hurting. But she showed me with such grace and gentleness that it is possible to lose the most important thing in your life and still stay present. Being the witness to her pain whilst she was willing to embrace it rather than trying to push it away was an experience that deeply and profoundly touched me.

Not everyone will face such challenges. In fact, when we make the switch, there may be times when life seems boring or uneventful. This is only because you refuse to buy into the drama that others want you to consent to. If you imagine your consciousness as being like a large lake, the water is constantly disturbed by events dropping in to your experience. Some of these may be small pebbles. Others are massive boulders. And if they are not on the plan, your inner peace will be disrupted. In a life of presence, you realise you are not just the lake but also the stones. Therefore your job is not to stop the boulders but rather to bear witness to the ripples on the surface. When you are no longer attached to the disturbance, even the biggest boulders seem to create only small ripples.

If you have been used to big boulders dropping left, right and centre, the peaceful calm of gentle ripples through your consciousness will be unfamiliar. You may long for a bit of excitement to shake your life up again. There is something addictive about dealing with crises that can give us a false sense of importance. But when you learn to ditch the drama and stay with the calmness, you will discover a natural and pervasive state of contentment that makes all the excitement and commotion pale in comparison. If I offered you an instant high that would last maybe a few hours or days or an enduring state of gentle joy that you could experience most of the time, which would you choose? The gift of more sustainable contentment is the product of a life of presence.

CHAPTER 2

Discovering Your Worth

If living a life of presence is such a wonderful experience, how do we ever get caught up in pursuit? We now know that everything we seek to obtain is really because of the emotional feelings we think the goal will bring. We have also seen that our feelings aren't necessarily dependent on achieving that goal. We can feel secure without the job. We can feel connected without the relationship. We can feel successful without the hefty bank balance.

And I am sure you have heard it all before. I can tell you that your feelings aren't dependent on your life circumstances and my guess is that you will probably nod knowingly and carry on with the pursuit of your dreams once more. I can say that with such certainty because it was the pattern I ran for so many years. Long periods of working too hard to reach my goals interspersed with temporary moments of undeniable wisdom that I was making my journey through life more complicated than it needed to be.

So, if on some level we know there must be an easier way to live, what keeps us locked into pursuit consciousness? I believe that as well as the more evident quest for happiness, we are also driven by an underlying need to feel worthy.

Simply put, we need to know that we matter and we will do almost anything to have to have this desire fulfilled. You only need to see examples of celebrities who are living painful and chaotic lives in the public eye to know the lengths that people will go to in an attempt to be acknowledged. You may not be like the celebrities sacrificing peace and privacy for external validation but if the rat race has its grip on you then there is a high chance that you aren't (yet) fully embracing your intrinsic value.

If you are questioning your worthiness on any level, you cannot feel a sustained sense of joy. No matter how much personal or spiritual development you commit to, life will continue to throw you curve balls that plunge you back into self-doubt again. It is a never-ending cycle that cannot be stopped until you finally cease doubting your inherent magnificence. The processes in this book will help you to re-connect to your worth but let's first look at how this pattern gets established and maintained. The good news is that your thoughts of unworthiness are a product of your own mind that has been holding you hostage without your knowing. You don't need to prove anything to anyone else; you just need to find new evidence to counter your own limiting beliefs. I want to show you how, as a child of this universe, you are already special and that your worthiness was never in question.

You were born whole, happy and complete. Perfect in every way, just as Mother Nature intended. This is your **True Self**. There were no thoughts of inferiority. You didn't look over at the next cot in the hospital and compare yourself to the baby lying there "*They have more hair, their rattle is better than mine, they slept for five hours whilst I only managed three!*" Such thoughts are ludicrous!

Not so ridiculous, it would seem, by the time we reach school. Now we are subject to the various scales of measurement – how easily we learn to read, how well we hold a pencil, our capacity for retaining and regurgitating information or our ability to throw and catch a ball. It's a never-ending process of judgment. A few manage to hang onto their self-worth but most of us, in at least one area of life, buy into the belief that we are not quite up to the mark. Responding to the opinions of those we look up to (literally), we are conditioned to believe our inadequate thoughts. And so a new identity is born. Let's call this ***False Identity #1***. It is a false identity because we have disconnected from the truth – the knowing that we are born from an originating source that provides us with inherent worth. Instead of being connected to our magnificence we now feel separated and in that gap we start to believe the thoughts of inadequacy and inferiority. This becomes our new identity.

What thoughts did you form about yourself in those

early years? Maybe that you weren't smart or sporty? That you were too emotional or too cold? That you were too talkative or too quiet? That you didn't measure up to your parents' expectations or a sibling's achievements? That you were destined to fail or would always live up to the role of the good child? Can you begin to see how, as the outer voices got louder, you lost the ability to hear the wisdom of the voice within? We lose sight of our True Self under a mountain of external "*shoulds*", "*oughts*" and "*musts*".

You probably won't find that unworthiness is a constant presence in your life. You may be happy a large proportion of the time. You may function exceptionally well in many situations. Yet, in those moments when your weak spot is revealed, you suddenly find yourself right in the middle of your unworthiness and believing the thought "*I am not good enough*" once more. For many people the discomfort of bumping into some inadequacies from time-to-time is never a big enough issue for them to want to tackle. But if those feelings are intense or frequent enough, the desire to change may win through and so begins the next stage of our journey – the quest for self-improvement!

Self-improvement can take many forms - goal-setting, therapy, self-help books, healing, workshops, or seminars to name just a few. Clearly there is nothing wrong with any of these approaches. I'm sure the quality of your life has been enhanced considerably with some of these tools. I hope you find some insightful moments in this book too. The real question is whether these tools are taking us back to the perfection of our True Self? If self-improvement becomes a mask for underlying inadequacy, we will find ourselves adapting to a secondary identity. We can call this **False identity # 2**. This identity is based on the presupposition that we have to live up to some illusionary standards of goodness or achievement in order to be an okay person. These may seem self-set but, more often than not, are measurements according to cultural norms or the expectations of the authority figures that have influenced our childhood development.

A familiar analogy may help here. Imagine a diamond immersed in dirt and grime. Rather than cleaning the dirt, self-improvement is the equivalent of trying to cover the muck with nail polish. We are trying to make it look pretty without realising the spectacular beauty at its core.

Examples of a False Identity #2 might be "*as long as I don't lose my temper then I am okay*", "*as long as I am achieving in my career or have money in the bank then I am okay*" or "*as long as I am putting others before myself then I am okay.*" Can you spot how these thoughts are designed to keep us from dropping into the inadequate thoughts? We are living in some kind of suspended state of being known as "*as long as I...*" One mistake (anger, redundancy or selfishness in the examples above), and we will plummet into the pit of unworthiness once more.

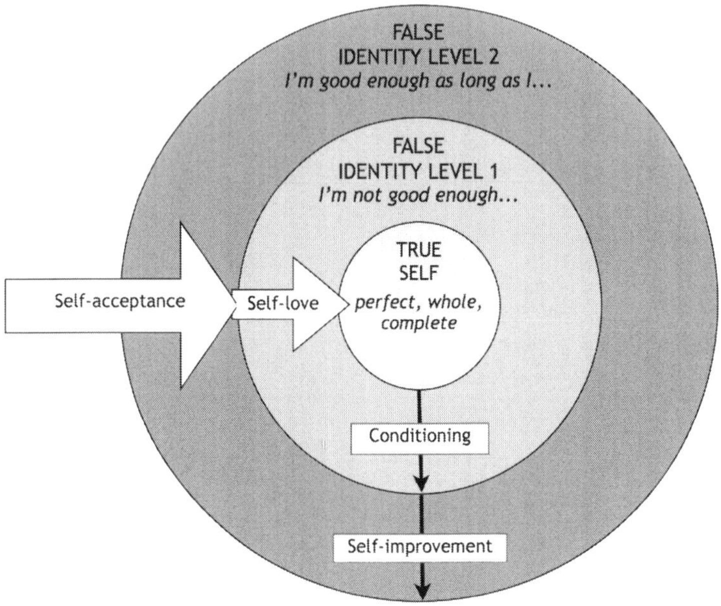

People can live out this False Identity with absolutely no awareness that it isn't their truth. Having our buttons pushed is a great way of finding out where we are fiercely defending ourselves from a thought of inadequacy. We are likely to react strongly to anyone who challenges this protective False Identity. As an example, I remember someone once saying that my decision to leave a party early was disrespectful. The intensity of my reaction towards the word *disrespectful* was a pretty clear indicator that I had "*as long as I am respectful to others then I am okay*" in my repertoire!

Take a few moments to recall any experiences you have had that may have been showing you your protective beliefs. What challenges or feedback have you reacted most strongly to? Where have you found yourself actively defending or explaining your position? What is your "*as long as I*" belief?

When living from this False Identity #2, we may be highly motivated but find that happiness and peace still elude us. There is a lot of stimulation and energy to be had when running away from thoughts of inadequacy. It propels you forwards. You are on a mission to prove your worth but this can't bring you the contentment and fulfilment you really desire. That can only come from dropping the false identities and connecting to your True Self once more.

Scratch beneath the surface of many a successful executive or entrepreneur and you often discover that they are terrified of their weaknesses being revealed. No amount of outward success can sooth a soul that feels inadequate. That is why this False Identity #2 is correlated with the pursuit consciousness. You are being driven by the quest for worthiness, not realising that your worth was your birthright. So it's not about trying to make ourselves better through self-improvement. It's about stripping back the layers of polish and grime and seeing what natural magnificence lies inside us.

Your True Self is the part of you that knows your inherent worth. It existed long before you succumbed to the opinions and judgments of others. Without the need to prove or validate your worth, it remains intrinsically connected to something pure, sacred and divine. Within the True Self, there are no rules or conditions to adhere to. It doesn't compare, criticise or analyse. It knows only one state of being – that of unconditional love. When it encounters a fellow being, it sees its own reflection. There is no separation or dissociation with others or with the planet. There are no defined boundaries. And if we are all one, how can there ever be a need to convince, fight or compete? We understand the perfection of the unfolding situation. There is no desire to improve or better ourselves. All is as it is meant to be.

Let's substitute the idea of self-improvement with self-acceptance. What if we were willing to embrace ourselves as we are, warts and all? Maybe you have some weaknesses. So what? Does that make you any less valuable or worthy? Of course not! We are all different. We all have unique gifts. We all have unique flaws. It's what makes you so perfectly you. With sufficient self-acceptance we may find ourselves right at the cusp of False Identity #1 once more. You are willing to stand in the presence of your inadequacies and not let them consume you. This allows you to approach your concept of self with a new attitude. Not with a sense of not being good enough but rather with a compassionate understanding of your authenticity. You know where you rock and you know where you don't but you are no longer attached to it being different to how it is.

Being accepting of our flaws is a good start but it isn't an absolute reflection of our authentic essence. What will move us right back into the core of our True Self? The answer lies in self-love. We don't just want to accept ourselves for who we are, we want to love our self without conditions. This is the art of recognising your True Self without the need for superiority – welcoming your weaknesses whilst seeing your magnificence and radiating your truth.

How can we know the difference between self-love and self-improvement? We only need to ask a question. Are we doing what we do because at some level we believe we need to fix ourselves? Our True Self knows that there is nothing to fix. We need to stop questioning our worth and be willing to embrace every aspect of our nature, no matter how scary it may seem. I promise you that all of the dark parts of your personality are really part of the light, they just haven't been allowed to shine. When you find the courage to look behind the doors that others have judged as wrong, you will find your magnificent self. It was there all along!

I wanted to share with you a short poem that I wrote some time ago. It was at a point when I was still firmly living from my False Identity #2. I woke one morning with words running through my mind and in a dozy haze, I grabbed my journal and recorded what I was hearing. I think it so perfectly illustrates this discovery of our inherent worthiness and it was completely outside of my conscious thinking at the time. Now, with hindsight, I believe it was a call from my True Self inviting me to come home.

This is who I am... I AM

This is me
Sometimes I am inspired, loving, compassionate, optimistic, trusting, elegant, gentle and joyful
Sometimes I am sad or angry or irritated or hurt or frustrated or fearful
But I am always, all ways me
This is who I am... I AM

I love the parts I describe as the best of me
I love the parts I judge as the worst of me
In fact I realise that I need to love myself even more when I need it most
Staying outside of my own judgments and condemnations I have about myself
For not being perfect or acceptable
Or some other mistaken view I hold
When I briefly forget the truth that this is all of me
This is who I am... I AM

And as I come to embrace every aspect of me
I give permission for others to love the whole of me

And I can reciprocate by loving all of them too
Even when their anger or hurt or fear is directed towards me
Seemingly unfairly or unjustified
I will remember
The universe is perfect just as it is
Every person is whole and complete just as they are
I am whole and complete and perfect just as I am
Because this is me
This is who I am...I AM

I continue to evolve and expand and change
Every day and in every way
Sometimes I delight and astound myself
Sometimes I am left bemused and bewildered by choices I make in the moment
when I am not in full alignment with all that I am

And even then, I shall look inside, take a breath
And remember
I am whole and complete and perfect just as I am
Because this is me
This is who I am...I AM

CHAPTER 3

The Joy of Presence

Living a life of presence is an ever-expanding and constant learning curve but committing to making the shift will pay enormous dividends to the quality of your life. It also allows us to make a greater contribution to the planet.

Up to this point, the world we live in has been driven by the acquisition of power, recognition and reward. Here in the West, we only have to look around to see the impact of pursuit consciousness. There's an *"every man for himself"* mentality. As a whole, we lack any sense of community and co-operation. Rather than feeling connected to our fellow humans, there is a pervading sense of separation and isolation. We watch the news and gasp in horror at the atrocities in the world and yet we don't notice the old lady dying of cold in our own street. We hear of chief executives taking huge payments out of the company while those lower down are surviving on pay cuts or facing redundancy. Everyone I speak to is working longer hours with higher demands on their energy. Stress and busyness are not only commonplace but now seem to be presented as evidence of the credibility of our personal worth. Maybe there is a belief that if we give our all day in and day out then we are too valuable to let go. But there is a big difference between commitment and workaholism. The boundaries are blurring and our individual and collective wellbeing is suffering.

But the world is changing. Epidemics, environmental crises and economic disasters are thrusting the world into uncertainty. It used to be that you could find security in your external world. You could get your job, buy your home and be set for life. These days no job is safe. The price of property is so high that even if you can afford to get a mortgage, your payments will be much higher over a longer period of time. With the collapse of financial institutions, even pensions and savings are no longer a secure option. This sense of insecurity is further added to by the threats of terrorism, natural catastrophes and the spread of new and aggressive diseases across the world.

I know this seems like a very depressing picture but can you begin to see how what is happening in the world is mirroring our individual journey from pursuit to presence. You will remember that the purpose of pointlessness was to create confusion and uncertainty. This phase released us from the grip of pursuit long enough for something new to emerge – presence consciousness. Could it be that this phase we are experiencing globally is a similar transition – an opportunity for us to collectively realise that the way we have been operating individually is not serving the whole? I believe we have a chance to move from the independence of pursuit consciousness to interdependence, working together collaboratively for a greater good. If you can't find security in your job, your home or the world, where do you find it? We have no choice. We must look within. Maybe the changes in the world are inviting us to awaken to this new consciousness. Perhaps the time has come to ask how we can better help each other?

The life of pursuit is an illusion. Pursuit has us believing that there is some imaginary place in the future where the you that has everything that you want already exists. It separates out *here* and *there*. Rather than being present to this point in time, we find ourselves living somewhere in between. Being in the gap between what you have and what you think you need can never be fulfilling. We are sacrificing our own inner peace and happiness for an imaginary future that we think will be better than what we have now. But this moment is where real life is happening. It simply isn't possible to exist anywhere other than now. You can't be present and fully experiencing life when your mind is trying to live somewhere else. You can't be awake and aware to the magic of presence if you are distracted by the busyness of trying to reach a future end goal.

When you stop chasing, forcing, pushing and driving, you drop into the open space of the current moment. Experiences deepen and broaden, pulling us into their richness and vibrancy. Presence is about learning to surrender — to release our expectations, our demands, and our fixed sense of self. As we let go, we open our hardened and conditioned hearts to new possibilities. Everything we need to know already resides inside of us, we have been too fearful to look there in case we stumbled upon our inadequacies and weaknesses.

The healing we have been trying to get through fixing, solving and sorting will only come when we allow ourselves to be vulnerable and receptive once more. Your True Self is accepting, forgiving and loving. This isn't a consciousness to aspire to or pursue, it is who you already are at the core of your being. We must strip back the conditioning that has us believing anything different.

We talk of love yet we really know very little about it. The pure unconditional love of an open and whole heart is a love beyond everything we think we know. We may tap into it periodically but we don't know what it is like to live from this boundless energy. Experiencing more connection, more freedom, more contentment and more love is the promise of a life of presence. The only question is whether you are prepared to open your eyes and your heart to it?

The table below shows some of the key differences in the qualities of a life of pursuit versus a life of presence. Language is extremely powerful in accessing your states of being. Some of these words may resonate for you. You may think of other expressions or phrases that fit better for you. It is worth noting your favourite '*hot words*' down. These will serve as useful reminders along the journey. You can use them to check in with yourself. For example, you might ask whether you are being led by your head or your heart in the moment or ask whether you are chasing experiences down or letting them flow.

Pursuit	Presence
Ego-centred	*Spirit-centred*
Chasing it down	*Letting it flow*
Fear-driven	*Love-based*
Limited and limiting	*Expansive*
In the past/future	*In the now*
Head-led	*Heart-led*
Seeker	*Sage (Finder)*
Striving	*Being*
Duality	*Oneness*
The achiever	*The Allower*

Hopefully a life of presence is an appealing proposition to you. No more fighting for inner peace, no more driving for results, no more running to stand still, no more berating yourself for not doing enough, no more effort, struggle and excessive work. These were never the routes to happiness. It is time to lighten up, loosen up and realise that we have everything we need to be happy right now, in this moment.

From Pursuit to Presence is a journey to connect with your True Self. Over the remaining chapters, I will be introducing you to a model for living from presence consciousness. Models by their very nature are limited and it is important to understand that we are taking a non-linear process and breaking it down into separate steps. Life doesn't operate in a continuous straight line and the steps won't happen sequentially but having the model will serve to simplify our understanding.

The Pursuit to Presence Model

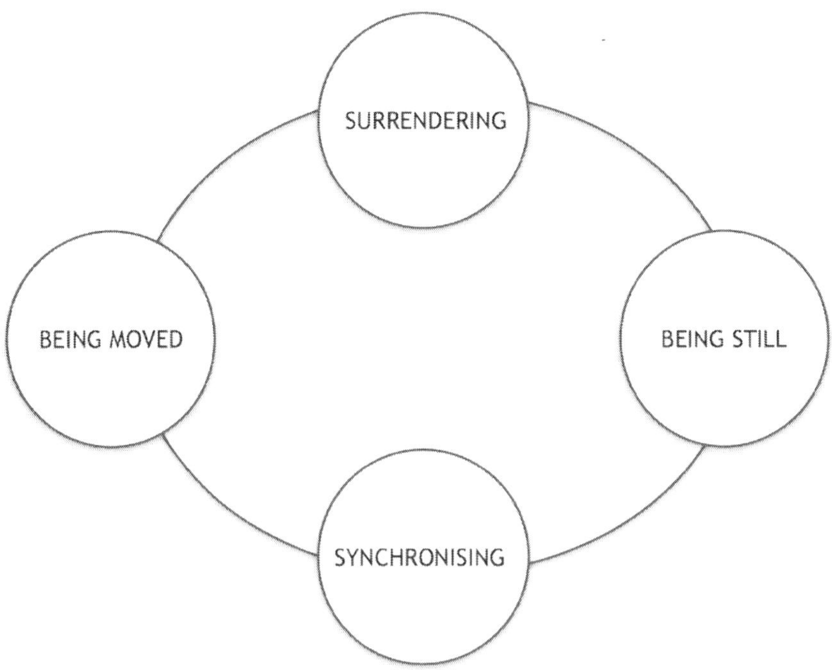

STEP 1: SURRENDERING

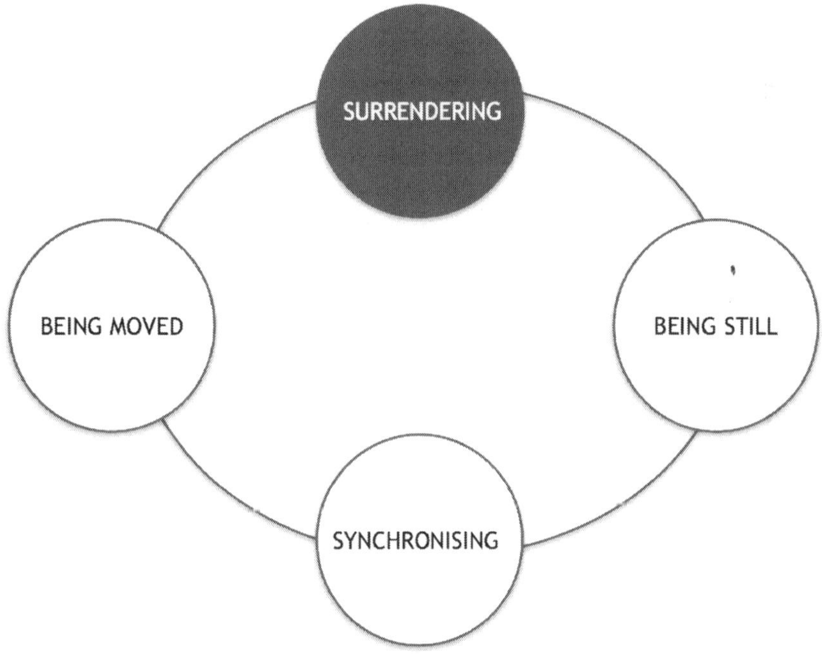

CHAPTER 4

Releasing Control

This section will cover four different aspects of surrendering. We are starting here because we have to liberate ourselves from pursuit consciousness before we can find a new way of being in the world. The first of the aspects that we will explore is the concept of *releasing control.*

In our current culture, the need for control dictates so much of our behaviour. When our happiness and sense of worth is tied to our achievements and possessions, we will pursue, protect and defend against losing what we have. It sets us up for a lifetime of struggle and, so long as we are fighting to be in control, we can't find inner peace or contentment.

Accepting that we have a need to be in control isn't easy. We use the word *controlling* in derogatory terms. No one wants to be perceived in such a light. We know we *shouldn't* be like this so we are going to resist the idea that there are parts of us that not only need to feel in control but are, in reality, *controlling* the direction and experiences of our lives. Until we are able to see and understand these parts, our existence will continue to be stressful. Where do you think any feelings of fear, anxiety or worry come from if it is not from the basis of control? Any scary thoughts about the future are really a part of us saying: "*I fear that something is going to happen that I cannot handle"*. Otherwise, you would have no need to worry about events that haven't happened!

I clearly understand this control paradigm now but that hasn't always been the case. I would have been willing to admit that I had attempted to control people and experiences in my youth. I could see that I had manipulated relationships to get my own way and done anything and everything that I could to defend against any perceived threats to my happiness or wellbeing. I got into screaming matches with lovers and friends when they refused to see the world my way and, if that didn't work, I would cut them out of my life permanently. With hindsight, it wasn't very difficult to see how controlling I had been. I was young, immature and didn't know better so I was able to forgive myself for my mistakes.

When I revisited the topic of control many years later, I was teaching others how they could improve their lives. I thought I knew more. I rarely got into conflict. I always took the higher ground. I believed I was influential rather than aggressive or antagonistic. Much of my self-worth was tied up with being an inspiring figure to others. My identity was someone who cared about people and wanted to make a difference in the world. If you had asked me then to see how I was attempting to control my life and my experiences, I would have risen strongly against such an accusation. It simply didn't fit with my sense of self. My self-image as this kind, loving and non-controlling personality was part of the False Identity #2 (discussed in Chapter 1). It was the shiny nail varnish covering the muck of unworthiness. To accept the concept of being controlling would mean facing that unworthiness all over again. That's why we will do anything we can to avoid it. But without the revelation of this truth, our understanding cannot evolve and if our understanding doesn't evolve, there cannot be the deep and lasting level of change that we need to experience sustainable joy and peace.

I now recognise those parts of me that do still want to be in control and I want to be as fully aware of them as I can be. I find it when I am demanding that people and events be the way that I want them to be. I find it when I feel frustration at my son for not keeping his room as tidy as I would like. I find it when I avoid difficult conversations or people who irritate me. I find it when I need to tell someone how they have hurt or upset me. I find it when I try to anticipate everything that I might need over the next year or two. I find it in every plan, goal and dream of how I think my life should be and I find it in every disappointment when the reality fails to measure up to my expectations.

Trying to get the world to conform to our expectations is always about control. You may not appear to be a demanding person but you will still have your own ways of wanting life to play out in a particular way. So before we go any further, just take a few moments and ask yourself what your version of control is? Do this with the willingness to see the truth rather than judging or berating yourself. Can you find the many ways that you are controlling your environment and your experiences? I promise they will be there because we all do it.

Why would we want to do this process? Facing up to these aspects of our self may not be comfortable but until we see this truth, we cannot be free or happy. We will continue to be locked into patterns of pursuit, protection and defence. And perhaps you can now see that all of these behaviours stem from our need to feel in control of our life.

Trying to get the world to deliver on our desires sets up a lifetime of struggle and anxiety. Needing the people, experiences and events to play out in a certain way puts us in a highly precarious position. When life is going according to our plans then we get to feel good but what happens if it is not? Have there ever been times in your life when, despite your best intentions and sound planning, things have turned out differently? We all enjoy the pleasant surprises but are not so keen on the ones that bring hardship or sadness.

Unanticipated curve balls seem to be the basis of our unhappiness but are they really? What if we had no expectations? Would we still suffer in the face of the unforeseen? We will explore this concept more later in the book but, for now, I'd like to just invite you to be willing to accept the idea that your expectations are really your attempts at controlling life and they may actually be holding you apart from the happiness you seek. If we want to fully experience the delights that life has to offer, we have to give up this need for control.

Who or what is really in control of our lives?

In powerlessness consciousness, we believe that we are victims of circumstance and therefore we give all our power away. That is why pursuit consciousness feels so good. We take back the power and get a sense of being in charge of our destiny. We have been feeling suppressed and depressed by what is happening to us and, therefore, gaining a sense of control is like a breath of fresh air. We can decide what we want, make a plan and go out and get it. And we think this is the answer to our quest for happiness. I see quotations and messages on social media that perpetuate this philosophy. We seem to love the messages about getting motivated, pursuing our dreams and refusing to quit.

But there are major flaws in these ideas. Yes, we have the ability to decide what we want and to take action but we have no way of guaranteeing that the action we take will bring us the results we seek. To go one step further, we have no way of knowing if, when we get what we think we want, it will *really* be what we want or need! It is always a best guess based on our experiences and knowledge to date.

If we were really in control of our lives, wouldn't we be able to set a goal and make that exact plan come into fruition? Wouldn't we also know for sure that the results we were going to get would make us as happy as we anticipate they will? If this isn't exactly how it plays out then there must be other factors to take into account. Who or what is responsible for those unwanted curve balls that knock us off track? And what could possibly cause us to *not want* the thing we get when we have desired it for so long? Surely there has to be something else that is really in charge!

For the answer, we can look to nature. Everything in the natural world has its own order of things. The acorn grows into the oak tree. As the weather cools, the birds migrate to warmer climates. The tides come and go. The seasons cycle through spring, summer, autumn and winter. We might not like the idea of the worm being eaten by the bird but we know that it is right and just. In fact, the worm is here to serve the bird's need for food and the bird serves it's purpose when it becomes prey for the fox. In nature we have a profound sense that everything is as it is meant to be.

What is the source of all creation found in nature? What manages the cycles and the tides in their perfect ebb and flow? What makes the rules of the food chain? There is some kind of indescribable energy that runs through nature and keeps it in balance. We have many different labels for this organising force – we may call it Source energy, the Quantum Field, the Universe, the Divine or God. Throughout this book I will refer to this as the Divine but please substitute this with the label that most resonates as truth for you.

We too were born from this energy, the source of all creation. We were given a body with which to explore this physical world and so we are also part of nature. We are therefore governed by the same natural laws. But there are two differentiating factors in being human. The first is that our consciousness allows us to be in a physical body whilst also perceiving our connection to the Divine. We can feel both the separateness of our physical individuality and the deep sense of connection to all that there is. The second is that this consciousness gives us a sense of self. That self-awareness seems to bring with it a sense of entitlement to have experiences go our way and to resist that which we don't like. Imagine if the trees refused to lose their leaves. Were they to interrupt the natural cycle, it would impact on everything in the surrounding environment. The flora and the fauna would be affected. There would be no seeds or berries to fall. Natural balance would be destroyed. The trees are part of nature and so there is no argument against losing their leaves. They elegantly bow down to Divine will. There is no resistance because they know this is their evolutionary process and the seasons will come round again.

Humans aren't quite so willing to leave things to Divine will. We attempt to control our environment to have it go our way. We so often find ourselves trying to defeat the elements, the weather and the seasons. We demand that the earth should feed and nourish us. If we look objectively at the human condition, can you see how we have mistakenly believed that we can control the natural world? But nature is the expression of the Divine and it will always find ways to restore the balance. Environmental disasters could wipe us out in an instant. We are here as expressions of the Divine but part of that responsibility is to serve the natural world. If we were more destructive than creative, there would be little need for our continued existence. Ultimately, if it came down to us against Divine will, who would win? Maybe we should ask the dinosaurs!

I share these ideas, not to paint a gloomy picture of the end of the world but rather to assist you in seeing how ridiculous our attempts at control really are. We are taking our little corner of the world and insisting that it matches our idea of perfection. But we are simply renting the space whilst we walk this planet and soon it will belong to those who follow in our footsteps. Ultimately it isn't ours. Our land *Lord* is the Divine, which has the final say about our lives. When we can see this bigger picture and realise that our controlling nature is trying to battle the governing force of

Divine energy, hopefully we can begin to see how pointless our attempts at pursuit and protection are. It may not always be fair (according to our man-made rules) but it is always as it is meant to be.

In presence consciousness, we are once more willing to give up the power. But now we no longer see ourselves as victims but rather as servants and children of the universe. We understand our preferences. We still have our wishes. Yet we know that we are part of a bigger and better plan. We can't know how things should unfold because we are only a tiny fraction of the whole system. Instead, we learn to trust the all-seeing, all-knowing governing energy because it has the fullest picture – about our lives as they stand right now, our history and our future. Would we really prefer to have our limited and narrow outlook be in charge? I am happy to hand over the leadership to that which has the broadest and wisest perspective.

Learning to release control is paramount to living a peaceful and content life. It doesn't mean that we become the passive doormats characterised in powerlessness consciousness. We remain active and engaged participants in an ever-evolving world. But we are no longer demanding that life satisfies our expectations. When we aren't asking our experiences to be different, we get to appreciate them for what they really are. Every creation is part of the Divine plan.

Endings

Part of this surrendering process is learning to accept endings. Everything that lives has a natural cycle and all cycles reach a point of completion. That which is born must die in order for evolution to continue. In general, we humans are fairly useless at endings! Death of any kind has become something to be feared and so we feel the need to hold onto as much as we can for as long as we can. We stay in unfulfilling jobs and destructive relationships rather than being willing to say goodbye.

But every death is really a transformation. Energy cannot be created or destroyed – it just changes structure. Even the concept of our physical death has been misunderstood for we will always continue to exist albeit in a different form. Our physical bodies may go on to nourish the earth whilst our spirit will find new ways of serving the Divine. If we can see birth and death as being part of the same process, perhaps we not only start to accept endings, we can also embrace them as the beginning of something new. And when we no longer fear endings, we are willing to give up the need to control.

When I have shared this idea on workshops, I often hear objections. How do we accept an ending when we are talking about the death of a loved one or a child? There is a clear distinction to be made here. Accepting endings doesn't mean that you have to like what has happened or that there won't be an intense emotional reaction. There may be great sadness and heartache. Experiencing deep emotion is part of what makes us human. In fact, disconnecting from your feelings will cause more damage – repressed grief leads to both physical and mental illness. But there is a key difference between not liking a situation and fighting it. There are circumstances that simply can't be undone, no matter how painful or seemingly unjust they are.

Ten years on and I still profoundly and deeply miss my father who died suddenly aged just sixty. There have been many times that I have wanted him here with me again. So many things I never got to share with him or say. But over the years, I have discovered new and powerful ways of re-establishing my connection with him. The most moving experience was feeling his undeniable presence on my wedding day. Although my brother walked me down the aisle, I could feel the energy of my father's arms around me. His physical form may be gone but the essence remains – the absolute proof I need that there is no real death, just trans-**form**-ation.

If you are ever struggling to come to terms with this concept, I strongly recommend you read Anita Moorjani's account of her near death experience in '*Dying to be Me*'[4]. The story she tells is not only deeply inspiring and moving but confirms that death is not *the* end but rather the ceasing of our physicality and the start of a whole new non-physical journey. Deaths of those we care about will always be the hardest to accept. We will never be asked to give up anything more precious than a loved one. However much we wish we got a say in this, we can't control these endings. Your fighting won't change anything; just prolong the pain and suffering.

Most endings will come in different guises – redundancy, divorce and bankruptcy to name a few. In fact, by default any transition needs an ending in order to have a new beginning. I wanted to share these ideas in this opening section as the shift from pursuit to presence will require that you go through endings – the end of chasing, the end of defending and even the end of some of your dreams. Releasing control sounds good on paper when we talk of ending the struggles. Who wouldn't want that? But if you are going to release control, you are going to find that some of those wonderful plans you had may not fit with your new level of consciousness and that is not always so easy to welcome.

It seems almost heresy to speak of giving up on dreams. Most people work with a coach to turn their visions into realities, not to give them up. I assure you that I have good reason for making this suggestion but I also recognise it was the part of the journey that I found the most challenging. When I was living in pursuit, I wanted to be an international trainer and author. I could picture myself speaking to big audiences and travelling the world. I imagined what the cashflow would allow me to do, the types of experiences I could create for my family and the quality of life we could have. There was never a doubt in my mind that it would happen. I invested a great deal of energy, time and money in my plan. I deployed every strategy I knew and studied with those who had successfully made the journey before me. It was big, juicy, exciting and inspiring. Who knows, perhaps if I had continued to pursue my dream, then it would have happened exactly as I wanted. So why was I prepared to give it up?

There came a point on my journey when I reached a subtle yet very significant turning point. My whole life was geared around my dream. There were many aspects of my world that were more important – my relationship, my family, my health and so on but they all merged together as part of this bigger life plan. I started to notice how many of my decisions were being fundamentally driven by this dream. In my mind I had a metaphorical checklist of what this perfect scenario would look like and I was building it up block by block.

That's what we have been taught to do isn't it? Turn our dreams into reality. If you have ever studied the Law of Attraction, you will have come across the notion that we are able to manifest our desires through the power of our thoughts. So having a dream and taking action to bring it to fruition seemed to make sense. And then I had a moment of absolute clarity. Here was I attempting to shape my world to fulfil a desire for the *perfect* existence while my life was happening around me. It was a dawning realisation that I was so busy trying to create an ideal life that I was actually missing the real one.

Let me give you an example of the two lives I am discussing. I am in an important meeting to discuss a potential work opportunity and my son's school calls to say that he is poorly and needs picking up. When I am living my dream life, my son's illness is an inconvenience. I may feel irritated or resentful that I have to walk away from the meeting. But if I am present to my actual life, the real opportunity is for me to care for my poorly child with love and kindness. My son and his illness are real in this moment. My dream life is an illusion.

There are so many ways in which we find ourselves living the illusion. Our dreams and desires can distract us from living in the now. Once I saw this clearly, I was completely willing to put an end to my master plan. Not because I no longer wanted it but because I wasn't willing to sacrifice the present moment for some imagined future. I came to see that the path in front of me is not a straight road. In fact, there wasn't just one route, but many, all representing the vast number of options that exist for my life going forwards. When I focused solely on the big dream, I was closed off to all other possibilities. I was living with my eyes on the horizon rather than allowing this moment to have the gift of my undivided attention. Now I don't have one perfect dream, there are multiple scenarios that I would welcome with open arms. Giving up my attachment to my plans has freed me to live fully in the present. Without desire or expectation, I can't be disappointed. There are no more endings to fear.

Sack the Storyteller

We find it challenging to release control because we have a preconceived idea of events and experiences. If I invited you to go out for an Italian meal tonight, you will probably start to run a mental movie of how things could play out. You might already be picturing the pizza or pasta! You don't have to actually be in the experience to imagine it. We can go there in our mind's eye. This is a useful skill to have in *some* contexts.

Let's say I asked you if you would prefer Italian or Indian cuisine. We make decisions by predicting the two scenarios, making a comparison and choosing the one based on our own criteria of evaluation. I could decide that I want Italian salad because I think it is healthy or that I want to taste the rich spices of a curry. Our own criteria will be unique to us. These are our preferences. When the decisions are simple this process may be so rapid that we have no awareness of the separate steps we go through. But if I was asking you what holiday you wanted to take next year or to select a house to buy, you may notice how you compare and contrast in order to reach your decision. Being able to predict future experiences is useful in decision-making, streamlining our lives and anticipating consequences.

But there is a downside. The mind not only predicts situations to help us make decisions or to keep us safe but it strives to be in control. Given the chance, it will take over the whole show. Gripped by our intolerance of uncertainty, we are prepared to listen to a mind that appears to know best. Like small and naive children, we keep asking how the story ends and the mind is more than willing to oblige with an answer. And so our mind fulfills the role of our **Storyteller** – making up tales that we tell ourselves to satisfy our curiosity. The truth is that our mind knows nothing more than anyone else. It's all pure fiction. We follow along blindly believing the stories, never knowing how bound up they are in falsehood and illusion. Without conscious awareness, we become dependent on our Storyteller. Like a habitual commentator, it follows you everywhere labeling events and judging your experiences as good or bad.

If you want to make the shift to being present, you have no choice but to release the control your Storyteller has over you. Having a story may bring you short-term comfort but it will always keep you from being present long enough to connect with what is real. Have you ever had someone reveal the ending of a movie to you before you watched it? Once you know what is going to happen, don't you lose interest in the movie? The same is true with our lives. Our attention wanes when we think we know how it will unfold. We don't realise that our Storyteller has made the whole darn thing up! We are not engaging in events in an authentic way because we have preconceptions formed from the ongoing commentary running through our minds.

I was recently working with my client, Diane who was facing difficulties in her second marriage. When she first visited me, she was feeling absolutely distraught that she had chosen the wrong man again. She had already visited her lawyer to discuss the divorce arrangements and talked about the whole situation as a fait accompli. As Diane talked me through her situation, it was painfully obvious that their relationship had just hit a bumpy patch. She was discussing divorce within a few weeks of her husband's redundancy from a long-serving position. What was most surprising was that she hadn't even raised her concerns with him. She had talked to a divorce lawyer before she had spoken to her husband! What emerged was that her first partner had gradually fallen out of love with her. Diane had watched with great sadness as he withdrew from the relationship while her own feelings had remained unchanged. When the day came that he asked for a divorce, she felt devastated and it had taken her years to recover from the experience.

Now her second husband was withdrawn and quiet and her Storyteller was only too willing to offer her answers. I imagine that the inner dialogue went something like this:

Diane: *"Oh no, my husband is not himself. I wonder what is wrong"*

Storyteller: *"Uh-oh, we have been here before haven't we?"*

Diane: *"Are you saying this is the same as last time?"*

Storyteller: *"Well let's look at the facts – your husband is quiet, there's clearly something that he is not telling you, he has that look on his face and he doesn't show you any affection. It looks exactly like your first marriage to me"*

Diane: *"Oh no. How does the story end?"*

Storyteller: *"The same as your first marriage. Better get yourself a divorce lawyer, hey?"*

It's obvious in this situation that Diane is drawing premature conclusions but our stories really are that powerful – they blind us to the truth. When Diane sat down and spoke to her husband, he apologised profusely for the upset he had caused and explained that he had withdrawn from the relationship because he didn't want to burden her with his fears about getting a new job. This situation that she perceived as the end of her marriage was actually an act of pure love. It doesn't get much more misguided than that!

You may be thinking that you would easily spot a misleading story like this one, but in how many ways does your Storyteller influence you? Every one of your automatic responses to a look on someone's face or a tone of voice is an example of you being led astray by the stories of your mind. And how often do you think you change your course of direction because you are told the ending of the story? This is an important concept to understand in our journey towards presence. We need to see how the Storyteller manipulates the truth. But how did the Storyteller ever assume such a dominant role in our lives?

When we are born we have no concept of self. There is no sense of separation, just this *me* who is experiencing the moment. If I am hungry, tired or unwell, I will cry. I don't explore my reasons for feeling that way, like trying to evaluate if it is real or emotional hunger. In fact, I won't actually know why I am crying because there isn't an observer separate from my experience that is able to make sense of my emotional state. I cry until something or someone makes me feel better, the suffering is gone and all is well again.

We live predominantly in this purely experiential world up until the age of about seven. But as we are growing and developing, we learn about our experiences from the authority figures around us. Let's say a child wakes in the night because of terrifying monsters in their room. They have no way of discerning real and imagined experiences. The monsters in their dream are as real to them as anything encountered in their waking hours. The child's cries awaken their mother who comes to comfort them. She explains that they were having a nightmare. If they are old enough and their understanding is developed enough to comprehend the concept, she has now given them an important reference point – dreams are not real. The next time the child has a nightmare, it may still wake them up but now they can recall their mother's words and know that it was a dream. The child that once screamed about the monsters in the room now tells the mother "*I had a nightmare*".

And so this process goes as we learn about events and experiences. But it is important to see how we are being *trained* to interpret our world. On a separate occasion, someone takes the toy that this child was playing with and they hit them on the arm. Their mother tells them not to be angry and to play nice. Now the child has a label for the vast array of inner sensations they are feeling (anger) and what they should be doing (playing nice). With the process of analysis and evaluation comes another feature – judgment. And judgment is the fuel for the Storyteller's fire.

As an adult, we no longer exist in that purely experiential world. As well as the *me* in my experiences, there is also an identified self, a sense of '*I*'. This self has been conditioned by all of our previous experiences to respond in automatic and unconscious ways. Now we are no longer responding to the events but to an illusionary tale that the Storyteller is proffering.

Perhaps we have internalised those well-intentioned messages from earlier childhood and believe we should be *nice* no matter what is happening to us. When things upset us, we smile through gritted teeth or reassure people that we are okay even when we are not. Expressing anger is just not something a nice boy or girl would do. Being inauthentically nice can cause us huge problems. We are unlikely to have healthy boundaries or genuine communication. It is difficult to create a deep level of connection in our relationships when we can't express all of our true feelings – whether that is love, joy, sadness or anger.

If we could see through the illusion of the story, we

would realise that anger is a natural human emotion. It would be evident to us that being angry and being nice are not mutually incompatible. We are being manipulated by the Storyteller who persuades us to continually believe the myths we were told in childhood. Just imagine if you could recall every *story* that you had been told in your life. If you could perceive them clearly, wouldn't you be able to observe the complex web of tales that locks you into your current life? We leak our stories in general conversation. Here are a just a few myths that I have heard over the years:

- *"It is disrespectful to be angry or upset with another person. I should keep my feelings to myself"*
- *"I have to answer the phone when it rings, no matter what is happening at the time"*
- *"I can't say no to an invitation. They might not ask me again"*
- *"I can't cancel. I would be letting them down"*
- *"It's impolite to ask for a pay rise. It might jeopardise my job"*
- *"I can't change my career at this stage. It wouldn't be fair on my family"*
- *"If I don't support my children in getting a good education, they will never amount to anything."*
- *"I need to be kind and loving at all times even if I don't feel that way inside"*

- *"I have to keep my partner happy or they will leave me"*

If you have been living by any of these stories, please know that they are not true. They are the result of your overactive and over-involved Storyteller. Make it a priority over the next few days to spot your own stories. You will find them in your automatic responses and reactions. This doesn't have to be an intensive exercise. Remember there is nothing to pursue or fix here. Instead it is something you can gently play with. Every time you spot a story that you are living by, just ask yourself whether it is serving you and if you want to continue believing that tale. You might want to keep a story that tells you things are always working out for you no matter what the evidence. You probably want to ditch a story that you won't have enough money to pay the bills at the end of the month because unless it is the end of the month and you are not paying your bills, you simply cannot know that it is true.

Without challenging our stories, we can't have a full and authentic response to our experiences. The Storyteller acts as a filter to life events and keeps us from being present to what is really happening. Instead, we are reacting and responding to a figment of our imagination. If we want to fully connect with the moment, we must release ourselves from the controlling grip of the Storyteller. Testing our stories against truth is liberating. When you realise how much of your life you have been giving away to the Storyteller, you will want to see through the illusions once and for all. Every story challenged dispels more of the drama and misery of your life. The reward for your efforts is greater peace, deeper connection and more pervasive contentment.

CHAPTER 5

Simplicity

Had you been living in the 19th Century your lifestyle would have been somewhat different. If you were lucky enough to own a house, it would have probably been heated by coal fires and lit by dangerous oil lamps as most homes were without gas and electricity until the 20th Century. Transport would have been by horse or carriage and it would have taken half a day or more to travel fifty miles. There were no supermarkets so your food would have come from local traders. Produce would have been only seasonally available, if at all. Diseases were rife and treatments included a change of air (trip to the coast), or laxative purgation together with bleeding by cup or leech to clear impurities from the body. Not surprisingly, life expectancy was just fifty.

Here we are at the beginning of the 21st Century and everything in the Western world has changed. The technological and evolutionary advances have transformed how we live. Life expectancy is now above eighty and not only do we have access to superior medical care but we can also buy over-the-counter remedies for most ailments. We are able to fly anywhere in the world or, if we'd prefer not to travel, instantly connect with anyone by phone or Internet using satellites. In winter we can have our home heated to the exact temperature we desire at the flick of a switch or cool it down in summer with air conditioning. From this perspective, it is difficult to imagine what else anyone could need but I am sure that our children and grandchildren will look back at this era with amusement at what they consider to be limited lifestyles.

We are really incredibly blessed with all that we have to make our lives run more smoothly. We only have to look to those struggling in less fortunate countries to know how much we have at our disposal. Let us never forget to appreciate a comfortable bed or a good meal. When we examine our lifestyles in this way, we know that living should be easy. Wasn't every invention designed to simplify our life? So why does everything still seem to be so unnecessarily complicated? The majority of people I meet are longing for a break from the ceaseless busyness of their lives. Trying to measure up to the cultural norms of everything we should be, do and have is exhausting and we see the damage it is causing in stress-related illness, debt, separation and divorce. If everything was meant to make our lives easier then why are we finding it quite so tough?

In this second aspect of *surrendering*, we are going to examine the concept of simplicity. When is enough really enough? And how do we create space in our lives to focus on the things that matter most?

What if we could just let it all go?

Imagine arriving at life's check-in desk only to find you are carrying too much baggage. As the clerk advises you of the fees for the excess weight, you begin to realise the price you are paying for traveling heavy. It's time to ditch the complications and simplify our lives. To find contentment and joy, we need space. Letting go of all that is weighing us down is an essential component to leading a life of presence. The challenge is identifying what you really need and what is surplus to requirements. The answers might just surprise you!

A lot has been written and said about the concept of letting go. If you are anything like me, you probably have a preconceived idea of what it means. Perhaps it conjures images of ruthless clutter clears. Maybe it has you evaluating the toxic relationships you would like to remove from your life or you think of the limiting beliefs and fears that you could most definitely live without. Yes, all of these are aspects of letting go but to really make the shift from pursuit to presence, I want to challenge you to go beyond your assumptions. Letting go isn't something you do when your thoughts and environment are cluttered – it is an ongoing process for delving into the depths of your attachments.

There was a point when I thought I knew what this thing called *letting go* was. I didn't just think that I understood it conceptually; I truly believed that I lived it. I was prepared to jump into the unknown – that was letting go, wasn't it? I was prepared to take risks before I knew what would happen – surely that was letting go? I meditated, turned my life over and asked the Divine to guide me in the right direction – that had to be letting go, didn't it? I was a letting go champion, wasn't I?

I couldn't have been more wrong. My version of letting go was being willing to swing on the trapeze of life providing there was a safety net below. Therein lies the issue. Whilst my mind was busy convincing me that I was mastering letting go, my fearful ego was making regular checks of the safety net. In other words, I was prepared to swing totally freely so long as it was within the confines of a carefully planned set of criteria.

Then things changed. I faced a personal challenge that I couldn't fix. I'd stretched myself financially by signing up to an extensive marketing training program. Rather than extending my portfolio of clients, the work that my business depended on began to dry up. Without cashflow, everything in my life seemed to be at risk. I wouldn't be able to continue my career as a coach and if I couldn't make the mortgage payments, I would also lose my family home. I was racked with fear and guilt.

I've always been great at solving problems. I'm optimistic and resourceful. There had to be a solution. I just hadn't looked hard enough or asked the right people or done enough meditation. I upped the ante! The problem continued whilst the clock slowly ticked by. Something was bound to change. I could feel it in my bones. More looking, more asking, more meditation and a sprinkle of praying. Yes, praying. I was sure that had to be the missing ingredient. So I prayed. Nothing changed.

But "*hang on*" I thought; I could do better than that. I'd been on this personal development path for years. I knew the Law of Attraction. Clearly I hadn't overcome this challenge because my focus and alignment was wrong. Ah-ha. That was it. I needed some affirmations; "*This problem is now resolved in ways easier than I could have ever imagined*". I said it every day. I said it morning, noon and night. I wrote it out. I told the mirror. I told anyone who would listen. But still the challenge remained! Eventually I had exhausted my tool kit of resources. I was out of options. For the first time in my life, I gave in to an unfixable problem.

Giving in felt as awful as I had ever imagined it could. Suddenly I was plummeting to the ground with no safety net in sight. Through the layers of my crumbling identity I fell. All of the self-protective shells I had created – being strong, being smart, being resourceful. Then into my fears, I passed by inadequacy, stupidity and shame. Still I kept falling. I wanted someone or something to make it stop, reassure me one more time that it was going to be okay and offer me a lifeline. Nothing happened. No one came.

Then, just when I thought I could take it no longer, my whole being was flooded with peace. I had been so afraid of my world falling apart and not being able to cope. My world was disintegrating but I was still here. I thought I was scared of losing everything. Really I had been terrified of discovering what I might find when the pretty accessories were taken away.

This experience taught me the truth about letting go. As we strip away the layers of conditioning, we find there is nothing ever to fear. When there seemed to be no other option, I had no choice but to surrender. Instead of losing everything, I found the ever-present and unquestionable sense of pure serenity in my soul. The voices of fear disappeared and were replaced by a delicious feeling of wellbeing. I could lose everything but nothing could be taken away. My outer world remained unchanged and yet I was totally transformed. When I stopped needing to protect my False Identity, I discovered something really incredible. Who needs a safety net when you know you can fly?

If you have ever had a moment of total surrender, you may resonate with my experience. For me, it was a *life-will-never-be-the-same-again* flash of insight. I now knew, beyond any doubt, how little I really needed in order to be happy. I dedicated the next few months to ridding my life of the unnecessary complexities that were weighing me down. Life became very simple.

Attachment breeds complexity

I'd like to invite you to take a moment and to reflect on your own life as it stands right now. Does it seem straightforward? Where are you burdened by complexity? If I insisted that you let go of three things in your life, what would they be? Write them down. Just notice how easy you found that exercise. Did you struggle to pick three things or could you have found five, ten or more? I'd like you to keep hold of that list and we will revisit it again for an exercise in just a short while.

I'd also like you to think about what you would be least willing to let go of. Don't worry, I am not going to ask you to give it up, but I would like you to observe your emotional reaction to the idea of releasing it from your life. The things that are important to us bring the most emotionally intense responses. It's one way that we are able to categorise the things we value in our lives. Perhaps it is your partner, a child, your career or a pet.

Anytime that we have a strong urge to hold onto something, we can be described as being *attached* to it. Attachment exists on a kind of invisible scale according to importance or significance. I am probably more prepared to part with a small amount of money than a member of my family! The greater our investment in a person or an object, the less easy it will be to give it up. And as we discovered in the previous chapter when we explored endings, saying goodbye doesn't come naturally to us. But the more that we are holding onto, the more complicated our lives become. Put another way, attachment breeds complexity. We are feeling tired and stressed because so much of our time and energy is directed at maintaining and sustaining our attachments.

A few months ago, my financial advisor got in touch with me to see if I could help another of his clients to develop a career in motivational speaking. He told me that he was a former marine who had been injured in action. His client wanted to use his story to inspire others and already had speaking engagements planned at schools and football clubs. I met Andy one morning for coffee and we discussed the plans for his business. When he told me his personal background, I was deeply moved. Andy had been severely wounded serving with 45 Commando, Royal Marines in Afghanistan when his colleague had accidentally triggered a trip wire attached to two improvised explosive devices. Andy suffered twenty-seven separate injuries. After receiving life saving treatment on the ground by his fellow marines, he was airlifted to Camp Bastion. He woke up two weeks later from a coma at the Selly Oak hospital in Birmingham. He was to stay in hospital for a further three months receiving treatment.

Andy always tells his story with playfulness and humor that I'm sure hides the true depth of the trauma that he and his family went through. But what happened after his injury is truly inspiring. Andy had lost a large proportion of his right thigh in the blast. Thanks to the care of the medical staff treating him, they were able to save his leg.

Requiring daily physiotherapy and rehabilitation, Andy found himself spending the next eighteen months in the Defence Medical Rehabilitation Unit, but unfortunately his leg failed to heal as was hoped. Of course, he was not the only one injured during service. He noticed other soldiers coming in with amputated legs. They were soon fitted with artificial limbs and taught how to walk. In contrast to Andy, they were literally up and running within a few weeks whilst he remained in the unit for months on end.

So Andy made the momentous and life-changing decision to have his leg amputated just below the knee. I don't know about you, but I can sense an attachment to my body parts! How does someone find it in his heart to give up something so valuable and important? On the day of his surgery, aged just twenty-two, Andy stepped into hospital knowing that he would never walk on that leg again.

What drove him to make such a huge sacrifice? He understood that to continue with the healing process would affect the quality of his life, perhaps forever. Letting go opened up a whole new world of possibilities. With the help of an expert team who have got him back on his feet, Andy now runs marathons, organises charity events and speaks of his experiences and a life beyond injury in schools and business. He has appeared on television, surfed in California and abseiled down The Shard in London. I'm not sure any of that would have happened had he still been attached to his leg.[5] When I think about the things that I have fought against giving up, they all pale into insignificance next to Andy's story. Knowing him has helped me to recognise how trivial my attachments really are.

How can we simplify our complex lives?

When I present these ideas, one of the questions I am asked the most is "*how do I let go*?' I have to say that it brings a wry smile to my face. There is a degree of absurdity that the subject of letting go requires techniques to help us. If you were holding a pencil and I asked you let it go, I'm guessing it would cause you no issue.

But surrendering our attachments in life is not so straightforward, especially when we have invested energy and emotion into something significant. It is why we hold onto something that no longer serves us. We may even know it is hurting or damaging us but admitting that we are on a dead end path may just be too much to bear. Like the addicted gambler, we think that one more spin of the wheel may help us recuperate what we have lost rather than walking away and accepting the gifts of learning from the experience.

But by now, you have probably guessed that simplifying our lives requires that we release our attachments. This doesn't mean that you should stop caring but rather permit the natural ebb and flow of life. If you held your hand under a tap, you wouldn't be able to hold onto the water that falls. You would simply have to let it pass through your fingers. A life of presence requires the same degree of fluidity.

One of the problems of our current culture is that the words "*want*" and "*need*" have become somewhat confused. When my children were small, they often used the word *need* excessively. I remember my son once announcing at the top of his voice in the middle of the supermarket that he needed a lollypop or something terrible may happen. This caused great amusement to fellow shoppers but for my son it really did seem like a matter of necessity and they were the only words he had to convey how important it was to him.

We may think we know what we need, but what if it's not true? What if these *needs* are preferences rather than essentials for our existence? It is difficult to argue that you need anything more than food, water and shelter. After all, there are numerous people in the world living with much less right now. There is nothing inherently wrong with wanting more, but if you mistake your desire for need, it rapidly becomes attachment. Our attachments eventually become burdens.

Think back to your list of things that you could let go of that I invited you to consider at the beginning of this section. What has changed? Are you able to now spot your attachments more easily? Can you find other things that you would add to the list?

Just knowing we are attached to things (and people) can be helpful. We see the web of complexity that we are spinning. But is awareness of the attachment sufficient for you to let go? Perhaps for the less significant things – for example, discourteous customer service might reveal your attachment to respect but why would it matter if that person has little influence on your life? An unjust parking fine might reveal your attachment to fairness but how far do you want to pursue the battle? It might just be easier (and take less energy) to simply let it go. Negative feedback or criticism might reveal your attachment to the good opinion of others but for how much longer do you want your sense of worth to be tied up to the subjective perspective of others?

Once you can recognise your attachments, the idea of holding on may just seem ridiculous and wearing. But when you think of the things that mean more to you, you may find that a part of you is still clinging onto the idea of need. Let's see if we can take it one step further and free ourselves from the chains of our deepest attachments.

When I decided to strip my life back to basics, I found the process of letting go invigorating. My bank account was still recovering from my business set back. I realised that if I let go of any unnecessary expenses, my path to financial freedom would be drastically and rapidly improved. With this awareness of attachment, I actually found it much easier to give up things that I had previously relied on. My lifestyle had been so busy that I had outsourced many projects and chores. As trivial as it seems, in all honesty, for a long time, these had been things I felt I needed. Otherwise how could I get everything done to fit with my ideals of the *perfect* businesswoman with the *perfect* family living in the *perfect* house? Making drastic cut backs in this area was not only easy, it was liberating. I found a new joy in taking care of my home and my family. I took back the aspects of the business that assistants had been handling and felt a greater connection to my clients. I cancelled my gym membership and took up running, walking and cycling. Now I had the benefits of being fit and connecting to nature on a regular basis. I kept stripping back my life and yet there was no catastrophe. I discovered I needed very little. Life continued and my bank account began to flourish.

And then I hit upon a stumbling block. On one level I knew it was totally absurd but every time I tried to face up to my attachment, something pulled me back. If you don't know me then you probably don't know that I measure 6ft 2' (187cm). There are pros and cons to being a tall woman; for example, I may stand out in a crowd but I can't get shoes to fit! When I was in my final year at school I was walking down the road engrossed in conversation with a friend and I accidentally knocked into a man coming in the other direction. We both immediately apologised, with him offering a polite "*Sorry mate*!" Had he left it there, I would have read nothing into his comment – "mate" is a common term of endearment in Liverpool. Unfortunately he wanted to amend his error by explaining to me how he had mistaken me for a man. I was an impressionable and insecure teenager and I took his explanation quite literally. I viewed his words as an insult. I spent the next few years of my life believing that I looked like a man until a friend called me "*a beautiful woman*". Her genuine sincerity was enough for me to see the truth – we are all beautiful in our own special way.

When I was releasing my attachments, I bizarrely found that one of my biggest challenges was letting go of my false acrylic nails. These had been a permanent fixture on my hands for the past twelve years. Every two weeks, the nail technician would come to my home to repair or replace them. Not only was it expensive but also time-consuming. I would have to squeeze my nail appointment into a busy schedule. By this point, I was doing more outside activities like gardening and canoeing, and my nails were not only unnecessary, they were also impractical. But I just couldn't bring myself to take them off.

When you find it easier to let go of a business that you have been building and developing for over ten years than false nails, it is a pretty big clue that there is something deeper going on! Lo and behold, when I tuned into my attachment, I saw the problem. My fear was that without nails, my large hands would look like men's hands. Like my son with his attachment to the lollypop, I needed those nails or something terrible might happen! Yes it is laughable to have a story like that keeping me stuck but, left unchallenged, these tales influence our experiences outside of our conscious awareness. Our attachments are fuelled by the stories that prolong and perpetuate them.

There are going to be things that you deeply and profoundly care about – like the thought of losing loved ones that causes your heart to ache. But you can care and still not be attached. My husband is my best friend and my soul mate. I spend most of my time in his company. Were anything to happen to him, I would be devastated and there would be a huge gap in my life. But on some level, as much as I couldn't imagine being without him, life would go on. I would want to live in a way that honored him and our relationship. Knowing

I *want* him rather than *need* him is liberating. I would never choose to let go of someone I love but, without my attachment, I realise that there is never anything to fear.

ⓘ ***Lesson 2** - Letting Go:*

Return to your original list of the three things that you could let go of. Now, I'd like you to take some time to expand your list to include everything that you think you couldn't manage without. Be ruthless and it will pay huge dividends. Work through each item in turn. What is the basis of the attachment? What is the Storyteller saying will happen if you dare to let go? Do you really want to continue your journey weighed down with burdens?

For each item on your list, ask yourself the following questions:

- What would stop me from letting go?
- What am I saying might happen if I let go?
- What might *not* happen if I let go?

Make this an exercise to play with and just notice what arises for you in the process. You may notice the needless complexities and choose to release them.

Every time you let go, you liberate yourself just a little bit more. Any time you feel heavy, simply ask yourself what you are holding onto unnecessarily. Seek out the attachments and challenge them mercilessly. This is the path of simplicity.

The hardest part of letting go is that it is a leap of faith. There are no cast iron guarantees. Anytime we do it to achieve an outcome, we can know this is holding on masquerading as letting go. The essential order of things means surrendering precedes anything new coming in. You cannot know how things will unfold. You are being asked to trust and have faith in a bigger plan. The Divine will only ever ask you to let go of something you have outgrown because there is something better waiting for you. It may not be exactly what you *want,* but it will be what you most *need.* You are not your possessions. You are not your experiences. You are the undeniable presence of divinity in human form. It doesn't get any simpler than that.

Once you understand the power to be found in simplicity, you will discover a new set of criteria with which to evaluate your life. What do you really need? Pick your complexities carefully. A life of pursuit keeps you trapped in cycles of overwhelm and burnout. When you see through the illusion that the more you seek brings added complications rather than happiness, then you realise how little is really enough. Traveling light is essential for presence.

CHAPTER 6:

Forgiveness

I am certainly not the first to write about forgiveness. Many self-growth and spiritual teachings offer forgiveness as a core concept for living peaceful lives. The fastest way to trample down your joy and happiness is to hold onto blame and resentment. You just can't feel good about life whilst anger or hurt is getting in the way.

The idea of forgiveness as an important spiritual concept is nothing new. I am sure even the mention of it probably generates an eye roll or two. Haven't we been there, done that, got the t-shirt? In the past, I would have probably been the first to make a flippant remark if it was suggested that I should do some more forgiveness work to find inner peace and contentment. I would have argued that I had let more than my fair share of people off the hook over the years.

And that is where we get tangled up in our story. Forgiveness is not usually practised in a way that opens the heart to presence consciousness. Even thinking that we have *let people off the hook* is really a cunning strategy deployed by the ego to keep us safely in our position of superiority. If we believe we have taken the higher ground and are passing our pardon on those that we deem deserve it, we are simply masking one illusion with another.

In this third aspect of *surrender*, I want to invite you to move beyond the patterns of hurt that are stealing your peace of mind and keeping you from presence. There may be a part of you that wishes to skip over this section – it is not always easy to delve into your painful story when your wounds are justified. But, on the other side of *real* forgiveness, true freedom awaits you. I would like to guide you there.

The point of forgiveness

Working as a coach, I have been privileged to hear many clients share their personal history. Everyone I meet has experienced trauma. Some have been subject to cruel and unjust situations that seem wrong on every level. Many years ago I was violently attacked by a stranger. I know and understand the pain that is inflicted and the emotional suffering that lasts far beyond the external scars.

When someone hurts us, it seems almost natural to feel hatred towards them. One moment we are tootling merrily along our path when someone does something to wound or upset us. Bang! Our joy comes crashing down. I am not condoning any unkind or offensive behaviour but it is my heartfelt wish for you that you don't continue to experience any unnecessary pain. Without forgiveness, you will simply prolong your own suffering. Are you willing to let someone come between you and your own heart? Forgiveness is a process that removes the blocks and reopens the heart. Blame and hurt will destroy our peace and ultimately injure us more than anyone else ever can. I've witnessed too many people holding onto pain and seen the damage it causes.

Bill was the CEO of a large company based in North West England. Over the years, I had supported him through some major work challenges. When I picked up an unexpected voicemail from him, I assumed that he wanted to book a session to explore an aspect of the business. As soon as we spoke, it was clear that something was seriously amiss. Usually stoic, Bill's voice wavered as he asked for an appointment as soon as possible. I agreed to see him the following morning. When we met, his appearance shocked me. He had lost a great deal of weight and his pallor was tinged grey. I knew something was significantly wrong.

He told me that had been feeling dizzy and breathless but dismissed the symptoms as meaningless. Having recently had the flu, he thought his low energy was just part of the slow recovery. It was only when he collapsed at work with chest pain and had been rushed to hospital that the correct diagnosis was made. Bill was diagnosed with a life-threatening heart condition. Naturally his family and colleagues were concerned for his health and wondered if the stress of his high-powered role was taking its toll. Hints were being made that he should step down as CEO. At only fifty-four years old, he was devastated. He wasn't ready to retire from a job that he dearly loved and found so fulfilling.

When I asked Bill what help he was seeking, he explained that he really didn't buy into the stress theory. His job was demanding at times but nothing outside of his capability. He believed he had good work-life balance and was physically and mentally fit. The opinions from those around him just didn't match his experiences. He wanted to get to the root of what was really going on.

As his mind was drawing a blank, I suggested to Bill that we asked his body for answers. I supported him in a relaxation exercise that concluded with scanning his body for any issues or niggles. Not surprisingly, Bill's attention was drawn immediately to his chest. He described a swirling black hole in the dark recesses of his heart. As he tuned into the energy, I asked if there was a particular feeling or memory associated with it. His face pained as he recalled an episode with his father when he was very young. Bill had accidentally knocked over a pile of paperwork that his father was working on. His furious father grabbed Bill and shook him violently while his mother, petrified with fear, helplessly looked on.

Bill had been so young that he had no conscious recollection of the event. But his body knew differently. He had been holding onto the trauma since he was a child. The memory was stored in his heart because it was there that he felt the pain of being hurt by someone who he knew was supposed to care for him. Now Bill had clarity about the originating trigger for his medical condition but he didn't know what to do with the information. Unfortunately, his father had passed away a few years previously as the result of a cardiac arrest so he couldn't get the apology he felt he needed. I asked him what he would say to his father had he been around and he only wished to know why he had done it.

I asked him to contemplate how his father might respond. Bill's body jerked suddenly and I was curious to know what had come to mind. With tears in his eyes, he said he had felt the response from his father in his body. Not only had he imagined his father apologising profusely for the pain he caused but he also told Bill, "*What I did was wrong. I did it without cause or reason and for that I could never forgive myself. I not only hurt you but I broke my own heart too.*"

Bill's story touched me deeply. Two men damaged by an experience that had been forgotten but not forgiven. Thankfully, Bill got the answers he needed and went on to make a great recovery. He's now back at work and thriving in his position as CEO. He told me that he won't hold a grudge against anyone. Nothing is worth the damage that it causes.

I'd like you to pause for a few moments and reflect on your own life. Are there people or things hurting you? Is the pain or upset you are experiencing happening right now or is it an experience from your past that you are replaying? We have a tendency to continue to rerun and relive mental movies of painful situations, torturing ourselves and extending our suffering. Do you still want to hold onto those stories? What will it cost you if you do?

In the next sections, we are going to explore what real forgiveness is. I invite you to go through this process, not as a means to let someone off the hook, but because you value your own health and wellbeing more. As we have seen, blocks to forgiveness can be highly destructive. Make the decision to clear everything that is standing between you and a joyful, open and whole heart. There is nothing worth falling out of (self) love for.

ⓘ ***Lesson 3*** *- Forgiveness:*

If you would like to try the exercise I did with Bill, I have outlined the process below. As it is easier to close your eyes, you may wish to visit the online workshop or have a friend guide you through the steps.

1. Find a comfortable place to sit where you can place your feet firmly on the floor. Allow your hands to rest comfortably on your lap so that your chest is relaxed and open. Close your eyes if you wish.
2. Take a few deep breaths. With each breath, allow your body to sink more deeply into the chair. Gently elongate your exhale, breathing out any toxins and impurities from your body.
3. As you begin to relax more and more, imagine that you are holding a body-scanning device. Beginning with your feet, scan the body upwards slowly and gently.
4. Your attention may be drawn to a part or parts of your body. If so, tune into the energy. You may experience a particular feeling or see an image. Notice if any memories come to mind.
5. If you discover you are holding onto pain or blame, ask yourself what you would need to fully release it right

now. Be open to every idea and suggestion. You may find you can converse with other people in the situation. Allow what will be to be.

6. When you are ready, gently bring your attention back into the room. Breathe deeply and stretch as you open your eyes once more.

Any experience that we have is valid. If you found this less than easy then you may want to repeat the exercise again at a later date. It sometimes takes practice to learn to tune into our bodies. If you had any intense feelings arise then respect and allow them. Our emotions are our messengers. We cannot be overwhelmed by anything that we welcome. We will be exploring how to honour our emotions in Chapter 10.

The 4 levels of forgiveness

There is a reason why we don't live with peaceful and joyful hearts. Each time we hold onto a negative experience, we cut ourselves off from our true and loving nature. To reclaim all of our parts, we have to forgive. The problem is that we haven't been taught how to *truly* forgive. In fact, there are four levels on the path of forgiveness and most of us never go beyond the first three.

Let's explore a typical example. Someone does something that hurts or harms you. It is likely that your first response is pain. *How could this have happened? How could they do this or say that? Why have they done this to me?* Any thoughts of unworthiness or inadequacy that you have been avoiding will surface and you are back at False Identity #1. If people are unreasonable or the situation seems irresolvable, you are going to feel helpless and powerless. This is the nature of hurt — that something outside of your control has happened and there is nothing you can do about it. This is the first level of the forgiveness diagram (*Level 1*). We are stuck and feeling like the victim.

FALSE POWER

LEVEL 1	I have been hurt. I have no power
LEVEL 2	I can blame you and hate you. I have false power.
LEVEL 3	I can pardon you. This makes me better than you. I extend my false power through my superiority.

REAL POWER

LEVEL 4	There is nothing to forgive. You and I are the same. You are my reflection, my teacher and my gift. I allow my heart to show me this truth. **There is nothing to forgive.**

No one wants to feel this way. Rather than staying present to our feelings of unworthiness, we do what we can to avoid them. This creates an additional reaction to our first response. We want to regain the sense of power that we feel we have lost. How do we do that? We assume the position of anger, blame or revenge directed at who (or what) we hold responsible for our suffering. We will make them pay for what they have done.

This is the first illusion of power. Now, instead of the shame of powerlessness, we experience the surge of energy that accompanies rage or hatred. It may feel a little better but isn't it curious that we would rather despise or blame someone than feel helpless? The problem is that any form of hate is the fastest way to close our own heart. It may give us a sense of control but in reality, we are moving away from our True Self. This is the next level in the forgiveness diagram (Level 2) but it isn't really forgiveness at all. Sadly this is where so much of the world is right now. Using their hurt as the justification for revenge that causes more suffering and simply perpetuates problems.

If you perceive yourself to be a kind or nice person, you may dismiss this idea that you get angry or blaming. It simply won't fit with your identity. But the process of reaching presence consciousness requires your utmost honesty. This need to regain power when we have been hurt can take different forms. Perhaps you suppress your anger and use your pain to manipulate someone into feeling guilty or you hide the seething resentment you are feeling behind patronising words. These passive aggressive techniques are still ploys by our ego to keep control. Be willing to observe your own patterns. Your awareness is the path to freedom.

Is there a situation where you are struggling to forgive? What would need to happen in order for you to find the place in your heart to release the pain once and for all? Don't you owe that to yourself? Why would you choose to suffer one moment longer? Forgiveness doesn't need to be complicated. It only takes one conscious decision to put your own happiness ahead of seeking retribution or the need to be right. The only justice your True Self needs is the understanding that nothing that has happened to you in your past has the power to dictate how you feel in the present moment.

Something inside of us always knows that we should forgive. Anger and blame are consuming – they take energy to be maintained. I have never met anyone who consciously wants to hold onto the pain of being wronged. It doesn't matter how much we have been hurt, we cannot ignore the nudges of our heart calling us home to love, connection and tenderness. We may not be ready to listen. We may not know how to do it. But forgiveness is an inherent part of our True Self and we can only ignore its pleas for peace for so long.

I am sure there have been many times when you have found the heart space of forgiveness. When you think back, what finally swayed you away from hurt, anger or blame? Perhaps it was an apology or a new understanding of the situation? Maybe someone or something else came along and made it easier for you to forgive? It may have just been the passage of time that gently healed the stinging wounds of wrongdoing. You can probably recall a number of occasions where you have been divinely guided towards healing and letting go of resentment and pain.

Every moment of forgiveness has the potential to be an act of pure love. But we don't always fully experience it that way. If I continue to view their actions as wrong; if I feel as though I am letting them off the hook; if I feel that I have some superior position that gives me the right to dole out a pardon, then I am still coming from a place of judgment. This is the next level of forgiveness (Level 3), and it is where most of us tend to end our journey.

The problem with Level 3 forgiveness is that it doesn't free us from our wounds. If we are walking around with a sense of superiority and patting ourselves on the back for taking the higher ground, we are still stuck in the account of what has been *done* to us. Any sense of one-up-manship comes from the conditioned self that would rather protect the False Identity than learn the truth.

Our True Self – the part that is connected to the Divine – knows that there is no place for arrogance in forgiveness. Real forgiveness cannot come from the mind; it has to come from the heart. It is the knowledge that the suffering we experience can only ever be a product of our own story. An open heart never has a sense of inferiority or superiority. Embracing this understanding, we exchange our false sense of power for the undeniable and unwavering power of love. This is the only real forgiveness (Level 4).

Let's take a look at a specific example. Claire discovers that her husband, Jeff, has had an affair. Understandably, she feels devastated (Level 1). As she questions her husband on his motives, Jeff explains that he felt that they had drifted apart, that Claire had seemed disinterested and when he found a connection with another woman, he found it difficult to resist. Claire is furious. How dare he blame her for the situation! She had also been finding the relationship tough but hadn't jumped into bed with another man. She lists all of the things that Jeff has done wrong in the relationship. She tells him to pack a bag and leave the house. As terrible as the situation feels, she now has some sense of control. Rather than experience any feelings of inadequacy or unworthiness, she can direct her anger and blame at him. There is a small degree of comfort that comes from moving into Level 2.

Over time, Claire's wounds begin to heal. The intensity of the emotion begins to subside. Jeff goes to great lengths to prove his love to her. Once more, he woos her as he did at the beginning of their relationship. In the face of so much warmth and affection, Claire's heart begins to soften. She realises that she wants her marriage with Jeff to continue and to do that she has to forgive him. For the sake of her relationship, she agrees to pardon him. She is willing to take the higher ground and grant him another chance (Level 3).

She allows Jeff to move back home. Everything on the surface appears resolved. But if Jeff is home late from work, she worries and has to call him to find out where he is. If he doesn't answer his phone, she frets until she can get hold of him. Whenever an area of conflict brews between them, she reminds Jeff of how she forgave him for the affair. She constantly tells him of how she suffered and what it cost her to take him back. Jeff is wracked with guilt that slowly eats away at his self-esteem. Every time Jeff does anything to upset her, Claire is tortured by the familiar feelings of pain and hurt. In this example, can you see how Claire is still trapped by the story of what happened?

Unconditional forgiveness requires us to go beyond our perceptions of a situation. Only from here can we find the inner peace and freedom that we want. There is no story at Level 4. The tricky part is being willing to seek the truth and not settle for the illusion that our Storyteller offers us. Without unconditional forgiveness, Claire cannot move on. The slightest wrong move by Jeff plunges her back into insecurity. And so long as Jeff feels guilty and responsible, he is trapped with her. He may stay there or eventually tire of the burden. We can only imagine the pain that Claire will experience if Jeff can't cope with the guilt and decides to leave her.

This example is created for the purpose of explanation and clarification but I have heard similar accounts from clients many times. The saddest part is discovering how long people have suffered unnecessarily. There is no escaping the fact that affairs can cause pain. But how the story unfolds after an affair can be very different if we are prepared to stay with the experience long enough for the revelation of something new. Situations like these *can* be fully healed but only when we are prepared to reach for a new level of consciousness. So what is the real truth?

The reality is that the only enemies we will ever have are within. Everything that exists only has the meaning that we assign to it. A tree is just a tree. Sky is just sky. Behaviour is just behaviour. Whether we judge that behaviour as being acceptable or unacceptable is down to our own values and criteria. We observe the actions of others and we set the rules. Nothing is inherently good or bad except what our thinking tells us. No enemy lives outside of you. Your enemies are your own thoughts about people and experiences. There is no such thing as bad weather. There is no such thing as a bad day. And there is no such thing as a bad person. It only exists in you.

The art of unconditional forgiveness

Now you might be thinking "*hang on a ring-a-ding minute, I'm not buying into this rose-tinted view of the world*". So let me be clear; I am not asking you to condone any behaviour that causes another to suffer, but I am inviting you to shift perspective so you can release yourself from your own limiting stories. You can't fight an enemy without contributing to the stress and suffering. Wars are self-perpetuating when both parties are fixated on being right. Defeating your enemies only comes from dropping your armor and weapons and allowing your True Self to reveal what the moment is showing you – not about them but about you. To make the shift to level 4 forgiveness involves welcoming the revelation. The heart knows that at the soul level we are all deeply intertwined. Every experience is a co-creation that requires the involvement and engagement of both sides. Instead of seeking to point the finger of blame, we can ask for Divine wisdom to show us where we are continuing the battle.

Let's return to the story of Claire. Remember that we

want to suspend our judgment of right and wrong in order to discover a new truth. Our True Self does not assign blame but seeks to know that which that prevents us from living in presence consciousness. When we find that, we will transcend our limited story. Claire's husband had an affair. That is an undeniable fact. But with a pure and unconditional heart, can we really judge him as bad? What was Jeff seeking when he fell for another woman? Love? Affection? Connection? In a misguided way, he was seeking the love that his soul yearned for. Could he have spoken with Claire about his feelings? Yes. Could he have recognised his feelings without acting upon them? Yes. There are hundreds of permutations to how the story could have played out. The reality is that Jeff did what he did because of the situation he found himself in at the time. We cannot judge his behaviour as wrong without making an enemy within us.

Exploring the situation with an open heart and mind might bring Claire to a new understanding of why Jeff made the choices he did. But that information is not sufficient to free her from the story. Only unconditional forgiveness can release us from our suffering. Jeff was a character in her tale but it was still her story. To work through the levels, we must be prepared to ask what the story shows us. If Claire can sit with the hurt she feels for long enough, she opens up to a new discovery. What was the situation revealing to her? Perhaps she can see the degree to which she was disconnected from her own feelings. Maybe now, she can understand how she was withholding love and affection from Jeff and also, more significantly, from herself. She may still feel the pain but rather than closing off to the world, the hurt she has experienced can be the doorway to immeasurable self-love. She only receives this gift if she can suspend her story and let her True Self guide the way.

Choosing to allow pain to reveal the healing that needs to take place is one of the most challenging concepts we will ever be asked to do. Our human nature is to avoid pain at all costs. But when embraced, our hurt can bring a heartfelt message. Now we can see that person who did me wrong is merely my reflection – my teacher – my gift. They are showing me the areas in which I have been neglecting love. My work is to find ways to learn from and appreciate the message rather than to despise the messenger.

In the earlier exercises, did you find areas where you have yet to forgive unconditionally? Are you willing to go there in the name of freedom? Do you want the revelation of the truth? Do you want to discover what it means about your relationship with yourself? If so, the first step is to identify the judgment you are making about the other person. What do you perceive as bad or wrong about what they have said or done? For example, you may be thinking that your boss micro-manages your work and you have no space to breathe. If I asked you to judge the behaviour, you might describe him as controlling.

Level 3 forgiveness might say something like, "*My boss does the best he could. He's not done as much personal growth work as me*". Can you spot the position of superiority? Our True Self knows better. To shift to Level 4, we have to see our judgment as perception and not real truth. Remember that behaviour is just behaviour – we are the ones adding the meaning. You don't need to do anything with this information. Simply bring your awareness to the situation so that you can see how you are holding onto your story.

If we want to be free, we must allow the situation to reveal something about ourselves that was previously hidden. What does your story uncover about your own inner relationship? If I say my boss controls me, then I can ask, "*How I am controlling myself?*" Perhaps you can begin to see the *match*. This person who has hurt or upset you is showing you the areas you have yet to heal.

When the moment does reveal a new truth about you, welcome it with an open heart. It is pointing you towards an outdated strategy you have been using to protect your False Identity. We are on the journey to re-connect with our True Self and this is Divinity showing you the way. Embrace every revelation with self-acceptance and self-love. Judgment of anyone (including ourselves) belongs to the self-serving ego and has no place in a life of presence. When you see the truth, make a conscious decision to love yourself. This is a time of vulnerability and compassion. You need your own kindness.

The next time you feel hurt, do not stay in powerlessness, do not seek revenge and do not try to let them off the hook. Instead, turn your attention gently within and ask the light of your heart to give you the gift of self-awareness. When we learn to forgive unconditionally, we realise that there is never a need to manage or manipulate the world. Every situation is about us. It has to be because we tell it through our own story. If I perceive someone as controlling, it is because controlling lives in me. If I see the world as unloving, it is because I lack love. When I witness the truth in my heart, I collapse the myth that I believed to be true and the past can no longer influence anything in my present moment.

When I talked about these ideas on one workshop, a delegate asked indignantly whether she had to now revisit all the relationships where she *thought* she had already forgiven them. My answer is simple – only if you want the absolute freedom that comes from living fully in this moment without preconceptions or limitations. Only you can know how important that is to you.

I want to conclude this section with a brief note on self-forgiveness. Often we find it much harder to be kind to ourselves than to others. But if you ever find yourself regretting something you have done or said in the past, it can only be because you have learnt from the situation. Hindsight is a wonderful thing. Guilt and remorse are simply the evidence of your evolution. Any self-blame will take you back into your conditioned thoughts about your lack of worthiness. Judging yourself for past mistakes only proves that you are listening to the Storyteller rather than connected to your True self. There is no blame or guilt in the True Self – only love and acceptance. You will make mistakes. Everyone does. But I can promise you that the more loving and kind you are to your self, the less you will hurt or offend others. Healing your own heart and allowing love to permeate your soul is one of the greatest gifts you can bring to the world.

CHAPTER 7

Allowing

So much of our lives are spent not wanting experiences that have already happened. Instead of embracing the current moment, our attention is firmly fixed on what has gone before. But we don't drive whilst looking in the rear view mirror. Your life isn't happening in the past – it is what is occurring right here and right now. The ultimate surrender is when we allow ourselves to yield fully to the present moment.

Driven on by our judgmental Storyteller, we are consistently categorising events as good and bad, wanted and unwanted. When things don't go the way we want them to, we object and argue. If life is not playing by our rules we set about fixing it – believing that we can only feel happy when things are in order. How much of your life feels like problem solving? It's a never-ending process of reordering, resolving and reworking. No wonder we feel so tired and stressed.

In presence consciousness, you cease fixing and reordering. You start to better understand your role in the Divine plan, not as the controller of life events but as the participant. We start to realise that *our* order is not the same as *Divine* order. Your job is to allow the gentle unfolding of the path before you with childlike curiosity and interest. You begin to see the perfect arrangement of life that no longer demands intervention or meddling. All that is required is your fullest attention and surrender to the present moment as it arises. In this chapter, we are going to explore how we can allow (and enjoy) life without demanding it to be different to how it actually is.

Ditch the drama

My husband and I used to watch a UK television soap opera called *Hollyoaks*. Set in Cheshire, it is a mystery why any of the characters would choose to live there as it has to be one of the most dangerous places you could find. Bombs, fires, murders and robberies are practically a daily occurrence. Marriage should definitely be avoided. Most weddings have ended with the bride or groom in a body bag! In all honesty, we rarely made it through an episode without a fit of giggles. The over-dramatic story lines are so far fetched as to be ridiculous.

If we watch a TV show or a movie, we know that it is purposefully dramatic. The plots are meant to capture our attention and engage us. It is all done in the name of entertainment. But when it comes to our own lives, we aren't always able to see how we are creating our very own dramas – and when we take the starring role, it is not always so funny!

So what is wrong with a bit of drama in our lives? There is nothing inherently wrong with having an *event-full* life. We do need a degree of stimulation to do even the simplest of things – like getting out of bed in the mornings. The real issue is that many of the events that fill our lives really comprise of unnecessary anxiety and self-invented stress. We are so caught up in the endless drama that we can't even discern what is real and what is a story.

In pursuit consciousness, we are simply passengers on a runaway train. We rush from problem to problem with hardly a moment to draw breath. It can feel as though we are a human punch-bag, scarcely finding our feet before the next blow knocks us down again. Drama convinces us that all the good stuff happens on the outside. Rather than staying centred and alert to our inner world of thoughts and feelings, we are more likely to seek external things to engage our attention. Pointless traffic jams occur when cars have a minor bump and drivers slow down to see what has happened. Celebrity gossip magazines fight for readership by outdoing each other with the most shocking headlines. Theme parks launch bigger and more thrilling rides, pushing our bodies to their absolute limits and scaring us silly!

We are drawn to these external pulls because fundamentally we want to know and feel that we are alive. If I offered you a life of adventure and excitement, or one that is endlessly dull and mundane, which one are appeals more?

In our current culture, fast and furious is favoured over slow and steady. We want to *feel* deeply and intensely and we will seek satisfaction wherever it is offered. Why do you think that news programmes and papers cover the most appalling and scandalous stories? We are misled into thinking that *the News* is a fair representation of reality when, in fact, all that is good in the world far outweighs the troubles. For things to continue as they are, we have to buy into the drama, but at what expense?

Firstly, we give away our peace of mind. Emotionally arousing or highly stressful events cause a surge of the hormone adrenaline (epinephrine) to flood our bodies. This stimulates the heart rate, contracts blood vessels, and dilates air passages, all of which work to increase blood flow to the muscles and oxygen to the lungs ready for fight or flight. These physiological changes and the accompanying high are often known as the adrenaline rush.

Following the surge of adrenaline, the body is left to cope with the after-effects. Adrenaline releases glucose into the blood stream, raising blood sugar and giving the body additional energy with no outlet. As the body attempts to reset the system to handle the excess adrenaline, you will feel restless, irritated or despondent. To escape these feelings, we need time for our bodies to recover but many people have become reliant on another hit of adrenaline. So begins a cycle of dependency on stressful events. Far too many of us live this continual rollercoaster pattern as part of our normal day-to-day functioning. A life of pursuit is characterized by cycles of thrilling highs followed by devastating lows.

Living this way, we have learnt to anticipate difficulties and troubles, placing us in a constant state of high alert. This has an enormous impact on our physical, mental and emotional well-being. Stability and tranquility will elude us. We can't live on an even keel whilst feeding our addiction to drama. Drama prevents us from experiencing the gentle beauty and wonderment of our inner world. I'm not for one moment suggesting that you should stop doing things that you enjoy. Pick your own adventures for life. But do notice that there is a big difference between consciously choosing to participate in an event that excites you and being constantly on the receiving end of anxiety and challenges. If you are fuelled by drama, your subconscious mind will be creating crises out of problems just to ensure you get your next hit of adrenaline!

When I first met Patricia, she was convinced that she was in a cycle of bad luck. Having been made redundant from a job that she loved, she had struggled to find another position and eventually set up as a freelancer. As the funds were running low, she was doing her best to spend as little money as possible. Yet she seemed to be plagued with unforeseen expenses. She was involved in a minor car accident and, although not her fault, the other party was driving without insurance leaving her to foot the repair bill. Both her washing machine and fridge had stopped working on the same day. The final straw had been an unexpected tax bill, which more or less matched her remaining savings. In a last ditch attempt to regain control, she had booked a business planning session with me. She was fairly desperate to create an income stream as fast as possible, and was prepared to do whatever it took.

Patricia was locked into the pursuit consciousness cycle. Surrounded by problems and crises, she could only find one solution – to make more money as quickly as possible. With the best of intentions, she was driving, pushing and fighting for control of her life. Rather than bringing her the freedom that she wanted, it was simply pulling her further and deeper into the drama. Like a tangle weed, drama grows and wraps itself around our roots, eventually strangling our sense of peace and stability. The only way to be free is to cut off the weed at its source. Instead of jumping into the business plan, I wanted to invite Patricia to ditch the drama in her life.

The problem with drama is that it is both addictive and suffocating. Human beings are generally very resourceful so we can handle a great deal of challenges and difficulties before we hit breaking point. The downside is that we get sucked into self-defeating patterns of behaviour long before we are aware of the signs. So how can you know if your life is fuelled by drama? The easiest way to spot your own patterns is by asking how you handle unforeseen events. How do you react to an unexpected bill or expense, or to the news that someone has said something cruel or mean about you behind your back, or to last minute delays to your travel plans? If drama is running your life, your response will be out of proportion to the situation. Feeling stressed or anxious, you may immediately launch into taking defensive action to resolve the issue – phoning to query the bill, challenging the person who said the unkind words or marching up to the travel company's customer service desk to complain (the fight response). Alternatively, you might actively avoid difficult or challenging situations and simply worry, fret and have sleepless nights about what has happened (the flight response).

In presence consciousness, we learn that life is never as it seems. When the unexpected happens, we are more likely to be curious or intrigued. We allow events to unfold, recognising that energy is eternal and so nothing can ever be final. We might be interested in what is happening but will never sacrifice our inner peace and contentment for the rush of adrenaline that the Storyteller is peddling. We learn to suspend our judgments and assumptions about the situation and the people involved, knowing that all meaning resides in us.

Even when we have made the shift, people around us will still ask us to buy into the drama. I once commented on a social media petition I had been asked to sign, saying that whilst I fully supported the intent of the protest, I didn't want to join something that placed me in opposition of the original cause. For example, I will actively support charities that help young, single mothers but I wouldn't protest against lowering the age of sexual consent. This is a personal choice because I want my energy to flow towards something constructive rather than defending or fighting for a position.

When I made my comment on Facebook, I faced an enormous backlash. It was suggested that my ambivalence was part of the original issue. One lady went so far as to say that with my attitude, women still wouldn't have the vote. This is the drama cycle at work. Others may want you to react as they do and it can take some awareness (and initial investment of energy) to sidestep the hooks.

Contrary to that lady's opinion, I do care deeply about what is happening in the world. Avoidance is as much a part of pursuit consciousness as attack and defence. I have learnt to care without being caught up in the drama. Are there huge atrocities in the world that need to be addressed? Without a doubt, but if I allow the story to consume me, I disempower myself to make any meaningful contribution. We simply can't be of any service to another if we are unhappy, fearful, angry or stressed. There is a huge difference between speaking and acting upon your authentic truth and being caught up in the story. You experience freedom from the drama when you are able to witness events with compassion and understanding whilst staying centred enough to make the right choices in the moment – no matter how much others may disapprove.

In Patricia's one-hour session, I helped her to perceive the self-defeating cycle that was holding her captive. Instead of trying to fix and resolve the problems she was facing, I encouraged her to explore other meanings and possibilities. I didn't want her to come up with specific actions but rather to view the issue from multiple perspectives. Part of the process of releasing our drama stories is to make peace with all eventualities. Together we uncovered Patricia's worst-case scenario of losing all her money. Like so many of us, Patricia had been vividly imagining such an outcome and already had a clear idea of what living on the street would be like. That's how drama locks us in. It presents an image so awful and horrendous that any indication of its forthcoming appearance has us desperately fighting for control or fleeing for safety. We start to believe the story. Every bill that landed on Patricia's doorstep was the evidence of her worst fears coming true.

Exploring her nightmare scenario wasn't easy or comfortable for Patricia but, when she did, she could find other possibilities that she hadn't been able to see when drama was in charge. It dawned on her that she would be entitled to income and housing benefits and she knew her friends and family would support her if needed. Would she want to rely on these sources of revenue? Absolutely not. But if that helped her to get back on her feet, it was a temporary situation that she could live with. Now her current challenges could be seen as they really were. Disruption and inconvenience, but nothing worth losing sleep over.

When we step out of the drama cycle, things start to change. Patricia contacted me a couple of months later with some good news. She had secured a freelance contract a couple of days per week. She had been able to purchase a new fridge and washing machine on an interest free credit deal. And what had surprised her most was a letter explaining that an error had been made and the wrong tax code had been assigned to her account. The upshot was that she didn't owe the money that they had originally asked for.

I like to think of these happy occurrences as the joyful by-product of ditching the drama and living with presence. If we do things in an attempt to control the situation, we just submerge ourselves more deeply in the story. The only thing worse than having things go against you is when you invest considerable energy and effort into attempting to create a pleasing outcome and it still doesn't go your way! Ditching the drama has to be a full release of expectation and control

– the absolute willingness to yield to life's events exactly as they are. It is a conscious decision not to give away your peace and happiness, no matter how contrary the evidence may seem.

Once you break free from the drama cycle, life will respond accordingly. If you no longer need the adrenaline rush to sustain you, you will find a more gentle and delightful energy source that comes from being the curious witness to a wonderful world that knows how to rebalance and restore itself naturally without your intervention. In a life of presence, the unwanted will still happen. Bills will come, people will talk about you, delays will occur, but you choose not to make anything of them. Instead of consuming your attention and energy, they just pass through with gentle acknowledgement and compassion. Without your meddling, life will unfold in many unexpected and delightfully surprising ways.

My husband and I witness this magical process consistently. Issues arise but we know that they will self-resolve. To give you just one example, we joke about our ability to attract free meals. If we find ourselves in a restaurant and our food is poor quality or delayed, our bill is always taken care of. We don't have to cause a scene, just gently and politely inform the waiter of our experience and the manager cancels our tab. It has happened too many times now to be coincidental. So we don't buy into the drama – we have delicious food first time around or we get a free meal – either way is better! Recently my friends experienced a five-hour delay to their weekend trip. The compensation they got was actually greater than the cost of the original flights. It may not always be exactly what we want or how we want it but life always re-compensates you in some way – it is part of the natural rebalancing process.

We will explore the idea of non-meddling later in the book when we look more closely at the concept of taking action. For now, let's complete this section with a short exercise on ditching the drama.

ⓘ ***Lesson 4*** *- Ditch the Drama:*

I'd like you to take a fresh piece of paper and make a list of all of the challenges and difficulties you currently face. As you fully consider each one, I'd like you to rank the level of drama it creates in your life on a scale of 1-5. If it is a mild irritation (perhaps a difficult phone call to make) then you would give it 1 point. If it consumes enormous amounts of your attention and energy (maybe an ongoing relationship or job problem) then it would score the full 5 points.

Depending on the length of your list and the assignment of points, you will be able to see more clearly whether drama is controlling your life. For each of the items on the list, I invite you to answer the following questions:

How much does this matter in your life?

If it isn't important, then you may choose to simply let it go, using the processes outlined in the earlier chapter on simplicity. If you can't simply let it go, then continue with the questions below.

What is this problem evidence of? What's the story you are telling yourself?

Without censoring, just notice your responses to this question. It will help to reveal any self-defeating patterns of thought.

What is the worst-case scenario? How will you deal with that?

This question may be uncomfortable but it is the fastest way to deal with unnecessary drama. Stay with the second part of the question until you find a place of peace with the scenario. If you struggle to find an answer, talk to a neutral friend or colleague for ideas – it is always easier to see beyond a problem when you are not actively involved in it.

If the worst-case scenario doesn't materialise, what might happen instead?
What else could happen that you have not yet considered?

How will your life be different when this is no longer an issue for you?
How you will be feeling when this is problem is resolved?

When you allow and trust divine order to restore the balance, you can sit with a problem without becoming over emotionally involved in the story. Enjoying a life free from drama may well become your new addiction – there is no substitute for tranquility and contentment. Only you can decide not to give away your inner peace unnecessarily again.

Practising non-resistance

I regularly hear people talking about how hard life is these days. In pursuit consciousness, there is no denying that life appears difficult. After all, you assume all responsibility for fixing problems and directing the course of your life. As we have seen, trying to maintain control is an exhausting and impossible task. In presence consciousness, we begin to realise that life is as tough or as easy as we choose to make it. This has nothing to do with external events but to the degree in which we *resist* our experiences.

This is an important distinction to make. Most of us think that contentment stems from having an easy life. But how do we define easy? I'm sure you know people who have highly complex lives and appear to be extremely happy. Then there are others who have relatively few demands and yet joy eludes them. Ease is therefore a subjective perception and open to interpretation. Some people find running long distances relatively easy. Some people find writing relatively easy. Some people find speaking in public relatively easy. Some people find stitching up a bloody wound relatively easy. And for each of these examples, there are many others who would consider such things to be pure torture.

If it is not the content of a situation that dictates the degree of difficulty or discomfort, there must be another governing factor. Our talents, skills and knowledge are core parts of the formula. But more than that, our experience will seem to be easy or hard depending on our attitude towards it. If it is something we want, we will find it easy to embrace. But if it is something we don't want, we will tend to reject or resist the experience.

Resistance occurs when we push against the flow – the greater the resistance, the more challenging the experience. You can check this concept out with a partner.

Place your hands out in front of you with your palms against theirs. Take it in turns to push against each other's hands. Vary the degree of force (resistance) that you use. You'll find that the more force the other person applies, the harder it becomes to push their hands. In life, our resistance to circumstances we enjoy will be extremely low and much higher to unwanted or unwelcome situations.

Before I met my husband, Tim the idea of pleasurable running couldn't have been further from my mind. I would happily run around a tennis court to pursue a little yellow ball, but running a 10k would have been my idea of living hell. Tim had a completely different mindset. Running long distances was his idea of clear space and time to think. One day, in a temporary lapse of sanity, I asked Tim to take me out for a gentle jog. It was somewhat validating to find that even running at a snail's pace was as awful as I expected it to be. I was practically hyperventilating by the end of our street!

Everything in me wanted to reject running. How could it be possible to find space to think when every inch of my awareness was focused on the pain of tiring muscles, the shortness of breath and the monotony of placing one foot in front of the other? But I kept listening to Tim's account of his enjoyment and I was a little envious. If I wanted to find the pleasure in running, something was going to have to change.

I started to play with my experiences and I found that

the quality of my *running pleasure* would change depending on where I was focusing my attention. It felt more enjoyable to run when I was looking a few yards in front of me rather than thinking about how much further I had to go. I learnt that if I paid attention to the tightness in my muscles, then they hurt more but if I tuned into the rhythmic nature of my breath, any suffering would dissolve. I discovered that when I gave myself permission to run at a pace that suited my body, then I could run further and faster than when I tried to beat my personal best time – my speed fluctuated more but overall I was quicker when I listened to my body's signals rather than forcing or pushing myself on.

I am sure this is common sense to any runner but for me it was enlightening. I now had a direct experience of running 10k and enjoying it. But what I really learnt from running was that the quality of every event is dictated by the degree of our resistance to it. When I resisted running, it hurt. When I relaxed, it was more pleasurable. The more we fight against an experience, the more we will suffer. The more we embrace it, the easier and more enjoyable it will be.

All negativity stems from resistance. In the moment that our reality fails to measure up to our expectations and we argue against what is happening, we are in resistance. If we find ourselves objecting to the natural flow of life, the only outcome can be anxiety, fear, irritation or grief. You can't stand against anything and not experience negative states. They come as a package deal. Any time we wish things to be different to how they are, we simply create more turmoil. Therefore, our task is to spot our resistance. With awareness, we re-establish choice. We can agree to life's flow or we can fight against it and experience the consequences. The decision is ours.

Once we recognise that our objection to life experiences is the source of our discomfort and pain, it seems only natural to want to surrender to what is taking place. This is the subject of many spiritual teachings – to understand that we can end our suffering instantaneously by finding a way to agree with what is occurring. If you always want what is happening in the moment then how can you ever be hurt? Acceptance offers an alternative to experiencing pain. That is what makes this concept of non-resistance so appealing.

Intellectually, we may understand that the path of non-resistance is the doorway to freedom. But, if I suggested that from this point forwards you welcome every experience unconditionally, my guess is that it wouldn't be too long until you found something else to object to. This is the flaw in the general strategy of practising non-resistance. We can aspire to embrace every circumstance but unless we are enlightened masters, the real experience is likely to be very different. Try it for a few hours and see how long you can go before your complaints or objections arise once more. It is even worse when you catch yourself in resistance and know that you are holding yourself apart from the freedom you seek. It is a bitter pill to swallow. Now you are resisting your own resistance. Try getting out of that one!

To be released from this trap, we need a new level of understanding that allows us to transcend the double bind. Firstly, we need to understand that we cannot defeat resistance. As with any other aspect of life, arguing against it won't set you free. In fact, it only amplifies the hold it has over you. It is impossible for anything that you hate to leave your life. Your ongoing attention to it makes it so. To truly transform resistance, we need to better understand its purpose and function. What can resistance show us that, without it, we could never see?

Resistance is our teacher. Rather than being something to try to avoid, it offers a powerful tool for our evolution. It will show us the self-imposed limitations that have been holding us back. We will finally be able to observe where we are trying to manipulate and demand conformity to our expectations. It won't be comfortable but it does offer a real opportunity to free us from our patterns of control.

Another way of thinking of resistance is as the refusal of a lesson. If we are rejecting an experience, what can we ever learn from it? Imagine sitting in a classroom with your eyes closed and your fingers in your ears. How much knowledge would you acquire? When we learn to bring the source of our resistance into our awareness, we are given a unique opportunity to uncover a new truth. For a brief moment in time, that which has lain dormant in our psyche is available for conscious processing. Hanging onto our illusion of control is the avoidance of evolution. Only by knowing the truth can you escape. A willingness to let the resistance teach you something new is the only way to break the cycle.

Where do you find yourself most commonly in resistance? Do you object to spending money or paying your bills? Do you get defensive in the face of negative feedback or criticism? Do you dislike an aspect of your work like paperwork or company politics? Does it irritate you when someone else tries to tell you what to do or advises caution on your big plan? Do you avoid difficult situations because you fear or dislike conflict? Do you rush to defend family members or friends from the accusations or judgments of others? Do unexpected circumstances or changes in plans send you reeling?

The first step in learning from resistance is to simply notice its presence. Where do you find yourself complaining, avoiding, defending, arguing, dismissing or being aggressive? These are the indicators of your resistance. Find a specific example of a situation that you have resisted in the last few days. Noticing it doesn't mean you are doing anything wrong, just that there is something new you are ready to learn.

So here's a question to ponder – did the resistance exist before the troubling circumstance arose? Put another way, is the situation that you find yourself in the cause of your resistance? This is where we are most likely to trip ourselves up. When something happens to disrupt our peace, we blame the situation rather than understanding that the point of resistance was already there inside us. The situation didn't cause the resistance; it revealed it. Our unconscious patterns of thought have now been brought into our conscious awareness. We can fight against the revelation or we can invite in wisdom and let it show us the obstacles that have been blocking our own peace of mind. Your awareness sets you free.

I love this quote from Pema Chodron[6]:

"When the bottom falls out of our life, we know we're in such a tender place. And we know that it is actually very rich. But it hurts so much, that the habits we've used in the past to keep ourselves comfortable are going to rise so strongly"

Be grateful that your limiting habits do rise up so strongly because in your observation of them, they can be released. Your resistance has shown you where you most need to heal. Now the therapeutic process can truly begin.

You are on the brink of transformation.

Underneath every point of resistance is a fear. If there were nothing to be afraid of, why would you feel the need to push back? You would simply let it pass by without your attention or acknowledgment. To give you an example, if I told you that I disliked your blue hair then, unless you actually do have blue hair, it probably won't bother you very much. There would be no attachment — and therefore no resistance — to what I said. You might laugh about my comment later but my guess is that you wouldn't give it another thought.

But what if I called you malicious or stupid? Does that create a stronger reaction? Such statements tap into thoughts of inadequacy and unworthiness created in childhood. Remember we learnt early in life that we had to be deserving of love and affection and that we should hide any aspect of our personality that didn't fit the standards others held. So now, when you are called malicious or stupid, your fears are triggered. Bad things might happen if you are not perceived as kind or clever. Rather than facing up to your *not good enough* thoughts, you get defensive or aggressive in an attempt to deflect the hurt. Can you see that the unworthiness already existed? The person making the statement didn't create those feelings, only triggered them. The comments that you now resist and defend against are actually showing you the limiting beliefs. When you embrace the revelation you can see that the real work is healing your thoughts of unworthiness, not disposing of the critic.

Every point of resistance contains the potential disclosure of your limited thoughts and fears. Your reaction to an unexpected bill might be showing you your scarcity beliefs. Someone making a negative comment about your child might highlight your thoughts of inadequacy about parenting. Being let down by a friend might bring up your feelings of isolation or loneliness. A last-minute change to a deadline for a project might reveal your time shortage thinking. There is a gift to be found in every moment of resistance. When you notice you are in opposition to an experience, simply ask yourself, "*What do I not want to know about myself in this moment?*" Your awareness will begin the process of transformation.

ⓘ ***Lesson 5*** - *Working with Resistance:*

Not all resistance is easy to pinpoint but there is a foolproof way to spot when you are allowing the natural flow of life and when you are fighting it. Our body literally reacts to resistance. Think of something that you would really like to happen and feels good to imagine? Notice how your body feels when you hold that idea in your mind. For example, I would like to live in a log cabin one day.

When I visualize that picture, I can feel my head, chest and stomach areas open and expand. You might notice something similar in your own scenario.

Now think about something that you really don't want to experience or happen. I can go there easily when I consider doing my filing! Again, notice how your body responds. You may feel heaviness in your body or find that you begin to hunch over. When we are in resistance, our body contracts. Think about your wanted situation again and observe how your body opens and expands once more. We can use this as an easy and effective way of tuning into resistance. Any time you notice the contraction, just ask, "What am I resisting right now?"

I would never want to appear flippant about resistance. For the purpose of explanation, I have used fairly generic examples to highlight the key points. Of course, there will be unwanted events and experiences that challenge us to the core of our being. It is not about defeating resistance; it is about being willing to learn from it. Guy Finley says; "*I have never seen a storm that doesn't pass*"[7]. Every storm is transient. How will it change you?

Surrendering our false identities

I began this book by explaining how we create false identities – that we internalise messages from well-meaning authority figures about our own inadequacies (False Identity #1) and then develop a protective self-image to keep the thoughts of unworthiness at bay (False Identity #2). Letting go of these masks isn't easy but if we want inner peace and contentment we have to move beyond the containment of our false selves. Without presence, the fearful ego will run the show. When we are relating to the world from a limited and bogus sense of who we are, how can we ever have authentic experiences or relationships?

The false self thrives on identification. Our protective nature (False Identity #2) loves to create a positive impression to portray to the world. It will reject or deny anything that threatens its self-image. It laps up positive feedback and encouraging statements from others if they are perceived as good (like kindness, beauty, wisdom, intelligence or toughness) but woe betide anyone who calls into question its strengths.

On the other hand, the self that believes it is inadequate (False Identity #1) seeks out evidence of our failings. In the moment that we are found to be wanting, this nature has the stick to beat ourselves with. When this identity is in charge, we know that we can never be good enough. Every criticism or mistake is further reinforcement of our weaknesses.

Let's be clear, both of these identities are illusionary. You are neither perfect nor a failure. Believing either thought fuels the ego but nothing more. When we make a statement that begins with "*I am...*", we are actually assigning a label to ourselves. As we speak the words or think the thought, we are identified with whatever follows the "*I am*". Whether I say "*I am rich*"," *I am strong*", "*I am smart*", "*I am weak*", "*I am depressed*", "*I am stupid*" or "*I am hurt*", I present myself as equal to that which the statement defines. When I say I am hurt, I am literally saying, "*I am my pain*". When I say I am depressed, I am really saying, "*I am my depression*". This is where we limit ourselves to being the label that the false self has given us. In that moment, you can't be anything different to your identification. When I proclaim that I am hurt, I can't be any more or less than my pain.

The ego-driven nature has many sub-identities – one for every occasion! It will happily locate a protective or inadequate sense of self for you to believe in depending on your circumstances. These identities are consuming. If you have ever found yourself in a rage and afterwards wondered what made you behave in such a way, you will understand how all-encompassing the False Identity can be. Like a body-snatcher, it takes over you. But it will only last for as long as the situation demands it or until another identity assumes control. Perhaps you can see how you are driven from pillar to post by the creations of your ego.

Bella was a client of mine for a number of months. Reserved and quiet, I always enjoyed the gentleness of our sessions. Bella prided herself on being seen as balanced, sophisticated and together. I soon discovered that a different persona would emerge on nights out. Given a few glasses of wine, Bella became the life and soul of the party, known for her propensity for dancing on tables!

The problem was that Bella disliked that side of her personality. She always hated hearing stories of her antics, even though they amused her friends and companions. Following her party nights, Bella would always say with complete sincerity and commitment, *"I'll never drink again*". But of course she always did. Time would pass. The pain and discomfort of embarrassment would fade and she would soon forget the promise she made to herself.

How can it be that in one moment we have absolute certainty that we will never repeat a pattern of behaviour and yet somehow we always do? We need to understand that our behaviour is driven by our sense of self. How we act will depend on which identity is in charge in the moment. Bella would go out and party hard when the fun-loving self was in charge, but regret it in the cold light of day when the sensible personality regained control. When she felt she had behaved outrageously, she would come down hard on herself. Her behaviour didn't fit with the person she believed (and wanted) herself to be.

To find peace and contentment, we have to de-identify with these illusionary creations of our ego. Otherwise every action we judge as unacceptable or inappropriate will simply cause conflict and suffering in our inner world. Remember that our True Self is always whole and complete. You are not your actions or behaviours. You are not your thoughts or feelings. You are not even the name that you give yourself. You are so much more than that.

ⓘ ***Lesson 6*** *- "I am" Exercise:*

Try this little exercise. Sit and contemplate the words "*I am*". In a gentle state of relaxation, see what words come up to complete the statement. Honour each response and breathe into it. Acknowledge without identifying with it. Allow this process to continue for a few minutes whilst staying in the curious observer mode.

Once you are settled into a pattern of acknowledging and breathing, I'd like you to expand the process by taking each response and asking, "*who am I that is more than that*?" Your process may go something like this:

- Response "*I am peaceful*" - acknowledge and breathe into it.
- Ask "*who am I that is more than that*?"
- Response "*I am energy*" - acknowledge and breathe into it
- Ask "*who am I that is more than that*?"
- Response "*I am a child of the Universe*" - acknowledge and breathe into it.
- Ask "*who am I that is more than that*?"
- Response .... And so on

Even if your words appear to be negative, do not be concerned. Just relax and breathe into each one. Remember you are allowing the process without identifying with it. All of the statements may contain some elements of truth yet none of them are real. Think of each response as a box that you are sitting in.

When we identify with the box – "*This is who I am*" – we have limited our sense of self. You can keep finding bigger boxes but each identification is also a limitation. Even when you introduce yourself with your name, you have boxed yourself with your own representation of your self. And you are always, all ways more than that!

This exercise will show you the subconscious messages that live within your identity. You will have a different experience depending on which sense of self is present during the process. It can be interesting to try it at different times and discover what lies beneath our conscious, every day thinking.

De-identification allows us to see the full relationship. We start to observe when we are being taken over by a false sense of self. We learn not to let ourselves be captured and held hostage by a particular identity. We begin to surrender who *we think we are* for the truth of *who we really are* – the indefinable and undeniable presence of Divine energy in human form!

STEP 2: BEING STILL

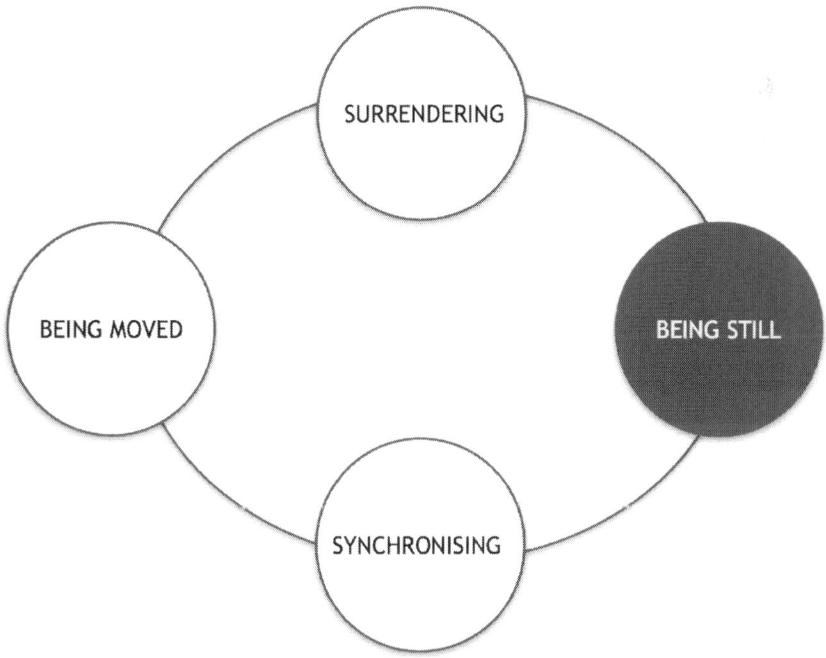

CHAPTER 8

Beyond distraction

One of the essential components of a life of presence is stillness. So long as we are consumed by endless distractions, our schedules are packed full of back-to-back appointments or we rush from one task to another on the to-do list, we can never fully experience the present moment. Our minds will flit from activity to activity with scarcely time to draw breath. Remember, this is the illusion of pursuit consciousness – that there is some imaginary point in the future where you will have got it all done and at last you will be able to relax. But that time will never come. Even if you are thinking of retirement, you can't hurtle at full speed towards a point of stillness and expect to feel peaceful when you arrive. It is much more likely you will feel restless, edgy and empty – hardly an appropriate reward for a life of hard work.

We have been deluded into thinking that the achievement of results is the name of the game – that there is some advantage to postponing relaxation and rejuvenation. Those who know how to take their foot off the gas and go with the flow are told that they lack ambition or are lazy. I don't believe anyone is lazy. If they appear to be doing nothing then it might be that they are lacking motivation but maybe they have figured out one of the secrets to happiness! Most of us refuse to lay ourselves open to judgments of laziness. Our worthiness depends on being seen as productive and useful and so we join the exhausting rat race to ensure we get the recognition and reinforcement that our self-value depends upon.

When you really think about it, how can constant pursuit possibly be a healthy way to live? Mother Nature knows that balance is key. Lions don't hunt all day. They stalk their prey in the cooler mornings and evenings. During the hotter parts of the day, they are most likely to be found basking in the sun. We seem to have a different mindset – to engage in the chase from morning to night with only the rudimentary fifteen-minute coffee break to obtain a caffeine fix needed to keep us going. We are no longer connected to what our bodies, minds and souls really need. The diet and nutrition industries are booming with contradictory advice because we don't have the space to tune into our natural, inner wisdom.

Stillness is essential to our mental, physical, emotional and spiritual wellbeing. Without it, we can't hear the voice of the Divine that whispers through our soul. If you are living in some imaginary future then there is no one home, here and now, to take care of *you*. The unfortunate by-product of pursuit is burnout, illness and addictions. If you aren't present to your own being, you won't hear the call of your body for respite, space and nourishment.

In this section, we will examine four different ways of releasing the pressing and demanding grip of pursuit so that you can finally slow down and find the peace and contentment you crave. Now is the time to commit to self-care. This section is about building the foundation for the *rest* of your life.

The myth of multi-tasking

The technological advances of the last decade have been incredible. When I was a child, we had one television in our house and only a landline telephone. If we wanted to correspond with the world through the written word, the only option was postal mail. Take a look at how far we have come. We can send messages at the push of a button by email and text. Your friends can know your every movement – where you have been and what you have been doing (and with whom!) via social media. And I can telephone you when you are away from home, even if you are on the other side of the world thanks to the international mobile network. I am a big fan of technology and I most definitely have an inner geek who loves to play with new ways to communicate and build relationships. I know that both my personal and professional network are vastly larger than they could have been had I lived in an earlier era.

But there is a downside. We are always available and constantly switched on. That has now become the expectation rather than the exception. Once, when I was coaching a group of lawyers, they told me that if they fail to respond to an email within fifteen minutes, they would get an insistent telephone call questioning the delay! All of this buys into the belief that we have to be at everyone's beck and call.

The biggest issue we now face is information overload. Just sitting at my desk, I am contactable in numerous formats – landline, mobile, fax, door-to-door callers, email, Facebook and Skype to name a few. How can we ever stay focussed on the present moment when so many communication lines are set up for immediate responsiveness? A proportion of your energy has to remain in standby mode.

We are constantly bombarded by a flood of information demanding our attention. The younger generations, born into this information-ready era, are better equipped to discern the important from the insignificant – at least by their own quality measures (which may explain why parental advice is so easily ignored!) Growing up in a world of text and Twitter, they appreciate the value of communicating succinctly with each other. Knowing we live in a hectic and overloaded culture, they are aware of the necessity for getting straight to the point. But for those of us who are still catching up with technology, we haven't yet quite worked out how to pick through the incessant white noise. We simply get bogged down in nonstop and unremitting attention demands.

Somehow we need to work out how to access information without it overwhelming us. Cognitive Psychologist, George A. Miller, a pioneer in cognitive learning, researched the ability of our mind to handle and process bites of information or *chunks*. Our capacity was shown to be dependent on our attention – what we can hold and process in our short-term memory. In his report, '*The Magical Number Seven, Plus or Minus Two*'[8], he stated that we can hold on average seven chunks with the typical range being from five to nine (the plus or minus two). This number was affected by both the subject and other external factors.

In fact, later research showed that the number seven could be misleading as it is often much closer to three or four chunks. However, this principle of a limited aptitude to handle information is still valid. Let's ambitiously assume we can handle seven chunks of information. According to Wikipedia, a chunk is "*the largest meaningful unit in the presented material that the person recognises*" so depending on your knowledge or understanding of a topic, you will have different chunks of information. For example, a five year-old child learning the alphabet for the first time would have twenty-six chunks. We may recall our own phone number in three chunks (e.g. 0123 456 789) – if you want to check out the power of chunks, have someone read your phone number out in a different pattern. It can be very disorientating!

Imagine that it is Monday morning. Notice where you are and what you are doing. What chunks of information do you normally have to process? When you feel pressurised, how many more chunks are you handling? What number would you be trying to cope with if you were feeling stressed or overwhelmed? What if, as you are already feeling overwhelmed, the phone rings? How do you respond? It is useful to explore the impact of varying numbers of chunks on our own neurology. Even the most adept multi-tasker will find that the limits to our chunk capacity are surprisingly low.

This exercise in awareness can help you understand the demands on our attention. Further technological advances are likely to increase this pressure even further. This means that even if you are able to cope with the increasing levels, there will come a point where you exceed your scope for handling information. Somewhere after that (or preferably before then) we are going to need to develop a new system and approach.

If we are being pulled in multiple directions and being asked to process more and more information, there is going to be an impact on our attention span. No matter how good you think your multi-tasking abilities are, you cannot spread your focus across numerous points and give them the best quality of your attention. For every additional aspect you are focusing on, you are diluting your attention proportionally. The result of multiple points of focus is not higher productivity but rather greater distraction.

Let me introduce you to Sally. Sally's alter ego was most definitely superwoman. In her forties, Sally is a successful and highly paid executive, married with four children. On the surface, Sally seemed to have it all. The perfect job, the large family and the big house in the country but, when she sat in front of me for her first session, she explained that she wasn't enjoying any aspect of her life. She loved her family and her job but knew she was jeopardizing both. Something had to give but she didn't know what that some*thing* would be. By the time we met, it was apparent that the breaking point was likely to be her health. She was already being medically treated for high blood pressure.

As we talked, it became increasingly evident that the problem was distraction. Even as Sally shared her personal story, she would flit between the worlds of work and family life. I asked her if she ever found herself thinking about work when she was enjoying family time, or found herself consumed by home issues at work. Can you guess what her response was?

Many of us are living precariously like this, just about holding it together but afraid at any moment that we might drop the ball. Do we continue to live on the edge or do we commit to making a change before our health, our relationships or our careers suffer? There is an answer to this predicament. It is called presence – that ability to bring our awareness fully into the current moment. We know when we are present because all of the distractions fade away and we are left with our total attention on the current situation. We are able to stay with the task at hand without being diverted by the rest of a to-do list. Sages and gurus have long talked about the importance of being present for ongoing contentment and joy but, in a culture built on the premise of achieving as much as we can before we pop our clogs, such wisdom is rarely counselled.

So how easy do you find it to be present?

- Do you wake in the morning feeling relaxed and calm or is your mind more likely to be racing ahead onto the activities for the day?

- Are you able to be fully present in discussions without your thoughts wandering onto other topics or what you want to be saying next?

- Can you stick to one project or task on your list or do you find your focus flitting between activities?

- If you are in a meeting and you become aware of your phone ringing, are you able to stay engaged with the current conversation or are you wondering or worrying about the call?

- Are you able to stay focussed on your own priorities or do you find yourself flitting between the requests from other people?

When we are able to give our attention firmly to the moment, we can spot the unnecessary demands on our time and energy. Not everything that appears to be urgent is really that important. We have just learned to react to the waving of the red priority flag without checking its validity.

Once Sally could understand that the main issue was distraction and overspill between aspects of her life, we began a process of re-evaluating her priorities. Every time the phone rang or an email arrived, she would ask herself whether it was important or simply a distraction. She knew she could just let go of anything in the distraction category without a second thought. If it ranked as important, she would check it against her current activity. For example, her business phone ringing during a family meal was less important than her relationships with her husband and children. When she kept this in mind, it was easy to allow the call go to voicemail where she could collect it afterwards. When she was in an important business meeting, she would have all of her calls transferred to an assistant. She then knew she would only be disturbed in an absolute emergency. Reassured that no interruptions only meant that all was well, she could give her undivided attention to the conversations in the room without worrying about what might be happening at home.

We are often so busy rushing between our various activities that we don't have time to connect fully to each event. This was certainly Sally's experience, still mentally at work while with her family, and vice versa. We can learn to pull our attention to that which is directly in front of us. Let's say you have been out at work for the day. You are driving home ready to cook your evening meal, care for the children, catch up on household chores and so on. If you rush home without pausing for breath, what energy will you be bringing with you? Ever wondered why the kids act out as soon as you walk through the door or your partner seems disinterested? Now you know why! Try pulling over and taking a few deep breaths before you arrive home. Learning to let go of one situation before we engage in another helps us to be fully present to the moment.

The power of focus

I have to confess that for many years, I prided myself on my multi-tasking ability. I had a very busy life bringing up my boys and running my businesses. Much of my worth was tied up in an illusionary sense of self that I perceived to be capable and resourceful. I wanted to show everyone how much I could do and the world responded appropriately with praise and admiration for my achievements. If you read my first book or listen to my earlier products, you may be able to spot this desire for getting things done. However, like Sally, my energy was often divided across multiple people and situations. I could be physically in the room and conversing with you but my mind was elsewhere. Even though I try not to regret anything about the past, I do actually feel a sense of sadness about this now. I was privileged to have some wonderful experiences with some truly amazing people but not all of me was there to *fully* enjoy it. In doing so, I short-changed the people I interacted with and deprived myself. Too many perfect moments that simply dissolved without the gift of my awareness.

But I do remember one moment in my life that completely absorbed my attention. I was a teenager travelling across America with my family. We had arrived in

Arizona the evening before and it had taken huge persuasion on my mother's part to have us get up before dawn to watch the sun rise over the Grand Canyon. I can remember the experience vividly. Still a little petulant at being woken so early, I was arguing about mindless nonsense with my sister in the back of the car. As we rounded a corner, my mother invited us to stop bickering and look out of the window. As I turned my head, I felt like I stepped into a slow motion movie. Passing time ceased. The magnificence of the landscape took my breath away. My grouchy huff disappeared and I was left suspended in the moment. I couldn't comprehend that the view I was seeing through my own eyes was even real. The shimmering light of the early morning sun lit the red rocks and deep crevices with spectacular effect. It seemed like a picture postcard. Even as I write these words, I can experience the sudden surge of emotion once more. I felt like the smallest being on the planet but totally connected to everything. I immediately wanted to share it with the world and yet I was totally speechless.

There is a choice to be made. You can spread yourself thinly across many points of focus and have diluted experiences or you can bring all of your attention to this moment right now and get the full-on, glorious technicolour, high-definition, masterfully-directed version! It is no coincidence that I can remember in such detail my Grand

Canyon experience. It captured and held every inch of my being in the experience of awe. I am no longer a fan of multi-tasking. I just don't want to miss any Grand Canyon style experiences. And they don't just come from the big and the daring adventures. Even the briefest conversation can touch us deeply when we are fully aware and awake in the moment.

I want my attention to be fully engaged with the situation. I don't want to attempt to hold important conversations whilst I am driving or cooking a meal. I want to sit and talk with my children without mentally listing all the jobs I have to do after they go to bed. And I avoid interruptions when I am busy working on projects – as I write this book, I have turned off my emails and phones and escaped to a writing space where I know I won't be disturbed.

So how far are you spreading your attention? Here's a little game that you can play that offers a twist on the traditional to-do list.

ⓘ ***Lesson 7*** *- The Power of Focus (The Car Park game):*

Take a piece of paper and divide it into boxes so that it has some resemblance to a car park. As you think about the day ahead, write in the individual boxes everything that you have to do. Be as comprehensive as possible and include anything that will consume your time or energy. Each time you write in a box, mentally park that task. When you are complete, take a look at your piece of paper. How busy is your car park? Do you have plenty of space for new activities or unexpected requests when they arrive? Or are you going to be cramming more in or even creating an overflow car park?

Remember that we only have the capacity to mentally handle about seven things. If you have more then any unforeseen interruptions are likely to send you into overwhelm. There simply won't be the capacity for anything else. Take a good look at your paper. Which vehicles have overstayed their welcome? Perhaps it is time to have them towed away! Personally, three is my comfortable number. I can move fairly seamlessly through this number of activities and know I have the scope to give each one my undivided attention. If something else arises, I still have sufficient space to evaluate what is most important. It's the difference between being stretched to the limit and taking things in my stride. I know I can contribute so much more when I have wriggle room. Perhaps you have a sense of your own limits. Be honest and frank with yourself. What number of projects or activities can you handle with ease? When I ask this question to my clients, I challenge their answers. We may not want to let ideas or projects go but if they all consume bandwith, it won't take much before the quality of your focus is diluted beyond a worthwhile level and everything else will suffer as a result. As we said in the simplicity section, remember to pick your commitments and complexities carefully!

Check back to your car park and decide what is the first priority. You can now mentally visualise yourself climbing into that car – this is what you will be driving for a while. If you find your mind wandering onto other parked topics, just gently bring your attention back to the car you are in. Ignore the irrelevant distractions. Keep your attention on the road ahead remembering how important focused attention is whilst you are behind the wheel.

There's a quote that goes "*Life is not measured by the number of breaths you take but by every moment that takes your breath away*"[9]. The breath-taking moments come from our willingness to dedicate ourselves totally to the moment. Beyond distraction there are many Grand Canyon type experiences to be had. But will *you* be there?

Attention Shifting

The ability to develop and hone our focus can be life-changing. If you regularly feel pulled in multiple directions, the chances are that you have acclimatised to poor quality attention. It's a by-product of our current culture. I remember eating out at an exclusive restaurant in London. The venue was exquisite with ambient lighting and spectacular views across Tower Bridge and the River Thames. After we had been enjoying great conversation and delicious food for a while, one of my party pointed to the table next to us. A group of young women appeared to be celebrating an eighteenth birthday. Slightly to our amusement, every one of them was holding their mobile phone, either frantically tapping in a text or engrossed in a telephone conversation. It was one of those moments where the ridiculousness of the situation highlights our own crazy habits. How many times do we find ourselves being distracted by side-shows and missing the main event?

Let's make a conscious decision right now not to settle for sloppy attention. If we want to have the fullest and richest life experiences, it is essential to stop caving into the endless distractions. Switch the television off. Let the calls go to voicemail. Choose to only check your email once or twice a day. Track the distractions back to the source and inform and educate those who are requesting your attention. For example, your voicemail or email auto-responder might advise people that you will return their call within 48 hours or you might let work colleagues know that you can't be contacted after 6pm at night. People may not like your choices but remember you are committing to bringing the best of you to each situation. Ultimately, it is in their best interests too.

I do want to make a distinction here between the hard and driven focus associated with pursuit and ambition (what we might call single-mindedness) and the soft, allowing and creative focus of presence (expanded awareness). To show you this, I want to offer you an exercise that you can play with to explore the qualities of different levels of attention.

ⓘ ***Lesson 8*** - *Attention-Shifting*

Begin by making yourself comfortable, either sitting or standing. Look in front of you and find a focal point to direct your attention. It could be a picture or a clock for example. Now I want you to really hone in on a fine detail. As I sit here, there is a light on the clock in front of me. Something like that will work perfectly. I want you to put all of your attention on that one spot and notice what happens. Have a go now and then come back to this section.

How did that feel? What else were you aware of? Often when we talk of focused attention, this is what we are referring to. But you may notice that it wasn't entirely comfortable. This level of focus is known as tunnel vision and it is associated with the fear response. It is priming us for our primitive fight or flight response. Absolutely essential if a tiger is hunting us down, not so great if we want to experience tranquillity. This is the variation of focus linked to single-mindedness. Rather than supporting us in giving our undivided attention to the task in hand, it is more likely that we will be distracted by unnecessary and unwelcome stressful thoughts. Feel free to have another go and check this out for yourself.

So now let's try something different. Put your attention back on the spot you were looking at before – in my case, the light on the clock. This time allow your focus to gently expand outwards. Keep your eyes and head still but do remember to blink, otherwise you will end up with very dry eyes and blurred vision! Continue to let this awareness widen so you can notice even more that surrounds the focal point. For example, seeing the numbers on the clock or the frame a picture. Keep allowing your viewpoint to extend even further. In fact, see how much of the rest of the room you can see without moving your eyes from the original focal point. Notice what you notice. You may be surprised. Try it now.

What was that experience like? How did you feel this time? What else were you able to notice? And what were you saying to yourself? This second way of focusing our attention is called peripheral vision and it is associated with the relaxation response. In other words, when we are calm, at ease and happy, this is how we are naturally. The problem is that most of us aren't relaxed very often. You may have noticed that the last question was a trick question. In fact, when we are in peripheral vision, the inner chatterbox disappears. It is impossible to be in an expanded awareness like this and still be having an inner dialogue. And without inner dialogue, you simply can't be distracted by stressful thoughts. Peripheral vision can take some practice to learn. You may want to repeat this exercise again over the next few days to get accustomed to it.

In expanded awareness, we are in this state of gentle yet focused attention. We give ourselves to the moment. We don't worry or fret about what we might be missing or the other tasks on our to-do list. Having evaluated our priorities and consciously chosen to do what we are doing, we let go of everything else. We bring every inch of our being to the project, activity or conversation. We refuse to compromise the quality of our focus for another's demands – not because they don't matter but rather because we care enough to never again short-change someone with a fragment of our attention. A life beyond distraction is something worth developing. Only through presence can the true wonder of each experience be revealed to you.

CHAPTER 9

Slowing down

A few years ago, we arrived home from holiday to a suspicious looking brown envelope on my doormat. It was addressed to my husband so as soon as we had managed to get our four children and luggage in through the door, he opened it. Inside was a notice from the DVLA (the organisation of the UK Government responsible for maintaining a database of drivers and vehicles) listing my husband's car in a speeding offence recorded by a camera just a couple of days before we went away. I immediately felt deep sympathy for my husband for being caught – that was until I realised that I had been the one driving the car! My pity disappeared and was replaced by a sense of rage. I had only been driving a small fraction over the speed limit for that area. It seemed so insignificant that I couldn't believe it had registered on the camera. What made it worse was the formal wording of the notice – something along the lines of '*notice of intended prosecution*'. Priding myself on being a law-abiding citizen, it challenged my sense of self and had me plummeting back into those *not good enough* feelings once more. It was much easier to feel indignant and angry than face up to the consequences of my actions.

We advised the DVLA that I had been driving the car at the time of the offence and I received a letter offering me two options. One was to pay a fine and take the penalty (three points on my licence). The other was to attend a speed awareness course – something my friend teasingly described as "*naughty school!*" Knowing that points on my licence would mean a huge increase in my car insurance, it made sense to take the course option. I paid the fee, accepted a place and then spent the next few weeks mentally disputing the punishment. It seemed so unfair and unreasonable that I had to give up my precious time for something so trivial. I wasn't happy!

The day of naughty school arrived and I took my desk alongside the other speed offenders. I listened to the others speak about their convictions whilst still refusing to take responsibility for mine. Taking it in turns, we had to answer a question about why we felt the need to speed when driving. When it came to my response, I found myself lost for words. I simply couldn't find a logical or rational explanation. Was I really constantly late for appointments? Was there always an emergency that I was trying to prevent? Did I think that the time spent driving meant that I was missing out on something better somewhere else? I didn't have an answer.

The purpose of the course was to raise awareness of the potential risks of speeding. By re-educating drivers – many of whom took their licensing tests when they were still teenagers – the DVLA aims to reduce the issues associated with driving too fast. As I am sure you can imagine, this did involve presenting us with some of the more traumatic situations, which weren't comfortable to hear. There was a point in the course when a realisation dawned on me. If I was driving even one mile over the speed limit and was involved in a catastrophic accident, how would I live with the consequences? I could never know whether that one-mile excess had been a deciding factor in the outcome. It just wasn't a price that I was prepared to pay.

Since my experience at naughty school, I have made a conscious decision not to speed. I choose to drive everywhere below the limit. Rather than having a negative impact on my life, it has been liberating and calming. I tend to schedule more time for travelling to appointments so I arrive early with plenty of time to relax and prepare. I no longer treat the driving part of my journey as a chore – it is the perfect opportunity to be present and observe the scenery. And I really enjoy the sensation of gently moving along – as though I have all the time in the world to get to where I want to be.

There is a distinct art to the process of *slowing down*. Sometimes, unexpected or unforeseen events do crop up and I find myself short of time between appointments. In the past, this would have been my cue to put my foot down. Now, I know it is essential that I travel with ease so I slow down even more. If I need to stop and make a phone call or send a message to explain that I am running late, I do so. I've learnt that anything that relieves the pressure and the urge to rush is a very good thing.

The world hasn't stopped spinning. I haven't missed out on anything. Instead, I have found the quality of my meetings and appointments has vastly improved. Because I am moving more slowly, I am much more able to be fully present. The cost of my fee and my time in attending the speed awareness course proved to be a very small price to pay for discovering the relief of letting go of rushing.

The pleasure in pootling

We live in a culture that extols rushing. We don't just find speeding on our roads and highways. It is a more pervasive issue of society. We rush into making decisions for fear of missing out on an opportunity. We leap into the intimate side of relationships before we really know the other person. We don't give events enough time to unfold before we are off looking for the better job, spouse or experience. We rush through our working week to get to the weekend. You don't have to look very far to find another example of the ways in which we speed through life. If you ever find yourself rushing between appointments or to get things done, let me ask you that same question I was asked on the DVLA course – why do you feel the need to speed?

What is it that pushes you to haste? It is worth taking some time to really delve into the depths of this behaviour. It is always underpinned by some sense of scarcity or lack. What do you fear might happen if you slow down? What are you scared of losing? Rushing is one of the characteristics associated with pursuit. We believe that life is some kind of race and so we measure the quality of our lives by how fast we accomplish tasks. For some, that may take the form of wealth and material gains. There is still a sense of kudos offered to the young millionaire. Others may benchmark their careers on how quickly they can climb to a position of responsibility and authority. We may even be evaluating our personal or spiritual growth according to the speed with which we seem to be reaching enlightenment. Who said this was a competition? Can you see the craziness of such thinking? Pursuit is a totally unnecessary waste of energy. What are you ever really pursuing other than the sense of worthiness that was your birthright? It doesn't live anywhere else but inside of you – your True Self was born that way. The irony of pursuit is that the only thing you are ever pursuing is yourself.

A life of presence is absent from haste. When we live in the moment, the only time is now. And without a sense of ticking time, how can there ever be a need to rush to the next moment? The wonderful author and speaker, Robert Holden, has created an analogue watch that, instead of numbers from one to twelve, simply repeats the word *now* on each segment of the clock face[10]. What a wonderful reminder not to rush but simply to live in the now!

Most of us haven't been taught how to move slowly and gently. How many times were you told in childhood to '*hurry up*' or '*to get a move on*'? I sometimes catch myself saying it to my children and then have to gently remind myself that there is nothing worth rushing for. It is a habitual pattern that has been passed down through the generations. It often reminds me of the White Rabbit in Alice in Wonderland[11], who appears right at the beginning of the book lamenting his lateness. If you have seen the Disney adaptation of the film, you may remember his little ditty "*I'm late! I'm late! For a very important date! No time to say hello, goodbye! I'm late! I'm late! I'm late!*" So many of us have an equivalent inner dialogue running on a loop through our minds. Not exactly a helpful affirmation if we want a life of presence.

Slowing down is an art form. To live peacefully we have to learn to dismiss the hurry-up taskmaster that only exists in our time-bound minds. A big part of mastering presence is becoming aware of the drive to haste and discovering the joy of ***pootling***. I use pootling as a way to describe moving calmly and easily through life without living under the dark cloud of a continual sense of urgency. Below I have listed a few top tips that may help you to enjoy and master the art of pootling. When you have read these ideas, come up with some of your own ways for slowing down and living in the moment.

Top tips for pootling:

- Where possible try to avoid scheduling back-to-back meetings or appointments. You may have noticed that even the seemingly simplest conversation can take much longer than you expect. Give yourself more space in between items in your schedule and you won't need to rush between appointments. You will bring a sense of calm to each event.

- Likewise, leave longer for traveling. If the journey is expected to take an hour, plan for double that. If traffic delays you, you will remain composed and relaxed. If you arrive at your destination an hour early then you have time to stretch your legs, grab a coffee, listen to music or read. Too many people claim not to have sufficient *me-time*. Here is your chance to do something just for you!

- Beware of squeezing things into your time. This was one of my habits. I'd have ten minutes before a coaching session and decide to catch up on my emails or clean the house. When you use those ten minutes to sit quietly or relax, your energy shifts to a more gentle and present form and the quality of your interactions and relationships will benefit hugely. Don't take my word for it. Try it for yourself and experience the difference. If your schedule doesn't allow more time then you are over committed to too many people/projects. The only solution for a life of presence is to simplify.

- Become more conscious of your inner dialogue. Notice if you are hurrying or chivvying yourself along. How does it feel when you pressurize yourself? In all likelihood your stress levels will increase, dramatically spiraling you into an adrenaline-fueled drama story. Remember that life is not a race. You probably won't get there any sooner by rushing and even if you do, the only prize is anxiety, stress and the longer-term negative impact on your health. Remind yourself that you always have sufficient time. There is no sense of passing time when you are present to the moment. The only time is now.

- Deliberately slow the pace of your walk. In city life, it is incredibly easy to get caught up in the hectic bustle driven by the need to get somewhere. Walk more slowly than initially feels comfortable. Then force yourself to slow down some more! You might notice your stories coming up – "*This is a waste of time*", "*I could have been there by now*", "*I'm holding other people up*". Gently acknowledge the message without identifying with it. When we have spent our lives learning how to rush, it may take a bit of time to get used to moving with less pace. Allow your resistance to slowness to reveal your limiting thought patterns. Taking your time is actually a deeply valuing and honouring process. You matter too much to rush your own life!

Over the next few days, start to really tune into your own patterns of haste. What causes you to speed up? What are you saying to yourself? How does your body feel when you are rushing? What would your life be like if you consciously decided to move slowly and purposefully, no matter how much urgency the Storyteller is forcing on you? Any time you find yourself rushing is the perfect time to practice pootling!

How movement affects the quality of our life

Observing how our body is affected by rushing can be extremely insightful. After practising slowing down, I am now very sensitive to the changes that the process of speeding up creates inside of me. Initially, I feel a rise in sensation in my stomach area, and my shoulders and neck tense up. I can notice that I am breathing more rapidly and less deeply and my heart is beating faster in my chest. Soon afterwards, my hands begin to tingle and I feel light-headed and slightly dizzy. If I don't take preventative action and slow down, the tension spreads into my head, which increases my susceptibility to a headache or migraine. My blood sugar levels also shift and I find myself reaching for a sweet snack or drink. What can you notice in your own observations?

I am entirely convinced that rushing affects our bodies beyond anything we consciously perceive. If I compare my own symptoms of rushing to the short-term effects of taking an artificial stimulant like amphetamines[12], there are many notable similarities including stomach irritation, dizziness and changes in heart rate and blood sugar levels. The longer-term consequences of taking amphetamines are reported as:

- Poor memory and concentration
- Lack of clarity/confusion
- Depression, anxiety and tension
- Increased likelihood of panic attacks
- Sleeping problems
- Paranoia and aggression
- Reduced immunity and increased susceptibility to

infections

- High blood pressure
- Rapid and irregular heartbeat increasing the risks of heart attacks
- Increased risk of stroke

How many of these are prevalent in our current culture? You may even be experiencing some of these in your own life at this time. Can this really be pure coincidence? There seems to be a degree of correlation between the accelerating pace of human existence and the rise in mental and physical health problems that we are witnessing in society. Is rushing really worth the damage to your body? I think I would rather be a few minutes late or not finish my to-do list than risk my own health! How about you? Facing up to the consequences of our ways of being in the world isn't always comfortable but when we are prepared to see the truth, we liberate ourselves from the chains of the story. We cease to be part of the generalised thinking that tells us that rushing, doing and achieving more are the paths to happiness. We understand that going too fast serves no one.

But I want to take this a step further. The way in which we move has a direct impact on the quality of our life. To begin this idea, here's a little exercise for you to play with.

ⓘ ***Lesson 9** - Movement:*

Wherever you are right now (if you can), I'd like you to take a short walk! For example, if you are in your house, you could walk upstairs/downstairs or to the other side of your home and back. If you are on a train, you could walk through to the next carriage. If you can get outside, that would be even better – just pick a small landmark or point about 25-50 meters from where you are. I'd like you to take the exact same route three times. On the first loop, just walk at your normal speed. On the second, I'd like you to consciously speed up to as fast as you can walk given your current circumstances. Finally, take the same route but deliberately slow down as much as possible. Take a few moments to reflect on your experiences. How did they compare? Which felt easiest to you? How did your body react?

There are no right or wrong answers to this process but you might find that your body knows what it likes! To be clear, there's a distinction to be made between what your body enjoys and what you are familiar with. If you are used to moving at a fast pace then slowing down may feel strange or alien at first. If you are a potterer, speeding up might feel different or unnatural. You may need to repeat this exercise a number of times over the next few days to really tune into how your body feels. Give yourself plenty of space to dedicate yourself to the adventure and discovery of movement.

ⓘ ***Lesson 10*** - *Space Flight*

Another exercise you can try (which is useful if you can't physically move around) is to imagine flying through space. Try simply closing your eyes and visualise moving through the darkness. Play with speeding it up and slowing it down. You can have the stars and the planets move quickly towards you and then more slowly. How does it feel to be whizzing through space at speed? What is it like if you are gently floating? Again, just notice what feels comfortable and what doesn't.

It is important to understand the impact of pace on our life because when we talk about being in flow, we are referring to the natural synchronisation of our energy and movement. When we are in our flow, life runs much more smoothly. We show up in the right place at the right time. Events unfold with a degree of effortlessness. Creativity and inspiration are accessed more easily. We have a more omnipresent sense of all being well in the world. We will revisit this topic of being in flow in more depth later in the book.

For now, recall a time when you felt anxious or

panicky. How were you moving? What about a situation when you were feeling stuck or overwhelmed? Were you moving differently in that scenario? When I asked myself these questions, I found that when I was feeling anxious, I had a sense that I was moving too fast. When I felt overwhelmed, there was very little movement or I had stopped completely. Bringing our awareness to the quality of our movement can be enlightening. You may find that you never want to rush again!

If we are in pursuit consciousness, we may be tempted to use this information to manipulate our experiences. For example, forcing ourselves to move more quickly when we are feeling overwhelmed or stuck. But in presence consciousness, this is about awareness (rather than control) so that you can bring more conscious choice to your actions. There is never a need to be driven to rush by the hurrying and demanding Storyteller. Just by being present to your experiences, you will start to recognise what is right for you. Be deliberate yet flexible and you will gain a much greater understanding of your body, your movement and the relationship between the two. Allow the moment to guide your movement.

Of course, this isn't just about your physical movement – you can apply it to other contexts too. Even as I am writing this book, I am very aware of the pace of my thoughts. If they come too thick and fast, the speed of my fingers on the keyboard can't keep up and I start to lose the trail of ideas. If the words come too slowly, it may feel as though I am forcing the concepts or I hit writers' block. Awareness of pace is helpful in assisting with our alignment to presence consciousness.

If you continue to move too fast, how can you ever fully experience the moment? If you have ever looked out of a train window travelling at pace, you will have noticed how little you can take in of the scenery. Each aspect of the view has passed before your mind has been able to absorb the details. To get the most out of life, we must slow down to comprehend the magnificence of the moment.

Practicing stillness

How long can you sit still for? This is not a trivial question. I genuinely want you to consider how long you can sit in one spot on your own without the distraction of a conversation, television or any other external stimulation. Right at the beginning of this book, I asked you to sit with yourself in total silence for five minutes. Was that easy for you? What if I asked you to sit there for an hour or two or three?

When I recognise that my client's are locked into pursuit consciousness, one of the very first exercises I have them do is sit in stillness for one hour and simply report back to me on the experience. A large proportion of them come back with a reason for not doing the task – *"there wasn't enough time", "I couldn't find any space away from the family", "I had too much going on at work"* and so on. On the surface these may seem like genuine reasons but they are really an avoidance pattern against spending time in stillness. When we are living in pursuit, we are so hooked into the story of rushing, chasing and achieving that we would rather do anything than stop completely. We fear what we might find if we stand still.

I was once working with a client who had a serious and life-threatening illness. Understandably, she was desperate to find a cure. Every time we spoke, the ideas would centre on doing less and being more. We would go from the frenetic pace of the opening conversation to something so much more gentle and honouring towards the end of the session. Each time, she would make the commitment to go away and practice stillness. But soon after leaving she would come across another new treatment or therapy on the Internet, and her focus would shift to the *pursuit* of that. I knew with absolute certainty that if she could stop and be still, then the voice of Divine intelligence would express itself through her inner guidance. Any of the approaches she tried had the potential to be the right treatment for her but unless she tuned into her own soul wisdom, each attempt would just be another shot in the dark. I could deeply empathise with her situation – she felt like her life was hanging in the balance – but snatching at ideas and opinions from other people is always going to be a poor substitute to the absolute truth of Divine wisdom.

This is how so many of us live. After I had been ill for a few months with liver problems, I rapidly gained weight. Having always found it easy to control my weight in the past, I signed up to a diet programme. I lost a few pounds in the first few days but then my weight just stalled. No amount of calorie counting or exercise could shift the number of the scales. All the experts I asked gave me conflicting ideas. Other well-meaning people offered unsolicited suggestions! It seemed as though everyone had an answer to what I should and shouldn't be doing. My head was spinning with advice. Every idea or comment simply distracted me from hearing my own inner voice.

So I did something different. I took myself on an inner retreat. I turned off all the distractions and I sat in silence for most of the day. Initially some less than helpful thoughts surfaced. I allowed them to circulate without being attached to knowing the answer. I became much more aware of my own judgments about what the extra weight meant. Having exercised regularly, I knew I was fitter than I had ever been so I could no longer hide behind the story of my weight being associated with my health and wellbeing. Like so many people who struggle with body confidence issues, I had been sucked into identifying with the additional pounds. I started to believe that I was fat and I felt ugly. I hated the way I looked in my clothes. I didn't want my husband to come close or to touch me. Seeing myself in photographs provided the concrete evidence of what I was seeing in the mirror. My mind was a haven for cruelness and unkindness and I was the willing envoy. I'm sure we wouldn't tolerate the harsh and nasty words we direct at ourselves from any other person.

I realised that by seeking the advice of external sources, I had been unconsciously avoiding the painful and dark thoughts that lived within my divided mind. I desired slimness with such longing and yet I was treating myself with very little respect or compassion. So I made the choice to stay with the thoughts rather than turning away from them. Without my energy to fuel them, they started to pass through my mind like small bubbles of cloud. Through the clouds, a new voice began to emerge. It had a different quality. It was kind and gentle but possessed a sense of authority and wisdom. It simply told me that this was how my body wanted to be right now. There was no disappointment in not having the golden answer I was seeking. The strong sense of knowing was sufficient for me to feel reassured. No more fighting, struggling or battling my body — just a willingness to be at peace with how things stood. That weekend I happily went out and purchased some new clothes in a bigger size.

Stillness is essential for learning to connect with Divine wisdom. Will you suddenly get the perfect answer to every problem you have? It's very unlikely. But I can promise you that as you release yourself from the need to seek the opinions and approval from others, you open yourself up to inner guidance. So your mission is to make stillness a part of your daily life. Initially you may want to commit to spending a period of time each day away from the distractions and stimulations of the external world. Whether you choose to do fifteen minutes, an hour or more, be willing to dedicate a proportion of your time to being with yourself. Stillness is not about meditating or trying to achieve a specific outcome. Rather, it's just being alone in the moment and meeting yourself wherever you are. If you are worrying and fearful, or happy and excited then meet yourself there. Don't try to change a feeling or fix a situation. Allow everything as it arises without avoidance or attachment.

Over time, you will find that stillness becomes integrated into your life. Pressing the pause button is now a fairly automatic process for me. I may find that I stop doing what I am doing and just sit for a few minutes, or I make a conscious choice to disappear into the woods and sit under a tree for a few hours. Stillness isn't something to do – it is something that you are. Allow it to invade your thoughts and actions. As we slow down, we connect to the truth about who we really are. As the Bible says, "*Be still and know that*

I am [God]."[13] In stillness you will meet your True Self and discover your relationship to the Divine. Stillness isn't about taking a break; it is a place to live from.

CHAPTER 10

Honouring emotions

As we step into stillness, we learn to meet with our authentic self. Our frantic and busy world leaves little time for connecting to our emotions. So many of today's cultural issues can be traced back to the disconnection of not knowing how we are feeling. We struggle to answer simple questions about our emotional states. How often do we hear someone describe their feelings in terms of their thoughts and actions? – "*Things are going well*", "*I'm running to stand still*", "*I'm wishing this situation hadn't happened*" are all genuine responses I've heard to the question "*How are you feeling today*?"

In general, emotions are seen to be the less than useful by-product of life. We are much more inclined to tell a story rather than express how we feel about the situation. We deflect, minimise and trivialise our feelings and then are surprised when we don't know what the sensations we are experiencing mean.

There is a societal acceptance of certain moods. It is perfectly reasonable to feel excitement about a forthcoming event like a birthday party or a wedding. Happiness and joy are appropriate responses to a new birth, exam success or a promotion. It's okay to get passionate about a cause or topic we firmly believe in. But other emotions are frowned upon.

We mustn't get angry with our friends or family. We shouldn't express our vulnerability at work. Girls shouldn't feel strong or powerful. Boys shouldn't feel fear or hurt. There is a full and diverse range of human emotions available to us but how many of them do we allow ourselves to authentically feel?

Before we go further, make a list of all the emotional states you can name. How many can you come up with? As you look at the list, how many of those have you felt in the last week, month or year? Which of those emotions do you experience regularly? Which ones do you enjoy feeling? Which ones are your no-go areas? This is nothing more than an awareness exercise. As you review your answers, what can you learn about yourself and the stories you have been believing?

If there were an *inappropriate* emotion, why on earth would we have the capacity to experience it? Why would the Divine or some other organising intelligence give humans the ability to feel something that was irrelevant to our existence? Unless you really believe that it is a type of punishment or some cruel trick, we surely must accept that there is an underlying purpose to every emotion in our range. We were given legs in order to walk, a brain in order to process information, eyes to see and emotions to feel. You wouldn't blind your eyes because you didn't like what you were seeing or have your brain removed because you couldn't understand something. Why do we make such futile attempts to cut off our feelings – especially those labelled bad or negative? This chapter is about honouring and learning from our emotions. Rather than being something to avoid, our feelings can be the doorway to our soul and a deeper relationship with the Divine.

What your body tells you

Part of my early career was spent as a corporate trainer. For the most part, it was a highly rewarding job – I enjoyed spending time with groups and helping them to explore their personal growth and leadership styles. From time to time, there would be some delegates who would have preferred not to be there and they would make their reluctance known. Although I was never one for keeping people locked in a room against their will, there were occasions when, due to organisational policy, it was a requirement for them to be on the course. Their attendance was compulsory but their co-operation wasn't! On one particular afternoon session, I was teaching time management to a group of executives who had spent their lunch hour in the pub. At the time I was young and a little naive when it came to dealing with the situation. As I tried to plough on with the content, I was ridiculed mercilessly. Plunged back into my unworthiness thoughts about being a '*not-good-enough*' trainer, I tried hard not to show the confusion and panic I was feeling inside. In all honesty, I wanted to run from the room but as I believed showing any vulnerability was an inappropriate emotion in a business context, I overrode my emotional state and did my very best to stick to the agenda. I can tell you that those few hours felt like a lifetime.

As I look back through my life, there are a number of events that have caused me to disconnect from my feelings. When an emotion is overwhelming, cutting off can seem like the best way to cope. Even during my difficult experience with alcohol-fuelled delegates, not experiencing my emotions seemed to save some face. Who knows how they would have reacted if I had allowed my true feelings to show?

But there is always a price to pay for not honouring our emotions. In this example, I felt drained and exhausted for a day or two following the training. But the price can be much more costly when we live from a disconnected place for a long period of time. Depression is the suppression of emotions to the point of numbness. In a culture that doesn't invite or allow us to truly feel our way through life, it is hardly surprising that one in five people are likely to suffer from depression at some point during their adult life.

When my eight-month old baby was diagnosed with a serious heart condition, I was overwhelmed with emotion.

We had an agonising five-month wait for his surgery to repair his heart. During that time, he was regularly taken ill and I spent many days and nights at the hospital with him. On one occasion he was so severely ill that his life hung in the balance and I really thought we might lose him. Even as I write these words, I can feel the rise of emotion and the sting of tears in my eyes. I am eternally grateful that he made it through that period. It still touches my heart beyond belief.

So how did I manage to get through that time in my life? The truth is that I went into autopilot. I simply wasn't willing or able to feel my emotions so I completely disconnected from what was happening. I went through my day acting as though it wasn't happening. Family and friends would often remark on how well I was handling it and I really believed that I was coping. One evening, just before I went to bed, I was brushing my teeth in the bathroom. I happened to glance in the mirror and saw a reflection. I say *a* reflection because in that moment I could not identify the image I saw as being me. There was literally no link between the reflection and my sense of self – just a vast space of emptiness and nothingness. As I touched the mirror and traced my features with my finger, I could feel the reconnection. The emotions passed like huge, breaking waves through my whole body. I spent that night sobbing on the bathroom floor. As dawn broke, I felt a deep sense of peace spread through my heart and my mind. I knew I couldn't control the outcome but I also realised that whatever happened, I wanted to feel my love for my son and I couldn't do that without allowing emotion. That's the problem with discounting our feelings. We can't cut off from the painful or overwhelming states without also losing all the feel-good ones like joy, contentment and love.

I meet too many people who have learnt to disconnect from their feelings. It is a pattern that is most often developed in childhood either as a result of trauma, conditioning or the overpowering emotions of people around us. We learn to be frightened of the sensations that intense states like anger or grief bring, and we would rather remove them from our life rather than run the risk of experiencing them again. The problem with cutting off from our emotions is that we don't find the peace we crave. In fact, we simply feel empty and numb, and life loses any sense of meaning or wonder. When I saw my reflection in the mirror, there was no aliveness in my eyes and no feeling in my heart. Disconnecting from our emotions is the equivalent of spiritual suicide.

Our emotions are the channel of communication from our True Self. When we allow our feelings, we bring ourselves into full engagement with life. You are meant to feel all emotions deeply and profoundly – anger, sadness, appreciation, love, despair, peace and joy – are all included in your repertoire for a good reason. When you hear a story of inspiration that moves you, that is the whisper of your soul reminding you that life is good, people are worthy and love is the only language that matters. Your True Self is your point of connection to Divine intelligence. When you take time to listen to your feelings, you will hear the loving voice of unquestionable wisdom. The door has to be open to let the Divine in.

When we honour and allow all of our emotions, our life experiences alter significantly. Recently I was working with a client who was struggling to find any passion or joy in life. She felt consistently bored and uninspired. She had attempted to shake things up by creating big bucket-list style adventures. Most recently she had swum with sharks and completed the highest bungee jump in Australia. But the adrenaline-fuelled feelings of euphoria had subsided too quickly and the monotony of daily life had consumed her once more. When she first spoke to me, her intention was to find bigger and better adventures. Instead, I invited her to do something completely different – to learn how to fully experience her feelings on a daily basis. We introduced exercises to support her in becoming aware of her changing emotional states and then I helped her learn to truly experience them. Within a few weeks, she was enjoying life once more. She no longer needed a big and thrilling adventure to feel alive. Living with feeling was all that it took to feel deeply fulfilled.

If we want to develop that sense of aliveness without the need for sharks or a 200 metre drop, we need to learn to fully allow and connect to our emotional states. No more pretending to be upset when what you really feel is anger. No more hiding your vulnerability beneath a veneer of toughness. No more suppressing grief when people or things leave your life. It's okay to feel sad or hurt or disappointed or guilty. In a life of presence, all emotions are valid. There is no need for pretence or phoniness.

So how do we begin to feel our feelings in their entirety? Our bodies can tell us everything that we need to know.

ⓘ ***Lesson 11** - Honouring emotions:*

Going back to the list you wrote at the beginning of this chapter, pick one emotional state and ask yourself how you know when you are feeling that way. It may not be a question that you have ever truly considered before — emotions often seem to live in a realm of mystery and confusion. But there has to be a way of determining the difference between anger or happiness or else you wouldn't be able to tell them apart. Tune into the way your body feels when you experience the emotion you have chosen. How does your energy shift? Do you notice any changes in your body tension? If so, where? How is your breathing affected? Is it slower or more rapid? Is it deeper or shallower?

Over the next few days, pay more conscious attention to how you are feeling moment-to-moment. Much of the time our emotional states exist outside of our awareness. The first thing we know about them is when we find ourselves shouting at a loved one or bursting into tears. Bringing our feelings into our consciousness allows us to more deeply connect with our sense of self. Rather than trying to figure out the causes of your moods, become the curious observer. Pay attention to the particular sensations and the changes in your body. What messages are they telling you? This is an ongoing process and it is worth the investment of your time and energy. When we are fully connected to our bodies and emotions, we need very little external stimulation to tap into the wonderful spirit of being alive.

The lies you tell yourself

Authenticity was one of the buzzwords that appeared in the past decade. I remember it cropping up in many personal development books and programmes. Each time I heard the word, it resonated deep within my being as truth. I understood it to mean showing up in the world without any pretence to being anything different. To be authentic means to know who you are and to be comfortable expressing it. Rather than adapting our persona to fit certain situations, there is consistency across contexts. The values that I hold to be true become a core part of the way in which I interact with the world. If I view myself as honest, caring or sincere then I would behave in a way that aligns with these qualities in every situation.

On the other hand, inauthenticity implies a lack of consistency. We adapt our behaviour to the people and situations in which we find ourselves. Just as I suppressed my vulnerability with the group of delegates on the course, perhaps we fear what might happen if we speak up. Maybe we believe we should hide aspects of our personality in order to secure the approval of others. Often we describe people who struggle with authenticity as *hiding behind masks*. If we want to live up to a certain self-image, we will present a best self by covering up the parts we don't like or that we think are unacceptable. Do these descriptions ring true for you?

So, in principle, this idea of authenticity seems straightforward. All we need to do is to know, own and express our thoughts, our emotions, our responses and our reactions and we can claim to be authentic. We can feel safe in the knowledge that we are expressing our real self. This is where most of us are in our understanding of authenticity.

But there could be an issue with our interpretation.

All of those ideas would stack up if it weren't for one major obstacle - the concept of our False Identity. Are we being authentic to our True Self, or to the identity that has adapted to those thoughts of unworthiness and inadequacy (False Identity #2)? Fully understanding this idea can be challenging to accept. Could it be possible that even when I own and express my thoughts and feelings, I am being deluded by the False Identity? How do I know if what I am experiencing is authentic truth or if I am being lied to by my own misguided sense of self? We have to be willing to delve a little deeper.

When Jack first came for sessions, he had been dating his girlfriend Jess for six months. When he had first been introduced to Jess, he had been bowled over and was taken by surprise when he found out that the interest was mutual. He couldn't believe that someone as beautiful and smart would take a liking to him. Initially, they had been inseparable and spent almost every evening together. But Jess also loved to go out with her friends and wanted to keep her girls' nights out. Jack said he was very happy for her to go but was concerned about her safety when she travelled home. He insisted on picking her up, rather than her taking a taxi. Jess was moved by his kind nature and that he was willing to put himself out to take care of her.

Each time Jess went out, Jack would worry

incessantly. He would hear about incidents that had happened in the area and use them to support the fears he expressed to Jess. She would do her best to reassure him. She was touched that he would so openly and authentically own and talk about his concerns of something happening to her and it brought them closer.

But then something began to change in their relationship. Jack would turn up at the venue sooner than planned, telling Jess that he had heard stories of trouble. He said he wouldn't interfere but would just sit quietly at the back to make sure he was available if she needed him. Over time, Jack would appear earlier and earlier, and it wasn't long before he was taking her there and staying all evening. Rather than feeling loved and protected, Jess began to feel smothered and paranoid that he was watching her every move. When they talked about the problem, Jack insisted it was purely because he worried about her safety. Much to Jack's confusion and despair, it all became too much for Jess, who ended the relationship. He felt he had been rejected for simply worrying and looking out for her.

Jack was living in a blind spot. From the beginning he had put Jess on a pedestal and feared he would never be good enough for her. Emotionally aware, he sensed his fear but attributed it to his concern for Jess's safety. In order to keep his image of being *good enough* intact, he was being lied to by his False Identity #2. Worrying about Jess and wanting to take care of her allowed him to feel that he was being a strong and considerate boyfriend. Had he been able to see the truth, he would have been able to admit to his authentic feelings of jealousy and inadequacy.

I'm sure in this example, it is easy to spot the lies that Jack was living by. But when we are protecting our False Identity, it is perfectly natural not to see the truth. Without really knowing his authentic feelings, there was no opportunity for Jack to learn from (or transform) the pain. The False Identity was masking the real issue and the opportunity for his evolution.

We all have this authenticity blind spot. We can be absolutely sure that we are expressing what is true for us and yet be totally unaware that we are being misled by a False Identity, whose main objective is to keep us from dropping into any dark feelings of unworthiness. As long as we claim this False Identity as authenticity, we will never really discover the truth of who we are. Beneath the layers of polish and refinement there are not only our feelings of inadequacy but also the secrets of our soul – the essence of who we truly are. We simply can't access that essence whilst believing the lie and protecting our false self. We've got to get down and dirty with our emotions.

What lies beneath?

Our emotions are not the unfortunate by-product of life – they are the messengers of our soul and to live fully involves learning to turn into them rather than away from them. I think it is a real shame that emotional states aren't taught as part of the traditional school curriculum. Which do you think will have the bigger impact on the quality of life, knowing the major rivers of the world or how to handle your anger?

There are many myths about our feelings – perhaps the greatest being that we shouldn't indulge them. Much of personal development/self-improvement is focused on learning to manage or change our emotional states. Public speakers and athletes are taught to control their nerves. You can take anger management or confidence building classes that teach skills and techniques to suppress your rage or your fears and feel something different in its place. I speak to many clients who are consistently blocking grief or sadness because the people around them think they should be over it.

I'm not suggesting that we act on our feelings but that we give ourselves permission to feel them without trying to fix them. Our greatest fear seems to be that if we allow our emotions that they might overwhelm us. But what if overwhelming emotions could actually be a good thing?

When I first began to work with my coach, John Overdurf[14], I was pretty masterful at deflecting and dismissing uncomfortable feelings. Any time an emotion got *too much*, I would simply disconnect from it. On the surface it seemed like a sound strategy for a happy life. I could avoid anything that I didn't like. But as we have seen with earlier examples, that isn't always helpful. Turning away from an emotion doesn't actually remove it but rather temporarily postpones it. And the next time it comes around, it is likely to appear with greater intensity. We simply end up constantly running from our own shadows.

John introduced me to a concept he calls '*Bailing at the Peak*'. He explained that when we sit gently with an emotional state, without doing or saying anything, the intensity lasts an average of 45 to 90 seconds. Rather like a wave, each feeling builds to a peak and then subsides all within less than a minute and a half. The problem is that if we dislike the feeling and try to avoid it, we never stay with it long enough for it to pass through and get to the other side. As the intensity builds, we bail at the peak. This becomes a repetitive and escalating habit as we learn to deflect an uncomfortable feeling as soon as we notice it arising. If we have a belief that we shouldn't get angry or feel upset, we will be fast-tracking in the opposite direction at even the hint of a wave of irritation.

So why is this a problem? Because the healing power

of emotion happens when it passes through our being and changes us. When we bail at the peak we only manage to avoid the therapeutic transformation. If we allow the wave, our True Self is revealed and we receive the gifts of Divine insight. You will discover the undeniable wisdom of your soul – the part of you that understands the interplay of your energy with the rest of the universe. It will tell you that there are no accidents. It will show you how everything in your life fits together. It will help you to understand your unconditioned nature and perceive your inherent wholeness and worthiness. It will remind you about who you really are beyond the illusions of the False Identity. So how do we use emotion to connect back to our True Self? We simply need to learn to move beyond the stories of the False Identity, invite our vulnerability and drop into the rawness of our authentic feelings.

On one of my retreat workshops, I asked for a volunteer who would like to clear a negative emotion so that they could live more fully in the present moment. A young lady called Gemma raised her hand. She explained that she had spent most of her life living under the dark cloud of an unresolved feeling. I asked her if she would be willing to come to front of the room and join me for a demonstration. Bravely, Gemma agreed. She shared with the group that before she knew she was pregnant with her first child, she had regularly got drunk and taken recreational drugs. Her daughter had been born with a facial disfigurement and every time she looked her, she blamed herself. Fighting back the tears, she wished that she could just know whether or not it had been her fault.

I checked with Gemma that she felt safe and was happy to do the process in front of the audience. With a cheeky smile, she said she was absolutely sure that now was the right time because she hadn't consciously raised her hand to volunteer and had been very surprised to see it in the air! I continued by asking her how she felt when she saw her daughter's face and she simply responded '*guilty*'. Instead of turning away from the guilt, I invited Gemma to just sit with it. Clearly it wasn't comfortable for her to do but she knew she had been avoiding the feelings for too long. I had her focus on her breathing and to notice any changes or contractions in her body. When I asked her what she might be resisting, she told me that she was terrified about finding out that she was to blame. Rather than protecting Gemma, this fear was destroying her life and her relationship with her daughter. It was time to stop avoiding it and to turn and face it.

I suggested that she did nothing else but just acknowledge the fear and breathe into it. When I asked her what she was picturing, she said she was imagining all of the drugs and alcohol in her womb damaging the baby. Again, I invited her to simply be aware of what she was feeling without trying to alter it. We discussed how the emotion felt in her body. Gemma explained that she had a sense of emptiness in her stomach and tension around her chest and heart. At this point, Gemma said she felt deep sadness. She began to sob and for a moment or two struggled to catch her breath. I reminded her to keep breathing through the emotion and to allow the wave to simply pass through.

When we face our demons, they can seem overwhelming. This is why we have hidden from them for so long. The closer we get, the more we start to see them as they really are – illusions of our false self. As Gemma continued to breathe, the wave of emotion subsided and a look of relief passed over her face. I asked her what the experience had revealed to her. Gemma gently smiled as she realised how she had been ignoring her daughter's beauty. She had been so busying worrying about the damage she had caused that she hadn't been paying attention to the sparkle in her daughter's eyes or the golden glow of her skin. The whole question of fault had dissipated and all she could see was how gorgeous her daughter looked. To complete the process, I asked Gemma how she had not been noticing her own beauty. She smiled and said that she realised how ugly her self-blame had made her. As we took questions and comments from the room, many people affirmed how beautiful Gemma looked now she wasn't burdened down by her guilt.

If you would like to try the process I did with Gemma, you will find it outlined below. In its simplest terms, every time you notice an emotion arising within you that is causing discomfort, breathe deeply into it. Often, especially if you have been avoiding the feelings for a while, you will find that the presenting emotion is a mask for something more deep-rooted. There is nothing to fear, simply continue to gently acknowledge your feelings and breathe into them knowing that the wave will pass through you. This advice is echoed by A H Almaas[15] in his book *The Unfolding Now*:

"Do your best not to judge the things arising or do anything with them, because true nature itself will transform them."

As Gemma discovered, on the other side of an intense feeling, you will discover the truth. Through sitting with our emotions and not trying to change them, we open the doorway for Divine intelligence to communicate with us. We see that there is nothing to be afraid of. The gentle wisdom will always come from a place of pure love. At last, you will be able to see what you were blind to before. When you honour your emotions, you transcend the conditions that were causing you pain. The difficult situation is transformed. A new you will be revealed. You are brought home to your authentic and unconditioned nature. This is your True Self.

ⓘ *Lesson 12 - Breathing Exercise:*

1. **Getting present**
    - Notice a feeling or situation that you are resisting or avoiding.
    - Bring your awareness into the here and now.
    - Give your attention to your breathing (without trying to change it).

2. **Exploring the Situation & Your Resistance**
    - Ask yourself "*What am I resisting*?"
    - Become the curious observer of any thoughts that arise.
    - What stories are you telling yourself?

3. **Understanding the Presenting Feeling**
    - As you think about the situation, how are you feeling?
      e.g. *frustration, anger, sadness*
    - Where do you feel it in your body? Is it warm or cold? Does it move or is it still? Does it have a colour or form associated with it?
    - As you are feeling this way, what are you saying to yourself? e.g. *He doesn't love me*, *I am a failure etc*
    - Allow all thoughts to arise without judgment or analysis.

4. **Experiencing the Pure Emotion**
    - Allow the presenting feeling to arise with intensity.
    - Breathe deeply into it. Allow it to overwhelm

you until it begins to dissipate. Keep breathing through.

- *Note: Some intense emotions cause us to hold our breath. This is part of the pattern of resistance and is why breathing can create such profound shifts. Keep breathing!*
- If any other feelings arise, continue to acknowledge their presence and breathe deeply into and through each emotion.
- When all the feelings have completely dissolved, a new truth will be revealed. Bring that into your awareness e.g. *I don't love me enough, I am failing myself.*
- Flip the original story (or stories) into an empowering question based on your new truth e.g. *He doesn't love me* becomes *How am I not loving myself right now? I am a failure* becomes *How am failing myself?*

CHAPTER 11

Nurturing and nourishing

One evening I was out with a group of friends. One of our party seemed a little withdrawn so I took a seat next to her to check in on how she was doing. It was clear that she was facing up to some of those *not-good-enough* gremlins. She told me how she felt like everyone else in the group was more attractive and glamorous than her. She went on to say that everyone seemed to have a better and more fulfilling career and that she was the only one who wasn't in a relationship because no one wanted to be with her. Her Storyteller had been running riot in her mind. I invited her to look back at the group and see beyond everyone's party persona. Did she really believe that there was anyone else in the group who never had a similar worry? The next time you are with a group, take a proper look into their eyes. Don't we all have that not-good-enough gremlin lurking somewhere in our psyche ready to pounce at the hint of a doubt or fear? Whether it dominates our life is not a question of *if* it exists but, rather, the degree to which we feed it.

Comparison is a nasty trick played by a false self to convince us of our worth (or lack of it). Any time you measure your own value against an imaginary benchmark that you perceive in others, you will either come up short or display superiority – neither of which reflect your true essence. Now is the time to ditch the comparison game. What can it ever give to you apart from a false perception of yourself? Comparison creates the need for approval seeking and self-judgment, which slowly eat away at your sense of value. If you require validation to know your worth, you will only ever be as good as the last opinion of you. Do you really need the applause of an audience to find the love in your own heart?

In evaluating who you *really* are, yours is the only opinion that matters. It is time to silence the critics inside and out and listen to the loving voice of your True Self. A sustainable sense of worthiness comes from within. We need to stop feeding the not-good-enough gremlins and instead nurture our body, mind, and soul. Knowing and experiencing our authentic self can only come from nourishing ourselves with kindness, compassion and love.

If we are living in our minds, trapped in the pursuit game, we will neglect or push ourselves to achieve more. To be present enough to connect to our True Self, we have to be in a relationship that honours our whole being. Essential components of presence are self-care and self-love. In this chapter, I want to take you on a journey to discover the many ways in which you can nurture and nourish your self more fully – in a way that is right for you rather than according to the opinions and judgments of outside influences.

The importance of self-care

When I speak of self-care, what comes to mind? How do you *care* for yourself? Is it something that you prioritise – or is it the thing that you do when you have finished the tasks on your to-do list or you are taken ill?

Self-care is a cornerstone to a life of presence. Perhaps you have been doing too much for too long. If you are showing signs of stress or burnout, then it is time to look after yourself better. Even if you feel like life is in balance, taking stock of how you foster your wellbeing is always a valuable exercise. Awareness of what nourishes us (and what doesn't!) can sustain us through periods of upheaval or challenge. It is all part of developing a deeper relationship with your heart and soul.

For some, the idea of caring for ourselves is regarded as being selfish. We are often taught that kindness and goodness comes from giving to others. But there is nothing selfish about honouring your wellbeing. You can't provide for others unless you have something to offer, whether that is your energy, your attention or your presence. We can be talking about our role as a lover, a parent, a friend, an employee or a leader. The greatest asset you can give is the *whole* of you and that is only possible when you are feeling emotionally, mentally, physically and spiritually well. That's why self-care and presence are so intrinsically linked. Rather than being an act of selfishness, taking care of our self allows us to be more present in our interactions with others and to add value in the world.

When I talk about self-care, I notice that many clients have a direct association with physical and mental health. Some view it as another item on the to-do list – a task that you tick off when you have been to the gym, eaten a healthy meal or had a full eight-hours sleep. They don't give it much attention unless problems arise. Getting injured or sick is seen as a problem to resolve. A trip to the Doctors or popping a couple of pills is often the fastest and most efficient remedy. There is no desire to stay connected to the issue for a moment longer than is necessary. We want to get fixed and move on. But without understanding the source of the pain or discomfort, we miss the learning opportunities and nothing of value can be gained. Every health issue is a message from our bodies. Unless we learn to listen and adjust what we do, we will just continue to run the same damaging patterns until a problem arises again.

Whilst some disregard their wellbeing, I work with many clients who do prioritise their health. Living in pursuit doesn't necessarily imply a neglect of our bodies and minds. In fact, I meet many people living a *full-on* life whose schedule includes eating highly nutritious food and working out regularly. They understand the connection between how they treat their bodies and their energy levels. To live at a fast and frenetic pace requires a good source of fuel. They recognise that to have maximum output requires measured and sustainable input. It all sounds like common sense.

But pursuit can often mislead us in our understanding of self-care. Rather than understanding the nourishment process holistically, it pretends to be caring while still having us strive for achieving ultimate energy, the perfect body or spiritual success. Pursuit mentality challenges us to achieve some type of illusionary end-goal. I've come across weight-loss challenges, meditation challenges and exercise challenges – all promising a desirable and appealing result at the conclusion of your investment of effort.

There is nothing wrong with any of these concepts, as long as we are aware when we have been lured into pursuit consciousness. Without a doubt, setting a goal can help us to experiment with and condition in new habits and behaviours. The real distinction is understanding the relationship between the challenge and the degree to which it *nourishes* you. Despite our best intentions, challenge doesn't always equal nourishment. In fact, the end goal can divert us from being fully immersed in the experience. We may get the *result* without benefiting from the process of self-care.

I witnessed this pattern with a client called Greg. Greg had found school incredibly hard. He was always the last to be picked in team games and had struggled with weight issues all through childhood. After he had left school, his mission had been to prove himself to others. With the help of a personal trainer, Greg had got into great shape. He had transformed his body by a strict eating regime and physical exercise programme. He had pursued and achieved the goal he wanted. He had shown his schoolmates that he wasn't the chubby non-athlete that they had labelled him to be.

Yet Greg was deeply unhappy. He was locked in a prison of fear. He was terrified of slipping backwards and regaining the weight. He was obsessed with what foods he could and couldn't eat. He worked out every day for hours on end – and his relationship with his girlfriend was being jeopardised because he had so little time to spend with her. Instead of feeling good about his achievements, he continued to compare himself to the other men in the gym and the images in health magazines. He still felt that he didn't measure up and he was toying with the idea of taking steroids to enhance his physique. He was tormented by a dark nature that told him he would never be good enough. His thoughts were so intense that they woke him up at night. When I met with him, he was suffering the effects of long-term sleep deprivation.

Here was a guy who, on the surface, seemed to prioritise his wellbeing above all else, even important relationships. But despite all his seemingly *good* practices, inner peace eluded him. Were his actions nourishing him? In all honesty, I think Greg was as much at risk (if not more) of a serious illness as someone doing absolutely nothing because of the intense pressure he was placing on himself. Can you see how pursuit can delude us into thinking we are practising self-care when, in fact, our actions can be highly damaging?

The difference in presence consciousness is that self-care goes much deeper than achieving a specific result. It isn't about the calorie counting, the number of times you go to the gym or how often you meditate. It is the understanding that there is no one path. Instead, it is learning how to tune into the signals from your body, day-to-day and moment-to-moment. In presence, we learn to recognise and honour the requests from within rather than striving to measure up to some illusionary model of perfection that our culture constantly conveys.

When we are connected to our inner needs, we understand our role as a channel for something greater than ourselves. We are a source of connection to the Divine. Your body and mind are not yours to own – they are a sacred but temporary gift that will one day cease to exist. This incarnation that you call *me* is the vehicle that allows you to play, explore and discover the world. There are no rules about what you can or cannot do with your gift. You can treat it with love and nourishment, you can neglect it or you can push it to the limit. There is no need to justify or explain your choices to anyone. Ultimately, we will all reach a point in our lives when we meet our maker and only then will be able to truly evaluate whether we think that we made the right decisions. Presence consciousness doesn't remove choice; it enhances it.

It would be easy in a chapter entitled *nurturing and nourishing* to start to list all the things that you need to do to practice self-care. However, I seriously doubt that you lack ideas about what a caring lifestyle might look like. There is a huge amount of information out there that will tell you what you should and should not do. You simply don't need another external voice telling you how best to nurture yourself. I want to invite you to stop seeking the answers out there and turn your attention within.

The biggest gap I see with my clients is that they may take care of themselves, yet they still don't know how to nourish their being. They may eat high quality, nutritious foods. They may be at the gym every day. They may meditate or practice yoga. But their minds are still riddled with the toxic thoughts generated by the Storyteller and so holistic wellness continues to elude them.

Self-care isn't something you practice for an hour or two a day when you are eating, exercising or meditating. It is the continual supply of self-compassion, kindness and love that flows through your entire existence. It is a willingness to spot and cease your self-defeating patterns like comparison, approval-seeking and judgment. It is the ability to make real time decisions about what you body is calling for and to respect and honour every request.

I want to invite you to really examine your own self-care practices. Are you truly looking after your mind, body and spirit? It's no good spending an hour a day in peaceful meditation and spending the other twenty-three hours berating and judging yourself. How will you embody self-care? You won't find the answer to that question in a mirror, on a set of scales or in the good word of another. In presence consciousness, self-care can only be evaluated by the degree to which you feel holistically nourished.

What your body really needs

There have been times in my life when I have desperately wanted to make changes. Usually triggered by a number on the scales or my clothes feeling tight, I've been absolutely resolute in my commitment to a diet and exercise programme. I never lacked motivation but sometimes the results didn't quite measure up to my expectations. When my efforts have failed, I have sought the advice of experts and found something very intriguing. For every piece of diet advice, you can usually find something contradictory. Don't eat carbohydrates/eat a full carbohydrate diet. Exercise as much as possible/don't exercise too much. Do cardio-based activity/stick to weights. It is easy to get lost in the minefield of information. Who has the right answer?

The truth is that everyone has *a* right answer. When someone shares their knowledge and expertise, it usually comes from their own experiences. Go to a bookstore and compare all the different diet books and you can know one thing for sure – this programme has worked for someone at some time. What you don't know is whether of not it is the right approach for you. Dieting is not an exact science.

The same is true in other contexts too. I once had the great privilege of interviewing two ladies who had been diagnosed with inflammatory breast cancer for my online TV show called *Share the Love*[16]. Gabby had fully recovered whilst Mel was still undergoing treatment. Both ladies had tried a number of different approaches to curing their disease and spoke with such beautiful wisdom and frank honesty about their experiences. They had undergone treatments like chemotherapy, mastectomy, Reiki, psychotherapy and raw food diets amongst many others.

Living with cancer is one of the biggest challenges someone can face. Not only are they dealing with the impact of the disease but also cultural preconceptions. We talk about cancer with fear and trepidation and we treat those that have been diagnosed with the disease as though they have been handed a death sentence. Someone seeking to heal their cancer is not only contending with the physical symptoms but also the collective beliefs of society. If we are prepared to look beyond the fearful stories, we will find many people who have successfully healed. Yet there isn't one solution. I've heard people attribute their recovery to the foods that they eat, their medical treatment and even comedy! If you or anyone you know has lived through cancer, you will be aware of how many different approaches are offered. The options can be both overwhelming and costly in terms of energy and money. Chemotherapy could be exactly right for one person. A raw food diet could suit someone else. There are no hard and fast rules. If there were, our understanding of cancer and other diseases would be very different. There would be nothing to fear if the answer was straightforward.

Can you see that throughout life, everyone is out there doing different things and getting different results? When we talk about truly nourishing self-care, you can find ideas and inspiration outside of your self but never answers. So how do you find what is really right for *you*?

The good news is that you don't need to rely on advice or suggestions from experts or authorities, only to learn how to hear the loving voice within. Your body already knows exactly what it needs to be nurtured in each moment. If you are thinking that you haven't heard any body wisdom, it doesn't mean that it doesn't exist. Just as you might need to dial in a radio to hear a specific station's broadcast, we have to tune into the inner voice to hear the message. And that is a skill that you can develop.

Throughout this book we have already begun to explore the messages from our body. You may have started to notice specific signals – for example, what a butterfly sensation in your stomach is telling you or what tension across your shoulders might mean. In this section, we are going to develop ways to get clearer on the signals. Some messages may be easier to detect and not require much conscious input on your part. Others may seem more confusing but there are ways to interpret the signals, especially in the beginning as you train yourself to pay closer attention your body.

Some of these techniques may appear weird or freaky as you first use them. I would love to tell you that it is a supernatural power but sadly the explanation is much less mysterious than that. It all comes down to your mind-body-spirit connection.

As you go about your daily business, you have your conscious, present-moment awareness (i.e. the things you are paying attention to at the time). When you say, "*I was just thinking*" then you are talking about your conscious awareness. Then there is everything else that makes up part of your experience that you aren't consciously noticing. Every detail of every moment is being tracked and faithfully recorded by your unconscious (or subconscious) mind. You may not be aware of how your left foot is feeling until I direct your attention there. Can you understand that the information was always available to you (you could have felt your left foot at any time), you just weren't focusing on it?

All the specific details are stored by the extensive filing system of the unconscious mind. This is why it is so wise. It knows everything about you. It knows how your body reacts to different substances like alcohol, gluten or chocolate. It knows which parts of your body are strong and which are weaker. It can measure the impact of every choice you make without you ever needing to be consciously there to oversee the process. It holds the information throughout our whole body. Do you remember the story of Bill in the chapter on forgiveness? He had no conscious recollection of his father hurting him but his body knew the pain he had suffered. How was he able to find out the cause of his own poor health? By tuning into the message stored in his heart. We can access this wisdom by building rapport with our unconscious mind. It can take practice to open the path of communication and get clear messages like Bill did but if we want to understand what truly nourishes us, it is a useful investment of our time.

ⓘ **Lesson 13** - *Muscle Testing (Part 1)*

One way of opening the communication channel is through muscle testing[17]. Your unconscious mind will show you what is (and what is not) assisting and supporting your body through the strength or weakness of your muscles. The easiest way to do this is with a friend or partner. Simply stretch your arm out at 90 degrees from the side of your body. Have your buddy **gently** push down on your forearm whilst you try to resist. This will give you a general benchmark for your natural muscle strength. Now have your buddy do the exact same thing whilst you hold your arm out and repeat the word '*yes, yes, yes*'. Was your arm easier or more difficult to press down?

Do the same thing for '*no, no, no*'. What do you notice? Play with the muscle testing for a while. Try saying your real name out loud and then compare it to a made up name. Or experiment with your correct age and then make one up. How do the results differ? When our mind and body are in agreement, we will get a signal of strength (it will be less easy to press the arm downwards). When they are in disagreement, your muscles will be weakened (it will be easier to press your arm downwards). Once you are sure you can tell the muscle responses apart, you can begin to ask questions with a yes/no answer and your body will answer.

Check out which foods your body responds well to and which it dislikes. Or test your unconscious alignment with a particular decision you are making by asking if a choice is in your best interests. Your unconscious wisdom will come through the answers generated by the strength or lack of it in your arm.

ⓘ ***Lesson 14** - Muscle Testing (Part 2)*

The good news is that you don't need a buddy to play with this idea. You can try a similar approach by pinching together your thumb and forefinger on each hand as though you were making the diving okay signal. Then take one of the linked thumb and forefingers and push them upwards through the circle you have made on the other hand. By opening the thumb and forefinger on the hand inside the circle you can judge how easy or difficult it is to pull your other fingers apart. The harder it is, then the more strength there is in your body in response to your question (i.e. a yes signal). If you find it easier to pull your fingers apart then it means less strength and a negative response to what you are asking (i.e. a no signal). This is a great one to play with whilst you are shopping at the supermarket. You can choose the foods to place in your basket based on the responses from your body.

For example, you may ask whether a particular fruit would be good for you or whether your body would like pasta for your evening meal.

ⓘ ***Lesson 15*** *- Pendulum Play*

Another way of building rapport with our unconscious mind is by using a pendulum. A pendulum is a small weight that hangs from a piece of chain or string. When it is held in a specific way, small nerve reactions occur in your fingers changing the direction in which the pendulum swings. Those reactions come from your unconscious mind in response to the different questions or ideas that you are considering. It can seem like voodoo or magic but really it is just the transmission of minute reactions through your fingers, down the chain and to the pendulum, which causes it to move. Your unconscious reactions are easier to observe this way because they are amplified in the swinging pendulum. Sadly, no great mystery but a great way of communicating with the part of you that knows your deepest needs.

To use a pendulum to communicate with your unconscious mind, you will either need to make one by adding a weight (like a fastening nut for a bolt) on the end of a string about twenty centimetres long. Or you can buy beautiful crystal or metal versions fairly inexpensively online. Drape the end of the chain/string over your first finger and thumb so that the pendulum can swing freely. Hold the end of the string lightly so that it won't fall but you aren't gripping it too tightly either. Gently focus your attention on the weight at the end of the pendulum. Let the pendulum swing until it settles down motionless. Continue to watch it and think about it coming to rest.

Once the pendulum has stopped moving, ask your unconscious mind to give you the signal for yes. Just say out loud or in your head, "*Please show me the signal for a yes response*". Keep observing the pendulum and it will begin to move. What direction is it choosing to swing? It may be back to front, side-to-side or diagonal. It may swing in circles and, if so, just notice the direction it takes. If the movements are small, you can ask your unconscious mind to increase the signals by saying; "*Please intensify the movement*". Treat your unconscious mind as you would a good friend. Be patient rather than demanding. Appreciate all of the signals, no matter how small or even if they don't seem to have an identifiable pattern.

Allow the pendulum to come back to a resting place (you can stop it with your other hand if you would like.) Now you can do the exact same thing and ask for a *no* response. Track which direction the pendulum moves to signal no. The important thing is to ask the questions as "*please show me....*" not "*can you show me...*" or "*will you show me....*". If it *can* show you it will give you the affirmative signal! You may also want to include a signal for "*I don't know*" or better still "*not consciously ready to know yet*". This allows your unconscious mind to make independent decisions on which information is useful for you to know and which isn't. It will always tell you the truth that is in your highest and best interests.

Just as with the muscle testing, you can now play with your signals. Begin by checking responses to things you already know like your name or your age. Then you can move onto asking specific questions about what will or won't nourish you. Always honour the signals from your unconscious mind and try not to overrule answers with your conscious thinking. If you are convinced the answer will be yes, you may jeopardise accurate responses. Sometimes getting signals can take some time. Much to my frustration, it took me quite a few attempts to get even a hint of movement. The most helpful thing you can do is to relax and be at ease without attachment to what happens. Given time and patience, the signals will come.

So we have begun to build up a channel of communication for our inner voice. As you are playing with these exercises, pay attention and tune into the other signals that you feel in your body. What else do you notice when you are getting a yes response? What is different when the response is no? Notice your breathing, areas of tension or sensations of movement in your body. This will help you to understand your yes/no signals without the need for testing. Your infinitely intelligent unconscious mind can now communicate with you through your body. It can tell you what it wants and what it doesn't. It can inform you on what is nourishing and what is not. Welcome to a whole new world of self-care!

Holistic nourishment

These activities are really warm-up exercises for a much deeper connection to your True Self. Of course it is helpful to know what foods nourish your body or whether you are making aligned decisions. But that is only a fraction of the story. If we limit the concept of self-care to just our mental and physical wellbeing, we are omitting massive areas of our whole being. We don't just want to care for our bodies, but to extend that nourishment to our minds, hearts and our souls as well.

So much of what we have already covered in this book

is relevant to the concept of nurturing our wellbeing. What damage are we doing when we allow a drama story to create a surge of adrenaline through our body? What is the impact of constantly seeking to control things that are beyond our realm of influence? How are we hurting ourselves when we hold a grudge and refuse to forgive? What effect does constantly rushing have on our bodies? Everything we do or don't do is either benefiting or harmful to our bodies. To embrace holistic nourishment, we need to pay closer attention to our choices. Do you think stillness is nourishing or not? What about comparison, attachment or judgment? How about forgiveness, simplicity or surrender?

There will be some generalisations that we are likely to concur on. I am sure you could write a long list of the things that you *know* to be consistently good for you. But there are no set laws. Living in presence is the willingness to allow the truth of the moment to reveal itself to you. I have found examples of this when I exercise. Some days my body wants to go for an energetic run. Other days it would prefer the gentle and allowing movements of yoga. When you pay attention to the signals as they occur, you find the best source of nourishment at that time. Presence consciousness knows that nothing is *all ways* right and nothing is off limits. It allows for the fluidity and flexibility of responding to what the moment brings. It is an ever-changing process that reflects the evolving you.

This is why stillness is so important. The more we cultivate a quiet and reflective space to connect with our True Self, the more readily we can access the requests from our body and soul. How can you hear your heart's desire to be in nature if you are engrossed in busyness and rushing? Dropping into the stillness of the moment develops the connection to our inner world. We hear the body messages before they manifest as illness or disease.

Our True Self has a channel to let us know when a choice or decision we are making is not in our best interests. Our hearts have a way of calling us home to love, to connection and to oneness. Holistic nourishment brings us into whole body alignment and, in that alignment, we are able to synchronise ourselves with something beyond our own being. Ultimately, our nurturing further develops our connection with the Divine and this is where the magic of presence really happens.

STEP 3: SYNCHRONISING

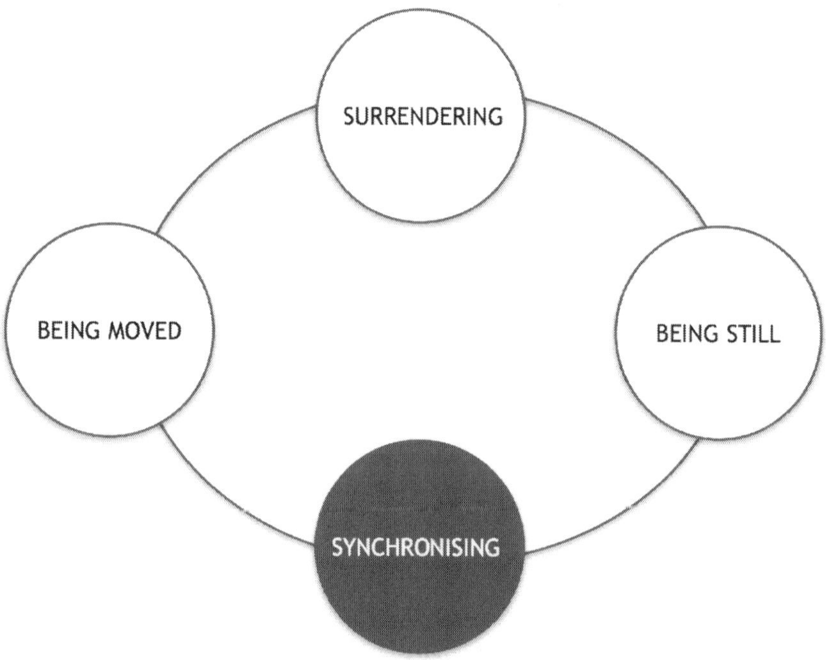

CHAPTER 12

Grounding

Up until now, we have been working primarily on our inner world. No amount of external change can bring you the peace and contentment you crave if, on some level, you still believe the thoughts of unworthiness and inadequacy. Like a house that is built on poor foundations, you can dress it up and make it look pretty but the instability remains. This is the nail varnish that covers the muck of the False Identity. Scratch the surface and the original issues reappear. It doesn't matter how many material gains you make, sustainable contentment will continue to elude you. A life of presence begins from the inside out. Your conditioned self has tried to convince you that the achievement of more goals was the answer to your quest for happiness. But only by delving into the dark recesses, where you have previously feared to go, will you finally find what was really missing. Once you challenge the demons that have been trying to convince you that you are not enough, you realise that the only things that have been keeping you from contentment are the stories created by a divided and unsatisfied mind.

You may find that you need to retreat from life in order to nurture yourself and to heal the patterns of inadequacy and unworthiness that have been holding you back. But human beings are not intended to exist in isolation. We are meant to live in community, to be an integral part of society, to build heart-centred relationships and to make our contribution to the world. Yet, we don't want to lose touch with the inner world that we have cultivated this far. Finding an optimum balance of being fully aware of our internal processes, whilst interacting and relating on the outside, is the practice of synchronisation.

Synchronisation is important because it gives us an expanded view of our experiences. Rather than being at the mercy of external events, we are the alert witness of our inner responses. When someone hurts or offends us, we are not taken over by a knee-jerk reaction. Instead, we can observe how our body responds, pay attention to any self-defeating dialogue and be aware of the judgmental nature that is keeping us separate from a world that we yearn to connect with. If your boss or a parent calls you dumb or incompetent for example, you are much more interested in your emotional reaction to the words than seeking to defend yourself or correct their opinion. Remember that your True Self knows your inherent worth. Therefore any doubts or questions that arise within are really the evidence of a false and conditioned nature. Is it more important that you challenge the imposter self or the person who has accused you? One will bring you greater self-love and self-acceptance; the other creates further conflict and insecurity.

The most meaningful and fulfilling aspect of synchronisation is the development of our relationship with the Divine. Imagine a life beyond difficult decision-making, exhausting goal-setting, dehabilitating procrastination, fear, anxiety, resentment and disappointment. When we learn to bring ourselves into alignment with something bigger, brighter and lighter than our limited human perspective, this imagined life becomes our reality. This section will take you on a journey towards contentment, inspiration and love.

A ship without an anchor

So much of Western culture is driving us away from our hearts and intuition and into our heads. Space is viewed as a luxury and yet our time is consumed with endless sources of low quality entertainment – newspapers, magazines, television, electronic gaming, social media. There is an expectation that someone or something should be constantly stimulating our senses. At the first hint of boredom, we are seeking out another fix to engage us. As a society, we eat excessively, drink alcohol, take mind-altering drugs and spend hours surfing the Internet. A sad by-product of our lifestyles is that our sense of aliveness comes from what we do, rather than our *be*-ing.

In this era of technology overload, our senses are bombarded with information that we are willing to absorb without questioning the source. We are giving away our intellectual and emotional capacity to an external authority. Some we may be choosing – like when we pick up a particular book or watch a movie – but how much is creeping past our conscious awareness unnoticed? How many times a day are your thoughts being manipulated by clever advertising or political positioning?

We have become addicted to being stimulated. Our quest for pleasure seems unending. Everyone wants to be happy but the concept of happiness is open to a very wide and diverse interpretation. What does it mean to you – contentment, fulfillment, excitement, bliss, elation? In my experience, very few people think of happiness as a place of peace. Instead, they describe a highly energised state of being that comes from the thrill of an isolated occurrence – it could be winning the lottery, meeting a new love, being awarded for your achievements or simply having a great night out. Whilst such events can feel wonderful as they occur, they are not enduring. How long does the buzz of success or euphoria last?

We also associate feelings like anticipation and excitement with happiness. But where are such states created? These feelings do not come from living in a grounded and connected body but rather are the product of the story-telling mind. In order to feel anticipation, we have to take ourselves to an imagined future. And what happens when the reality fails to measure up to our expectations? We come crashing down in a wave of disappointment. Would you swap the cycle of amazing highs followed by devastating lows for the serene simplicity of an even keel? Our over-stimulated minds are consuming our emotional states. Guilt, anxiety, fear, boredom, confusion, nervousness and so on come not from what is occurring in the present moment, but rather the story our minds are telling us about what could or has happened. The process of grounding brings us back into the here and now so we can experience events as they are, and not through the imagination of our Storyteller.

To do that, we need a solid and firm foundation for our life. Only then can we connect to something beyond our physical being and so become a conduit for energy from the higher worlds. Without that connection, we are like the unanchored ship being blown around by the biggest gust of wind. Have you ever been metaphorically *knocked off your feet* by the words or actions of another? Perhaps someone made an important decision that affected you without consulting you first? Maybe you have had a relationship end unexpectedly or without explanation? Maybe it was the shock of a medical diagnosis or a traumatic event like a car crash or burglary? Such experiences can destroy our sense of security and stability in an instant.

The feeling of being knocked off our feet (or *blown away, bowled over* etc) is a common experience that many relate to. If the focus of our energy is in our heads, how much easier is it to be tipped off balance? You don't even have to take my word for it. Have a friend gently push you when you are thinking about a problem or an issue and see how quickly you lose balance. Have them push you again with the same intensity whilst putting all of your attention on your feet on the floor. A simple illustration of how unstable we feel when we are living from our heads.

When I introduce the concepts of presence to clients who have been living in pursuit, they often ask, "*Won't I be bored*?" My honest answer is that you may temporarily experience some boredom – but that feeling is the detoxification from the endless sources of stimulation that you have come to depend on. Boredom is an impermanent and transient phase as you acclimatise to a new way of being. The reward for your willingness to see the detoxification through is an absolute and concrete knowing that your sense of aliveness is not dependent on anything other than your own breath. I breathe therefore I am. Breathe deep!

Our disconnection from earth

Can you imagine what earth looked like before human life took over? Modern humans spread from their African homeland some 70,000 years ago and now dominate every continent on Earth except Antarctica. Through the Stone Age, agricultural age and industrial age, we have gradually taken over the planet. We have claimed plots of land, erected boundaries and named the space as belonging to us. We buy and sell land as a commodity with vast sums of money exchanging hands for the right to erect and own homes, offices and factories on our exclusive plot.

Here in the United Kingdom approximately 63.23 million people[18] live on a small island totaling 243,610 km^2. We cluster around urban centres with the average UK plot size being just 295 m^2. Many people rarely venture outside of their towns and cities. There are children living today who have only breathed city air and never stood on anything other than concrete. The industrial and information ages promised so much but how many of us find ourselves locked in a prison – splitting our time between the small boxes we live in and the larger boxes where we work to earn a living? How much time in a day are your feet on planet earth? When was the last time you stood barefoot on a piece of undeveloped land? Perhaps only when we visit a park or go on a beach holiday? Our man-made constructions are now the barrier to our relationship with earth and we think of this as progress! The human race is wholly responsible for that disconnection.

There was a time when we grew our own food and exchanged or sold the surplus. We knew the history of fruit and vegetables we ate because we had witnessed it develop from seed to plant. We had been responsible for ensuring its growth and we consumed the rewards of our own endeavors. When we ate meat, we had hunted or nurtured it. There was a connection between the food we put in our mouths and its source. We knew chicken to be a feathered bird rather than pink-coloured flesh wrapped in polythene cartons. Take a walk around a supermarket and you will see how much of our groceries are now picked, packaged and processed miles away from our home and without much awareness on our part of the methods used. We are sustained by food that we have no connection with. A prepared ready meal, a chocolate biscuit, a carton of milk or even a fresh apple – do you know where any of them actually come from? Do you know how they got to your plate? Do you know anything about the people who prepared them for you?

Some aspire to restore their connection to the earth. There has been a rise in the number of households converting their small lawns to vegetable beds. More are keeping livestock like chickens to meet their dietary needs. There has been a significant increase in the demand for allotments and space to grow fruit and vegetables. Some are even escaping the rat race entirely and exploring ways to live off grid. They are finding their own sources of fuel and food in an attempt to break free from the dependency on the large corporations that control so many of our essential provisions. We can dream of sustainable living but the reality is that few have the capacity or the space to fully achieve their ambitions. We can try to get closer to the source by choosing to shop at local greengrocers or farm shops yet there is still a disconnection from the planet. We still complain when our root vegetables are soiled or we find a bug on our fruit. We expect everything to be clean, as though the original source is an inconvenience rather the essential part of the process.

This disconnection creates an interesting delusion – that in some way we own nature rather than vice versa. Imagine if we all started to claim ownership of the air that we breathe, the rays of the sun or the waves of the sea. We can see the ridiculousness of such an idea. Yet still we erect our boundaries on the land in futile attempts to protect our interests, our money and our property. We can never truly own the land. One swipe of Mother Nature's hand can remind us who is really in charge. It doesn't matter how spectacular your home is or how much you have paid for it, it could disappear instantly in a flood or an earthquake. We can feel afraid and take steps to protect our property or we can realise how egotistical human life has really become. We don't get to own earth because we are born from it. Like the parent that gives the child the autonomy to make mistakes, Mother Nature humours our efforts to take over. We believe in a level of control that only ever existed in our minds. Our need to control is destroying nature, community and ultimately life itself.

Let's take a different view – remember that we are being temporarily granted permission to reside in this space that we call home. No matter what the deeds to our house say, land can never truly be ours to own. Without the sun, life on earth would cease. The Divine is our landlord and our provider. We must drop our overinflated sense of importance and begin to treat the planet with the respect and admiration that it deserves – to be appreciative of our existence rather than demanding it. Everything that co-exists with us is part of the Universe. We are all born from the same originating source. The essence of the tree runs through each branch grown from the same original seedling. That which created you and me also created every plant, tree and wildlife. One day we will have no choice but to surrender our physical beings back to the earth. Ashes to ashes. Dust to dust. We will return to the same source from which we came. We are all part of the same family. Don't we need to take better care of our home?

I'm not saying that we shouldn't eat or live in buildings but we would benefit from a greater understanding and respect for everything that sustains us. Perhaps we can drop the sense of entitlement and honour things for what they really are – gifts from our provider. This is why having a sense of enough is so important. When someone gives you a birthday present, you don't demand more. You take time to acknowledge and appreciate it. Even if you don't like the item, you can still feel gratitude for the symbolic offering that the gift represents. Yet we hurtle through life using and abusing whatever we think we need to achieve our dreams and desires. Think of everything that you have consumed in the last week – water, food, electricity, petrol and so on. Aren't we incredibly fortunate to have a provider who offers us so much and begrudges us little?

Let us never take these gifts for granted. Yes, so much of what we use seems replaceable. We can buy new clothes or shoes. We can upgrade our smart phones as soon as the latest version is released. We can lease a car and get a new model every three years. In our current culture, new and glossy is favoured over repairing and recycling. I remember being in shock when I discovered that it would cost less to buy a new washing machine than to repair the existing one. New is often cheap. But what is the real cost that goes beyond the depreciation of our bank balance? If we keep consuming at the current rate, resources will run out. Even the best alternatives will require an adjustment to our lifestyles. We don't have to wait for that day to come. A simple change in attitude will transform our relationship with the planet. The earth has everything we need to sustain us if we stop our endless consumerism and begin to use it wisely. This is our opportunity to cease taking and to give back.

I'd like to invite you to just pause for a moment or two and fully consider your relationship with the planet. How deeply do you feel connected to the land on which you live? Is your partnership a mutual relationship of nourishment and appreciation or are you taking more than you are offering in return? This is not about feeling guilty or ashamed. Mother Nature doesn't judge or punish us for our choices. She will continue to provide as much as she can for as long as she can. That is why it has been so easy to get away with so much up until this point.

But now we know that our happiness is not dependent on the acquisition of more. Now we know when enough is enough. Now we know that simplicity is really the key to contentment and inner peace, we can let go of all of the unnecessary excess. We can take only what we need to sustain us. We can be a contributing force rather than a destructive one. We can make a decision to sidestep the lure of glossy advertising and promotion and to become more conscious of the consequences of our behaviour. Simply increasing awareness of the choices we make, opens our minds to new possibilities. Whenever I make a new purchase, I ask myself why I am buying it. I ensure that I really understand my choice rather than being lured in by shiny trinkets (sometimes a challenge for my magpie instincts!) I use my creativity to make cards and gifts for family and friends. I ask what I already have that could be upcycled into something different. I repair and recycle as much as I can and, when I no longer need an item, I pass it on to someone who could make use of it. In how many ways could you escape the pursuit trap that always promises *better – bigger – faster – more*?

Getting grounded

At the beginning of this chapter, I suggested that you have someone gently push against you whilst you considered a problem or issue and then compared the experience whilst putting your attention on your feet. You probably noticed how much more stable you felt when you were focusing on your feet on the floor. This is the essence of grounding. So much of today's lifestyle has our energy pushed up into our brains that we are walking around like disembodied heads. We simply cannot feel our connection to earth, to each other or to our own soul when we are cut off from the neck down.

Being grounded is absolutely essential for presence. Many spiritual practices are about opening our connection to higher realms. But we have a body for a reason. We are meant to explore our physical relationship with the planet. You may have met people on your journey who have cultivated a strong spiritual connection and yet appear floaty or scattered. Like a helium balloon that isn't weighted, it seems as though they might drift off into the atmosphere. Being grounded gives you the firm foundation for connection on every level.

When I begin working with my clients, I am always intrigued to discover how embodied they are. Although clearly not an exact science, there are some stereotypical patterns. Those who live and explore the world through their bodies are able to access emotional states, integrate information and process change more easily and rapidly. In fact, often the first necessary intervention for highly intellectual and *heady* people is teaching them how to drop into their bodies and ground themselves more effectively.

When I first met with Patrick, it felt a little like being with a human whirlwind. Initially I thought it was the stress of a project he was working on but it soon became apparent that this was a more widespread issue. He would begin the session with a list of subjects that he wanted to explore but couldn't stay focused on one topic for any period of time. He would ask a question but wasn't present enough to hear the response. When I asked him how subsequent ideas related to his original request, he seemed completely baffled. He couldn't remember what the first question had been!

Patrick was incredibly creative and his mind was swimming with so many ideas and possibilities that he just couldn't track. He was struggling to develop anything of any substance or meaning in his life. Relationships were fleeting

– arriving and departing from his life with incredible speed. His marketing business had the potential to be hugely successful. He had been recognised in the industry for his ability to think outside of the box and come up with totally unique ideas for campaigns. But his clients never seemed to stick around long enough for him to make a difference. Much of his time was spent finding and attracting new clients to sustain his struggling business rather than developing client projects. He felt frustrated and annoyed that he wasn't being valued.

But Patrick wasn't really undervalued. It was more that *he* was struggling to listen to his clients and loved ones. Even the simplest of conversations would spark yet another concept in his mind and he was off mentally exploring his latest inspiration rather than staying engaged with the conversation. If you have ever been around someone who is flitting from idea to idea, you will know that it can be mentally exhausting to follow their train of thought. People were distancing themselves from Patrick, not because they didn't like or appreciate him but because they just couldn't keep up.

Whilst it was important that Patrick allowed his creativity to flow, he also needed to develop a firm foundation. I had him learn how to pull his energy down from his head to his feet. He practiced grounding techniques to keep himself centred in his body. His fears that his creativity would be diluted proved to be unfounded. Instead of a decrease in ideas, he found that the inspiration kept coming and often the concepts were more relevant and viable than before. He could hold his attention on a two-way conversation and so his client relationships improved. They could now explain their specific business needs and he could offer solutions that really hit the mark. The number of referrals and recommendations shot up and his company thrived.

Patrick epitomised the ungrounded person living from his head. Massive potential remained untapped because there was no foundation to support all of the ideas and thoughts that ran wildly through his mind. It was extremely challenging to develop any kind of relationship with him because there was nothing solid to connect to. That is why grounding is such an essential component in presence. We want the ideas and inspiration to be connected to something sturdy and stable. Grounding our bodies keeps us anchored and in touch with physical reality.

ⓘ ***Lesson 16*** - *Getting grounded*

Here's an exercise you might like to try. You can find the recorded exercise in the online workshop or have a friend facilitate the process. Begin by standing upright. If you can find a place to do this where you are standing directly on the earth this will work even better. Imagine that the soles of your feet contain hundreds of small suction pads that grip the earth's surface. Put all of your attention on those suckers! Perhaps you can recall a time when you tried to detach a suction pad that was so firmly fixed that it was nearly impossible to pull apart. As you are standing there, strongly attached to the ground beneath your feet, feel all of your weight beginning to push downwards into your feet. Can you sense the gravitational pull? You may start to notice that your energy moves down from your head and disperses through your body. As it does, a quiet and peaceful calmness fills your mind.

Now imagine that in the centre of each of those suction pads are roots that are growing down into the planet's surface. Through the ground they extend downwards past the soil and the boulders that make up the planet's crust. Deeper and deeper they go through the molten rock right into the core of the earth where they connect with the creative and invigorating energy of Mother Nature. That energy begins to flow back up the roots, through the layers of the planet, through the earth's surface and up through the pads on your feet. Perhaps you can feel the tingling sensation as the energy rises up your legs, into your knees, your thighs and on into your hips. Take a few moments to breathe deeply into the experience absorbing any insights or inspirations as they appear.

Realising that you are able to move freely, now lie down in the same spot. Place your legs, head, arms and hands flat on the earth's surface. Really allow your body to relax and sink into the ground. Continue to breathe deeply. As you do, be aware of how your body is being supported by the planet beneath you. In this space, right here and right now, there is nothing else that you need. You are being held and cradled by the earth. Allow that sense of enduring and unwavering support to flood your whole being. No matter how many times you have fallen, the ground has always been there to catch you. Take a few moments to extend your appreciation to Mother Nature for everything that it provides to nurture you. Feel the relationship between you, your body and the earth. This is a connection that can never be broken or destroyed. You can turn your back and yet the support never ceases to be available. You are safe. You are secure. You are loved. How is your energy feeling right now? The power of this connection cannot be understated. The more that you practice living from a sense of groundedness, the more stable and secure you will feel. A deep-rooted tree can weather all elements.

There are many ways in which we can introduce grounding into our lifestyles. Here are just a few ideas:

- Walking in nature and simply standing on undeveloped land
- Getting our hands into the soil and growing flowers and/or food from seeds
- Camping out in the natural environment
- Hiring a canoe or paddle boat and taking a trip down a river
- Buying groceries from local farm shops or farmers markets (even better if you have to wash the soil from your vegetables!)
- Travelling outside (walking or cycling rather than using a car)
- Keeping chickens (there is nothing more wonderful than finding your first egg!)
- Swimming in the sea or paddling in streams
- Lying back and star gazing at night (outside of the light pollution from cities, you will be amazed at the number of stars you can see)

What else could you add to your list? How can you cultivate an even deeper relationship with the planet? How would your life be different if you lived from a grounded space rather than from your head? Being grounded opens your body and mind to sustainable and enduring nourishment, intuition and creativity. Now we have created space and built the foundations for an expansive and peaceful life, we can further explore the connections that characterise a life of presence.

CHAPTER 13

Connecting

Let's return to the question I asked in the *Letting Go* chapter about what you need in order to live. On a basic level, we require food, water and protection from the elements. Understanding our essential needs helps us to escape the pursuit trap. But is that ultimately enough to sustain us?

In the film Castaway, Tom Hanks stars as Chuck Noland[19], a Fed Ex employee stranded on an uninhabited island after the plane he's travelling on crashes into the South Pacific. As the only survivor and with no imminent rescue in sight, he is forced into survival mode. He begins his search for food and shelter. The plane was transporting a number of Fed Ex packages, so he opens each one hoping that the contents will contain provisions he can use. One package contains a Wilson trademarked volleyball which he throws to one side in disgust. As the days pass and still stranded, Chuck paints a face on the volleyball and starts referring to it as Wilson. His relationship with the volleyball develops into one of the most emotionally significant aspects of the storyline. Wilson becomes his best friend. At times he pauses and then laughs as though his imaginary friend was speaking to him. At desperate times, he argues and shouts at him. Towards the end, in a particularly touching scene, as

Chuck attempts his escape from the island on a hand built raft, Wilson is lost overboard. Chuck is overwhelmed by loneliness and is ready to give up the fight for life. Luckily he is found and saved by a passing ship. We are left with a sense of the deep significance that the relationship held and the role that Wilson played in his survival. Could it be that without connection, we would simply give up on life?

In a shocking human experiment, children in Romanian orphanages were deprived of practically all human contact and affection. The communist dictator at the time, Nicolae Ceausescu[20], was a zealous believer in technological advancement over human needs. He had boosted birth rates through incentive policies and established institutions to house any children that parents couldn't care for. When Ceausescu was executed in a revolution in 1989, the damage he had caused was finally revealed. The orphans were found exhibiting strange animal-like behaviour, rocking and grasping themselves in their cribs. Without connection, the children's emotional and mental development had been highly impaired. Some twenty years on, the UK's public broadcaster, the BBC, followed up with those Romanian orphans[21]. Thankfully, they found that with the correct love, affection and nurture, most had been able to readjust and recover from the destructive treatment in their formative years. As disturbing as this example is, we can understand from it that we are born with the need for connection.

We can't *truly* live without connection. Even though people may frustrate or infuriate you sometimes, could you really imagine a solitary life? In the absence of any relationships, for how long do you think you would maintain your sanity? Perhaps you, too, would be speaking to volleyballs or other inanimate objects. I'm sure many people do. Loneliness is a deeply rooted issue in society that stems from the breakdown in community and relationships. No one was ever meant to live in isolation.

Abraham Maslow described a hierarchy of human needs in his 1943 paper entitled *'A Theory of Human Motivation'*[22]. He claimed that after physiological and safety needs came the need for love and belonging.

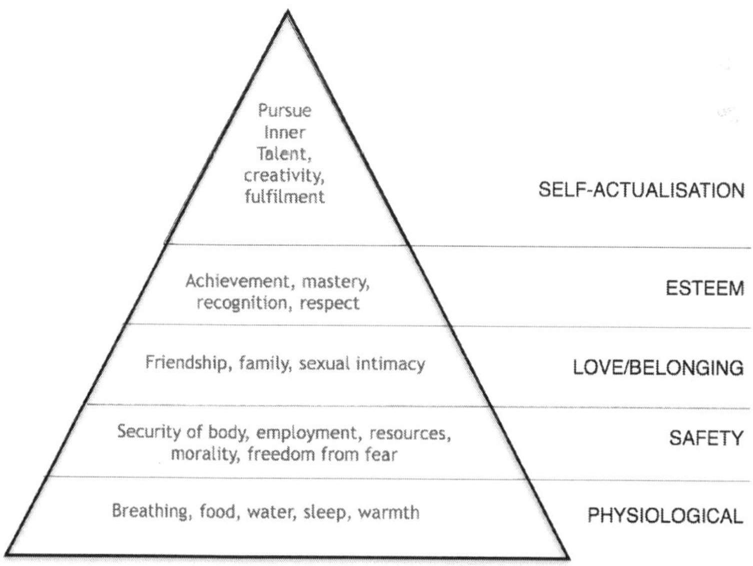

If connection is that essential to our mental, emotional and spiritual well-being, surely it's not a case of *if* we want to be connected but rather *what* do we want to connect to?

Disconnected and disillusioned

Before I go on, just take a moment to notice the connections that you already have. Some areas you might like to consider include your intimate partnerships and friendships, your relationship to food, your body or money, and your connection to something beyond this physical plane (whether you refer to that as God, the Divine, the Universe, the Quantum Field etc). Do you feel a deep bond of inspiration and fulfilment with your current level of connection?

The problem is that many of us are settling for a poor substitute. In the absence of what we need, we find alternatives to fill the gap. We have learnt to accept low quality forms of connection – like watching an unfolding tragedy on a television programme or seeing a car accident on a motorway. On some level, we know these are things aren't serving us but the drama-seeker won't let us turn away. Experiencing the negative emotion of a shared catastrophe is a poor type of connection but at least it is connection. In a twisted way, the drama can remind us of our humanity, which feels better than the emptiness of nothing. To be clear, I am not saying that we shouldn't know what is happening in the world but there is a necessary distinction between being informed and dwelling on the details. Many years after Diana, Princess of Wales was killed in a car crash[23], photographs taken at the scene of the accident were released on the internet causing a sudden surge on search engines. What purpose could seeing such pictures serve rather than to escalate the drama and create a greater sense of insecurity and fear?

In pursuit consciousness, we have chosen to be connected to the chase - some imagined future where our extensive plans come together. Every day I hear people describe the emptiness that comes with the drive for more. They have unknowingly and unwittingly sacrificed connection for the sake of their ambitions and achievements. Pursuit is not a real or meaningful relationship that can last. It is our version of Wilson the volleyball – simply a figment of our imagination. This is why so many of us feel disconnected and disillusioned when the plan doesn't seem to come together.

The transition from pursuit to presence isn't always easy. We would hope that it instantaneously brought us a deeper sense of connection. But letting go of our goals and ambitions can be followed by a period of huge uncertainty. In a culture that values productivity and performance, not knowing what to do thrusts us into unfamiliar territory. We haven't been taught how to handle the unknown and so we may experience the space as emptiness, loneliness, stagnation or boredom. But nothing could be further from the truth. Yes, you have disconnected from the drama, the story and the drive that defines so many human lives but that space doesn't have to *feel* empty.

The disconnection we experience is really a problem of separation. To understand that more fully, we have to explore one of the fundamental myths that our culture has been built on. When we look at each other, we mistakenly believe that we are two distinct individuals – There is you and then there is me. But is that really true?

To find the answer, we must begin by understanding relationships. Everything that exists does so in relationship to something else. We know darkness because we know light. We know warmth because we are familiar with cold. We know happiness because we can differentiate this from other emotions such as sadness or anger. I once worked with a client who had been struggling with depression for years. One evening, a friend had given her an ecstasy tablet in an attempt to cheer her up. For the first time that my client could ever recall, she had felt something different to the endless and enduring numb feeling that characterised her life. Now that my client knew what was possible, she wanted to find ways of experiencing those feelings without the need for artificial stimulants. She knew that she didn't want to become dependent or addicted to drugs so her sessions were focused on helping her to tap into her natural positive feelings.

The truth is that you can't know sadness unless you have experienced happiness. It is through the opposites that we are able to define and distinguish difference. The same is true of you. You exist in relationship to other people and things. Would you continue to exist if there was nothing for you to be in relationship with? If you have ever experienced being in the void, you may understand the relevance of relationships and connection!

The problem is that these differences we discern not only define us but also separate us. I am old and you are young. I am a woman and you are a man. I am short and you are tall. I am a counsellor and you are an engineer. Our Storyteller has us in a constant process of analysis and evaluation of our differences. This is how we form and maintain a sense of identity. Try answering the question '*who are you?*' and you will notice how you define yourself through opposites (*I am this but I am not that*).

Can you start to see the problem? We are born with the innate yearning for connection but then our lives become this eternal process of differentiation in order to understand who we are. No wonder we experience so much turmoil and conflict. We want to experience the merging sensation of connection, yet it always will elude us as long as we feel separate to everyone and everything else. Ultimately to feel fulfilled in our life, we must transcend the self-created barriers of separation.

In the book, *'Tuesdays with Morrie'*[24], Mitch Albem describes his encounters with Morris Schwartz in the last few days of his life. Morrie tells Mitch:

"If we saw each other as being more alike, we might be very eager to join in one big human family in this world, and to care about the family the way we care about our own. But believe me, when you are dying, you see it is true. We all have the same beginning – birth and we all have the same ending – death, so how different can we be?"

Our culture pays lip service to the idea of relationships and community but when the going gets tough, we can be too quick to distance ourselves from others or point the finger of blame. Wars are created around cultural and religious differences. It is too easy to agree to the righteous claims of the ego by seeing the faults in others.

Even well-intending self-improvement approaches often teach us that the solution to our relationship problems is separation. It is easier to maintain our self-esteem through making the other person wrong rather than assuming any personal responsibility. While I was writing this book, I engaged with a lady via social media in an interesting conversation about goal-setting. She sent me information on her current approach and how she was helping people to gain clarity and go after what they wanted. I could see that it was a very comprehensive and effective system and I was open to exploring ideas. I shared some of my thoughts about goals and how in this book I was examining ideas about non-action. Her response was very discouraging and she pleaded with me to not write my book as without sharing her approach to goals, I would be damaging the lives of my readers. What would have been your reaction to such an email?

In all honesty, my first urge was to put her straight! Her comments were an invitation for me to revisit my unworthiness. *Who was I to write a book? Why should I stick my head above the parapet if I was just going to get shot down? Better to play it small and safe, hey?* The easiest way to avoid such feelings would be to make her wrong. I could feel the desire to use clever language and arguments to show my authority on goal-setting. I could tell her that *she* was the one who didn't know what she was talking about. I could defend my position and explain my arguments further until she got it. It's easy to see how a power struggle could have been created between us! Less connection. More separation. More suffering.

I decided to do nothing but thank her for her response. The two positions of unworthiness and superiority battled in me like rebounding ping-pong balls. Still I did nothing. As the veil of frustration and anger subsided, a new clarity began to emerge through me. This was an opportunity for me to experience connection. I asked to see the parts of me that felt the need for superiority and I welcomed any thoughts of unworthiness. In seeing the individual aspects of my nature, I became much more aware of the whole. It was no longer about the lady who wrote the email. It was all about me. I was the judge and the judged. I was also the judgment. An expansive sense of peace washed through me. Allowing the conflict to transform into understanding and compassion created a deeper sense of connection to all that there is.

A few days later, I was at a workshop and we were invited to talk about things we were learning on our personal journey. I explained that, after this experience, I wanted to master staying with the inner conflict without trying to fix it. I knew that this would assist me in further releasing my judgmental nature. One of the ladies in the group offered me some well-meaning advice. She suggested that I should see what had happened as being '*her problem*'. That was when the penny dropped. Every time we perceive a problem as belonging to someone else, we simply extend the degree of separation and we miss out on the opportunities for our own personal evolution. Yes, seeing criticism and negative comments as being someone else's 'stuff' is a useful strategy to release us from powerlessness – it will move us out of victimhood and to a more resourceful place. But it won't ultimately connect us to our True Self unless we are prepared to go within and reconcile our own negative thoughts and beliefs. When you know that any cruelty or projection is the doorway to your own healing, all fears of criticism and disapproval completely dissolve.

Our world is built on illusion. Rather than know ourselves more fully, we take the easy route out and simply project our unworthiness on to others in the form of judgment. But while the feelings of inadequacy continue to exist in us, we will always find it in other people. Our natural reaction is to move away from the source but distance won't solve anything. You can leave the job or relationship but you can't escape who you are. Wherever you go, there you will be. The difficult people will just keep showing up again and again. Instead of turning away, turn into the discomfort of what you see in others and allow that awareness to heal your own separation from your True Self. This is the path to inner peace.

The problem with *spiritual* concepts is that they aren't always welcomed with an open heart and mind. There are many negative associations with types of dogmatic religion that only further separate and divide us. Some schools seem to have an arrogance that spiritual people are in some way better than those who aren't spiritual. Or that certain practices are better than others. Some use spirituality as a way to distance themselves from relationships and reality. These are all the ego's attempts to protect the self from meeting the thoughts of unworthiness.

We are not meant to disconnect from life. Nor are we meant to disconnect from the spiritual realms. The two are meant to live inside us in perfect integration. As above, so below. It is only in the divided mind that we see in opposites – black and white, hot and cold, right and wrong. Separation is the illusion of the False Identity. Our True Self makes no such distinctions.

In her book *My Stroke of Insight*[25], the American neuroanatomist, Jill Bolte Taylor, describes her experience of having a massive stroke. A bleed in the left hemisphere of her brain caused her to lose the ability to walk, talk, read, write, or recall any of her life. During the stroke, she described feelings of total connection and merging with the universe. She couldn't discern where her body ended and everything else began – making it difficult to perform even the simplest of activities like dialling for help. At one point she recalls feeling as though she was floating above her body and wondering how this immenseness she was experiencing would ever fit back inside that tiny little body. With the rational logic of our mind suspended, the ability to perceive distinctions and opposites is removed and we are left in a sense of oneness that Jill Bolte Taylor calls "*Nirvana*". It took her over eight years to recover from her stroke but the experience profoundly changed her. Her message of connection now helps others to learn from her *stroke of insight*.

We could go so far as to say that it isn't strictly true to describe ourselves as connected. Even the idea of being in relationship with someone or something else perpetuates a sense of separation. I might be in an intimate relationship with you, know your innermost thoughts and feelings, share your life journey and yet still sense a disconnection. Any split is still the product of our divided mind. We are not separate. We are not even intrinsically linked. We are one.

We were all born from the same source. It doesn't matter what you choose to name it. There is a creative energy that brought forward you, me and everything else that exists in the Universe. With all of the technological advancements we have, we still haven't managed to create another planet Earth. We can manage, manipulate, create and destroy life but cannot claim credit for where it all began. When we look at the branches on a tree, can we see where they came from? The twigs, the bark, the leaves, the berries, the trunk are all 'tree'. They grew forth from a tiny seed that no longer exists but that contained the possibility of that tree long before it physically manifested.

Maybe it would help our sense of connection to remember that the originating source existed and held the possibility of all of life, long before any human being came along. It still does. This oneness is the true essence of connection.

"*Heaven and earth and I are of the same root. The ten-thousand things and I are of one substance.*" Zen Master Seng- Chao/Sojo (384-414)[26]

What do you want to be connected to?

So let's return to the question "*What do I want to be connected to*?" We don't have to limit our thinking to enhancing and improving our relationships but we can widen our intention to know oneness. We can stop seeing ourselves as individual human beings having separate experiences and understand that everyone is a part of us (not apart from us). This is the journey from pursuit to presence – to move beyond the separation of the False Identity to the place of interconnectedness of the True self.

In the previous section, I said that space doesn't have to be empty. But it would be more accurate to say that space is never empty. Observe two people in conversation. Notice how they appear to be divided by physical space. Is it not true that the space that divides them is also the space that connects them?

ⓘ **Lesson 17** - *The Space in Between*

If you'd like to have an experience of connection, you might want to try this with a friend or loved one. If you don't have anyone close by, you can also do this process in your mind's eye by simply imagining a partner in front of you. Face each other standing a few feet apart. Take a few moments just to breathe deeply, being aware of each other's presence. As you begin to relax, put all of your attention on the space in between you both. See how the space connects and bonds you together. If you'd like, you can flood the space with thoughts of love and affection. Be appreciative of everything that they bring into your life. As you continue to stand together, notice everything that you believe about the other person. Ask for the wisdom and guidance to see those same aspects in yourself. Observe how you have been denying your best qualities and judging yourself and them for their perceived weaknesses. Allow this understanding to permeate your being, realising that there is no need to identify with any passing thought. Everything passes like clouds in the sky. Begin to see the space as being pure and undefined. It is a place of pure possibility for a new level of connection – oneness. You may want to end the exercise with a token of appreciation; perhaps a few kind words or a simple hug.

What was your experience of this exercise like? When we do this on workshops, many people report being able to sense something beyond the physical relationship. Not only do they feel the bond between themselves and their partner, but a deeper or higher connection is present too. It is as though, when they start to pay attention to the space, they become more aware of who they really are – their True Self.

Our true and expansive nature is revealed through our connection to something beyond that which we can tangibly know. We do not need to label or name it, just allow our awareness to extend beyond our physicality and into the unknown, the sacred, the Divine. In Huna[27] teachings (derived from the ancient Hawaiian practice of kahuna), harmony is sought between the three levels of consciousness or selves. These three levels are the unihipili (subconscious or unconscious mind), the uhane (conscious mind) and the aumakua (higher consciousness).

Our sense of oneness comes through the alignment of these selves. This alignment releases lower energies, negative emotions, fixations, complexes and false identifications and it frees us to connect to a higher consciousness. Now we are ready to fully open to that connection, bring the higher vibrational energies into the physical world and allow it to balance the opposites (male and female, fire and water, yin and yang). The following exercise will assist you in developing this integrated connection even more fully.

Lesson 18 - *Connecting to Love*

Find a place where you can sit comfortably, feet on the floor and arms gently resting in your lap. Take a few moments to breathe deeply into relaxation. Allow each breath to centre you more firmly in your body as you observe the thoughts as they pass through your mind.

As the calmness expands through your body, drop your awareness into your feet. Imagine that you have roots growing down into the centre of the earth. In the core of our planet is the warm and reviving energy of *unconditional love*. This is the essence of all creation and life sustained by the wonder that is Mother Earth. Allow the energy of unconditional love to rise up along the roots, through your feet and up through your body until it reaches your chest. There it blends with the love of your own heart – the energy of *self-love*. You may notice a particular sensation, image or colour naturally arising.

Now imagine a golden cord growing out of the crown of your head. This cord grows up through the room and building you are in, through the sky and out into the atmosphere. It continues to expand upwards through space. This time the cord connects to the energy of *Universal love*. The energy travels back down the cord and into your body, once again flowing into your heart. It now blends with the energy of unconditional love and your own self-love, merging and intermingling into a ball of adoring light. Again, notice anything that naturally arises – images, colours or insights.

Allow your attention to return gently to the room. Breathe deeply and reflect on your experience. Taking all the time that you need, you may just want to ask yourself the question once more, "*What do I want to be connected to?*"

I love this quote from Martha Beck: "*Whether you've seen angels floating around your bedroom or just found a ray of hope at a lonely moment, choosing to believe that something unseen is caring for you can be a life-shifting experience.*"[28]

Oneness becomes the lens through which you see the world

"*Often quantum change seems to connect or reconnect the person directly with that which transcends them and which unites them with all of humanity and life. Consequently their spirituality is not isolated, not separate from the rest of their life. Rather it becomes the lens through which they now perceive all of life.*" William R Miller & Janet C'de Baca ~ Quantum Change[29]

There is widespread belief that spiritual practices are what you do to cultivate divine connection in your life. Examples might include meditation, chanting or yoga. Whilst all of these are approaches can help us to raise our consciousness, ultimately it is the ability to live from our True Self (the unconditioned nature) and bring about a harmonious reconciliation with the higher and lower realms that creates a state of oneness.

In Huna wisdom, the lesson of life is seen as developing the ability to ascend the physical body and realise we are so much more that we think we are. The mastery of life is to take that inspiration and ground it in reality to make the world a better place.

We can think of this state of oneness as grounded spirituality. We find it in the daily moments of life. It is the picturesque sunset on a cold winters evening. It is the intense flavours of a delicious meal radiating on your taste buds. It is watching the grace and ease with which a swan lands on a lake's surface. But it is also the screaming toddler in the supermarket pram. It is the pouring rain that drenches you on the way to an important meeting or interview. It is the unexpected bill that arrives on your doormat. It is all one.

There is no separation between you and everything else that exists. It came forth from the same source and, therefore, at the deepest level it is also part of you. You don't have to like what is happening but you will not benefit from pushing it away. Oneness means finding you in all that you encounter and being willing to let the discomfort (and even the pain) reveal the healing work that is yet to be done. Turn into it rather than away from it and it will transform you.

Connection in the spiritual sense is nothing to fear or to be intimidated about. It gives us the chance to connect to the higher realms and then to bring that wisdom to our daily experiences. It brings the most wonderful position of seeing both the magical and the ordinary in perfect unison contained within each and every moment.

"Before I had studied Zen for thirty years, I saw mountains as mountains and waters as waters. When I arrived at a more intimate knowledge, I came to a point where I saw that mountains are not mountains and waters are not waters. But now that I have got it's very substance, I am at rest. For it is just that I see mountains once again as mountains, and waters once again as waters." ~ Fritjof Capra, The Tao of Physics[30]

Through seeing the world through the lens of oneness, we see the futile attempts of our divided mind to keep us separate. Now we know that the only connection we were ever missing was our connection to our source.

CHAPTER 14:
Intuition

Living a life of presence brings many rewards, not least a deeper and richer connection with all that is. The issue with writing about a particular way of being in the world is that it can create unrealistic expectations. The journey to awareness and illumination is rarely sudden or spontaneous. More often, it is a long and winding path with multiple attempts to navigate the twists, turns and frequent dead ends. When we make the commitment to live in the now, there may be days when it is completely effortless and other days when it feels like a constant struggle to get present. On the more challenging days, it is easy to fall back into the old and familiar patterns of pursuit.

You may have heard the story of the Cherokee teaching his grandson about life. As the legend goes, the grandfather explains the inner conflict going on inside him. He likens it to a fight between two wolves – one represents darkness (anger, guilt, pride, ego and so on) and one that symbolises the light (joy, peace, love and compassion). The Cherokee tells his grandson that the same fight exists in everyone. After thinking for a few moments, the grandson asks, "*Which wolf will win?*" His grandfather simply replies, "*The one that you feed*".

We can think of our journey from pursuit to presence in a similar way. Pursuit and presence are the two wolves. The wolf of presence has a caring, compassionate and kind energy. In contrast, pursuit is bold, loud and demanding. It screams out to be fed, making it easy to miss the tender appeals of presence. Every time you hear a statement that starts with "*You should...*" or "*You must...*", you are hearing the demands of pursuit. It will tell you to fight harder for what you want. It will plead with you to hurry up. It will silence the requests from you body in favour of the mind's orders. It will show you where you are failing to measure up to illusionary standards, plunging you back into the thoughts of unworthiness once more. It will consume your personality with a false and dark nature. This is how it maintains control over you. Observe the requests of pursuit as they arise, but avoid feeding the wolf.

Presence only asks two things of you – being and breathing. How simple would your life be if these were your primary intentions? Everything else that is required will reveal itself in the moment. No need to push or drive. Simply wait for the revelation of the next thought, idea or feeling. Your True Self is there to guide you but you have to be inwardly quiet enough to hear the words. This is why your awareness is your greatest asset.

Let's not get caught up in a myth that presence means perfection – not as we think of it in any case. Perfection often implies that everything has been sorted into distinct categories – right and wrong, wanted and unwanted, success and failure etc. Such concepts are not only man-made but also hugely variable depending on perception. At the time of writing this book, capital punishment is still carried out in 32 states of the USA whereas in Europe is has been abolished in all countries, with the one exception of Belarus. Interview Americans and Europeans on their opinions and you will get wildly different views that don't necessarily concur with the laws of their nation. Everyone believes that his or her perception is the right one. If the human race can't agree on such a major topic as the death penalty, how can we possibly see eye-to-eye on the finer details of life? Let's agree now that any thoughts of perfection are mistaken and misleading.

Striving to achieve a deluded fantasy of perfection will only keep you locked in the prison of pursuit. Human beings are imperfect. We make mistakes. We get things wrong. We hurt the people we are supposed to love. We get hooked into our own selfish ideals at the cost of others. We can't be perfect. We will always fall short. But we can do our best to be awake to ourselves *in our imperfection.* We can be willing to see our flaws with compassion and where possible to amend our ways. Choose not to hide behind your imperfections but rather make them transparent. When you hurt someone, apologise. When you let someone down, take steps to rectify the problem. When you have been unkind or cruel, repair the relationship. Never argue that you can't change something that is under your own influence. Own your humanity with humility.

The only perfection that really exists belongs to a higher realm – to the Divine organising intelligence. Only this omnipresent energy knows absolute truth. Don't ask for perfection because in doing so, we immediately relegate ourselves to only knowing our human perspective. Instead, ask for the guidance of infinite wisdom to assist you in releasing your False Identity and tuning into your True Self so that you can be an open channel for the insights of the higher worlds. This gift is offered through our intuition.

Living in the flux

Earlier in the book, I stated that the world was largely uncontrollable – that despite our best attempts (and all that we know about setting and achieving goals) we cannot make life conform to our ideals. How did that idea land with you at the time? Has your opinion altered or changed in any way? If so, how?

There is a big difference between an intellectual understanding of uncertainty and the absolute willingness to immerse yourself in the unknown. When I sit with my business clients and discuss strategy, it is obvious that they have a strong preference for knowing what is going to happen. Any action plan has to assume some degree of prediction. If I decide that I want to create a new product, I will probably carry out extensive research and test the idea with my market. Then I'll go through the design and development phase to produce the product before finally launching it. I may have elaborate sales and marketing campaigns to reach my target audience. Every calculated step is a part of building the overall strategy. And things often look really good in the design phase.

But the biggest issue with business planning these days is that those ideas simply can't fully account for the unpredictability of life. The best research in the world can only provide evidence of past trends and a synopsis of the current state of play. No prediction is ever guaranteed. Even when we can see it coming, avoidance is not always an option. We still find ourselves amidst an economic crisis that began five years ago. We have seen the total collapse of big name businesses, the bailout of banks by the Government, downturns in stock markets, climbing unemployment and the depression of the housing market. It doesn't matter how good the plan, not all situations are rectifiable in the way that we would like!

You may not want to entirely let go of your plans but there are advantages to embracing uncertainty rather than attempting to control it. I want to share with you how living in the flux can actually bring you more closely into the present moment and open you up to creativity, flexibility and possibility.

Let's go back to our business planners. To develop their plans most will use a deductive process. That is, they will begin with some sense of their overall aims and objectives and break those down into tasks, action steps or milestones. We were taught to learn this way in school. Our lessons were divided into subjects and each topic was broken down into smaller components – for example, in Geography we might be shown a map of the world that could be sub-divided into continents, countries, capital cities and so on.

But when it comes to life, we don't learn that way. Think about some of the earliest things you mastered like walking and talking. Did your parents or carers sit you down with a blackboard and map out the action steps? Perhaps if they had, the conversation may have gone a little like this;

"Right today we are going to learn how to walk. The process of walking involves putting one foot in front of the other with the aim of moving your body to a particular location. I would like you to pull yourself up using that table leg until you can get your body into a perpendicular position. Then I would like you to release your hands from the table one at a time until you have located your centre of gravity and achieved balance. I would then like you to begin the process of moving your left foot approximately fifteen centimetres

in front of you and then bring the right foot another fifteen centimetres further forward. I would like you to continue to alternate legs until you reach your final destination."

It's a ridiculous example but it does serve to illustrate the point that some of your best (and for the record, most rapidly learnt) skills didn't come from deductive processing but rather from the intuitive understanding of life through experience and example – a process known as inductive learning. So how is this relevant to a cultivating a life of presence?

In the Western world, by the time we have reached an age of understanding grown-up communication, the opportunities for inductive learning have dramatically decreased. By the age of ten, our ability to learn through our experiences has been superseded by the requirement to learn in a structured and organised format. I have had the pleasure of meeting amazing teachers who keep the inquisitive and openly curious nature alive in children but, in a world that favours logical and intellectual explanation over intuition and hunch, it can seem to be a losing battle. I remember one conversation with a client, who explained that in business meetings he could automatically perceive a solution to a problem. He didn't try to figure out an answer or calculate an approach; it just came to him as a flash of insight. As he worked with other managers who favoured the deductive approach, he found he had to work backwards to construct a theory that he could break down to the group to support his idea. He actually feared that his process might be discovered and, therefore, future concepts would be discounted as not having their basis in rational thought. Every solution worked but he couldn't share how he came up with the answers in case he lost credibility. Doesn't that seem a tad crazy?

But if we take a look at what is happening around us – the crises in the economy and the environment, the breakdown of relationships and community, the international power struggles and the threats of war and terrorism – aren't we ready for a big change in the way we do things?

Being present to uncertainty is very different to intellectually comprehending it. In pursuit consciousness, there is a general recognition of the unpredictable nature of life. We are able to tolerate the uncontrollable because it appears that there is more we can manage than not. As long as are able to hold on to the illusion of control, we feel safe and secure. When faced with unwanted or unexpected problems, our main focus is resolving the situation and regaining our power as quickly as possible. We soothe ourselves by imagining a future where the problem is no longer part of our lives.

Of course, there are situations where it feels fun to play with the idea of uncertainty. When we don't know what the future holds, it can be exciting to imagine possibilities – we call these our dreams. From pursuit consciousness, we are extremely comfortable with visioning all of the things that we would like to happen. In fact, believing in our visions can be what keeps us going through the darker times.

I think this is where people have struggled so much with concepts like the Law of Attraction, originally described by Abraham Hicks but now mainstream in the field of self-help. The Law of Attraction really describes being in a place of absolute non-resistance to the present moment – so that in the instant of discerning something unwanted, the perfect and opposite solution is created in potentiality. It is like a perfect relationship of unfolding and evolution. But rather than fully understand this idea, we tend to use it as a tool for overcoming our aversion to uncertainty. If I don't like this current moment, I can instantly change my experience of it by putting my attention on some imagined point in the future when this moment is how I would prefer it to be – I have money, I am in a relationship, my health is recovered and so on.

We have avoided the discomfort of the presenting situation by our projection into the future but that doesn't mean we have handled our resistance to the current moment. We think if we just keep focusing on our wants and keep our attention away from our problems that the manifestation will occur. But our resistance continues to block our desires. When our dreams don't show up, we have to wish for something bigger and better or convince ourselves that we just haven't got the techniques right yet. Can you see how emotionally exhausting this can be? Our understanding of the Law of Attraction is blighted by our need to feel in control of the future. But in doing so, we further separate ourselves from the present moment – the only place we can ever feel anything real.

Living in the flux is something very different to pursuit mentality. It is being willing to sit in this moment, fully embracing what it offers, whilst in a place of pure anticipation of what will happen next. Notice that I said *of what will happen next*. Not what you want to happen. Not what you think will happen. The pure anticipation of *whatever* chooses to happen next! This is an essential and potentially life-changing clarification because you have no way of knowing what will happen next. You can't plan for it; only experience it as it unfolds. It may seem wonderful to you. It may seem horrendous to you. You cannot know until you arrive at the next moment. Being wide open to each moment means that you don't have to control life to conform to certain expectations. You don't need to carefully manage or manipulate situations to bring you what you think you want. You choose to release all demands and to live in the space of the unknown.

We have to be aware of the pursuit trap. We can recognise our need for certainty and be eager and willing to release control and yet still find a part of us working behind the scenes to stay in charge. Think of this part of you as being your inner security guard. You'll let ideas and concepts wander through you unopposed but at the first sign of trouble the shutters come down and you revert to safety practices. Feeling out of control in a chaotic situation is not a naturally comfortable place to inhabit. That desire for predictability will raise its head once more.

But what if the only problems you have are actually labelling issues? Remember that your Storyteller has an answer for everything. It claims to understand every detail of your experience and offers suggestions based on prediction and judgment. An argument with a loved one might mean the end of your relationship. A lean period at work might mean a threat to your position or to your company. A red rash or an unexplained lump might mean something is seriously wrong with your health. We are living under the burden of these labels every day. And the Storyteller thrives on the drama.

But this is where we get to assert our influence. We can stop believing the unquestioned authority of labels. What if you simply stopped describing or thinking about things as bad? Maybe there is no such thing as bad weather, bad food, a bad day or even a bad person. What if you didn't have a word that represented "*problem*"? Would you only know solutions? What if you weren't able to label the past or the future? Would you only know this moment?

Would this change the factual content of what is happening? Not necessarily. We can't make reality fit our ideals. But it would alter our perception of a situation and subsequently our reaction to it. In fact, we are never responding to truth but to our interpretation of it. Perhaps without naming things we would be a little less caught up in the label and a little more present to the experience. Why would we want to move beyond our labelling issues? Because beyond what we think we know is the place of pure possibility.

Opening to possibility

Amy came to see me on the recommendation of a friend. It was obvious that she wasn't entirely enthusiastic. She started by saying, "*I have had depression for twenty years but that's not what I am here about*". I was instantly curious. Why would she mention something that she didn't want to address – especially when these were the very first words out of her mouth? She went on to explain that she was having relationship difficulties and she was hugely frustrated because her partner didn't understand her illness. As someone who suffered frequent bouts of depression in my early part of life, I know how difficult it can be to live with the condition. It's a place of numbness that eats away at your soul and gradually consumes every part of your life. So how could anything be more important than *un-depressing* yourself?

When I posed that question to Amy, she somewhat reluctantly explained her life story. After a couple of people very close to her had died unexpectedly and around the same time she had been forced to move with her job, she had suddenly felt very isolated and alone. With no one to share her feelings with, she had become more reclusive. Her energy had plummeted and she took no pleasure in doing anything. When she had been made redundant from the position she had sacrificed so much for, she lost all desire to leave her home. Her day consisted of doing chores and watching television until her partner came home from work. Soon she had stopped doing the housework. It had all seemed completely pointless. She rarely left the house.

Amy's partner was deeply concerned for her wellbeing. He asked her if she thought she might be depressed. He bought her a book on depression to see if that would help her. Finally, in a last ditch attempt to help, he asked the Doctor to visit. The Doctor agreed that Amy was depressed and prescribed anti-depressants. That had been just under twenty years ago and very little had changed since.

Amy's issue now wasn't really a problem of depression (although that was how she was experiencing it); in consistently labelling her condition, she had inadvertently created a secondary and more pervasive problem of certainty. When we know that something is true, we discount all other possibilities. We are certain of our knowledge and there is no space for anything new or different to come in. We become attached to our beliefs and will defend against any perceived threats or doubts. That's the problem with certainty. What if what you *know* isn't factually correct? There was once a time when everyone tenaciously believed that the world was flat. Where might you be so attached to your certainty that you aren't allowing a broader or more informed perspective?

Let's examine how Amy's problem developed. Her troubles started when she lost two people in close succession and then had to move to a new location. She knew that before this time, she hadn't felt depressed. When the feelings began, she didn't understand them. Her partner had helpfully suggested that she might be depressed, offering her a label for her unwanted state (the beginning of her certainty). He had bought her a book on depression and she related to the symptoms (creating more certainty that she was depressed). The Doctor supported the diagnosis (agreement from an authority figure adding to the certainty). And since then she had taken anti-depressants every day for nearly twenty years (a daily reminder of her condition). No wonder she thought it was irresolvable! Can you see how what had started as a feeling had become a problem of certainty? There was no escape from the label of depression.

But if we track it back to the beginning, was it more likely that Amy was experiencing the very natural emotional state of grief about letting go of close friends and her home? What if someone had pointed this out to her? Would her experience have been different? Grief is a natural part of human life. We expect to grieve over loss. I believe that her problems were due more to the labelling of her situation than her experience of it. Every reinforcement from her partner and the Doctor only confirmed the label. Now she was certain that she had depression and that it couldn't be helped. That is why she was asking for support with her relationship difficulties rather than addressing the real issue.

When I reflected back these ideas to Amy and asked her if she thought it might have been grief, she seemed totally baffled. This was closely followed by a wave of anger! As Arthur Schopenhauer is famously quoted as saying: "*All truth passes through three stages. First, it is ridiculed. Second, it is violently opposed. Third, it is accepted as being self-evident*"[31]. Amy had been absolutely certain that for the past twenty years she had been depressed and now I was challenging that belief. But as long as she had certainty about her condition, there was no possibility of her experiencing anything else. As she gave me a piece of her mind, I gently asked her how she was feeling. She told me that she was absolutely furious. With a twinkle in my eye and a compassionate smile, I said, "*so you aren't feeling depressed right now*?" She opened her mouth to say something back and instead broke out in a fit of giggles. "*No, I guess I'm not*" she replied.

Of course, this wasn't the end of the journey for Amy. She had some deep-rooted and conditioned beliefs about her illness to overcome. But each time she was willing to question a thought, she opened herself up to new possibilities. With those new possibilities came opportunities, ideas and feelings – not all of them exactly as she wanted but distinctly different to her experience of depression.

That's the problem with certainty. When we know that *we know*, we leave no room for anything else. In simple terms, if I ask you what flavour ice-cream you want and you are sure that the answer is chocolate, you have discounted every other flavour in the parlor. You'll get your chocolate ice-cream if it is available because that is what you were certain that you wanted. But what if the parlor stocked mint chocolate, chocolate-chip, triple chocolate and so on? You might end up with nothing. This is equally true of life. When you are certain that you want something in particular, that is the only option available! In fact, other opportunities might come your way but you will miss them because you are focused on getting your chocolate ice-cream. Amy had been expecting depression for twenty-years and every day she had got to be right.

Even as I am writing this book and the word count tells me that I am close to 70,000 words, I am still not certain that this will ever be a book. It sounds bizarre when I have written so many words. But what if I suddenly decide that I would like to record these words on CD? What if I choose to present the ideas as a workshop or online course? What if it becomes something different or it ends up being nothing at all? This is the essence of possibility – open to all ideas without attachment to any one concept. Sometimes my mind wanders to other things that I would like to do in the future – people I would like to work with, other books I may write, workshops I'd like to run. But I remember that each one of these is just a possibility at this stage. I stay with what is right in front of me whilst being open to inspiration. If I were certain that this is a book, I would not be allowing any other ideas to flow through me. The next concept might be even more fulfilling and joyful. Why would I want to ruin the chances of that?

There are so many areas of our life where we scramble to make things certain as quickly as we can. When uncertainty rears its head, we beat it back down by making a decision or coming up with a new plan of action. What if we didn't fear the unknown but welcomed it as the space of opportunity? Presence offers the wisdom that when nothing is certain everything is up for grabs. Certainty kills possibility. Contained in every present moment is the gift of pure potential? Are you willing to not know long enough for something new to emerge?

The gift of intuition

Learning to open to pure possibility brings the gift of intuition. Remember the business client who just knew the best solution to problems? How would your life be different if every next step, every idea and every answer came to you as a flash of brilliant insight? Again, this isn't about striving for an idea of perfection but rather a gentle and easy opening to the voice of infinite wisdom.

Intuition comes when we allow ourselves to be an expansive channel for Divine energy. It requires us to suspend our intellectual knowing in favour of possibility. As we embrace uncertainty and learn to live in the flux, without the need to force a decision or an action plan, we encourage deep wisdom to speak through our soul.

In pursuit, we have ideas and inspiration. We are able to play with theories and come up with new concepts. Some of these may be highly motivating. Some may be hugely successful. But ultimately such plans can only be limited because they come from a capped source – our intellectual reasoning. Albert Einstein said that problems cannot be solved with the same level of thinking that created them[32]. The mind will try to convince you that it always has the answer. That is part of the pursuit trap. It wants to keep you under control to ensure that it continues to run the show.

There is a very different quality to the gift of pure intuition that comes with presence. Intuition is a whole body experience. It doesn't feel as though ideas have been created within us but rather flow through us. I have heard people describe this in very diverse ways – as a hunch or gut instinct, as an instant download or package of information that just appears from nowhere, or just a gentle and definitive nudge in a certain direction. Initially, it can feel confusing or even slightly overwhelming, especially if it requires us to rise up and meet an idea that may seem beyond our current capacity or capability.

One of my favourite questions for cultivating intuition is the question posed by Michael Bernard Beckwith on his Life Visioning programme. He simply asks, *"What wants to be born through you?"*[33] I adore the way that question is posed. It so beautifully describes the process that is beyond our calculation and reason. This is why the synchronisation process is so important to presence consciousness. As we ground our roots in our origins (Mother Nature) whilst opening our whole being to the energy that lives beyond our physical realm (Universal energy), we become this receptive channel for intuition and creativity. The process of inviting intuition into our lives is incredibly straightforward – ground, connect, open, receive.

I remember clearly the first time I heard the question "*What wants to be born through you*?" It instantly sent my mind into searching for an answer. But rather like a computer that hunts for missing data, consciously I was drawing a blank – file not found! As I was freed from the intellectual processing, it felt as though my body was being lifted up. I received two very clear responses to the question. The first was to create a retreat centre for developing a community based around love in Phoenix, Arizona. Such a thought was beyond any concept I could have come up with at the time and yet I received huge amounts of detail instantaneously. No amount of attempted idea generation would have led me to that creative conclusion. Quite frankly, it was a little bit overwhelming. The second idea I received was to create a folder of laminated exercises to support my personal growth. I fully considered both options and pulled out my laminator!

Since that experience, receiving intuition beyond my rational thinking has become a regular occurrence. Sometimes it comes to support and extend my current ideas. Sometimes it feels like a sharp turn in my course of direction. But I have learnt to listen to the voice of wisdom that I know goes far beyond the limited capacity of my conscious processing. Even yesterday, as I was working on some concepts for my new website, I received a *download* that I needed to do it very differently. My mind instantly came up with the objections; "*but you've already started with this idea*"; "*you've paid money that you will lose if you change it now*"; "*you are messing people around*". The mind will complain and resist – our job is to see it as a last-ditch attempt to regain control. When we understand that our intuition always has the bigger and more informed picture, we learn to trust the wisdom rather than attempt to silence it because it doesn't fit with our plans.

I am yet to create the retreat in Arizona. If I am honest, there are times when I have thought the idea is just crazy. All of the "*how will I do it?*" questions seem unanswerable from my current vantage point. And yet, the concept continues to live on and grow inside me. I know it is subtly influencing many of my choices. Sometimes I can join the dots and see how my actions are taking me down a particular path. More often, I have no conscious comprehension of the plan. It is why releasing control and attachment is so essential. In the old model of pursuit, bringing such an idea to manifestation would require an action plan. In presence consciousness, you only need to be in the moment making the right choice for now. I realise that in all likelihood, only with hindsight will I be able to truly understand the unfolding steps.

So here is my question to you; "*What wants to be born through you*?" There is no need to decide right now. You may already have a sense of the answer; it may come to you at a later point. If you think you *know*, continue to be open to all other options, even the ones that seem like a sharp change of direction. Remember the question, *are you willing to not know long enough for something new to emerge*? If you would like, you can simply add the question to the end of the connection exercise in the previous chapter. Follow the process – ground, connect, open, receive.

Stillness is the birthplace of intuition. When you are locked into the busyness and drive of pursuit, there is no space, no opening for the wisdom of the higher realms to communicate with you. Without intuition, life is less simple and more forced. Learning to be present to the moment opens the channel of creativity. We embrace the flux because we know it to be the place of pure potentiality. Pursuit will tell you that it is your job to make things happen. Presence knows you only need to invite life in. Pay attention to the voice of infinite wisdom when it speaks. When you choose to be guided by your intuition rather than your rational thinking, you are allowing yourself to be led by the Divine. In the higher realms, there is only ever one meaningful journey – the path to unconditional love. Let your intuition take you there.

CHAPTER 15

Love

When I first contemplated writing a chapter on love, I was hesitant. The word has such diverse implications and interpretations. We use it to describe the intense infatuation we experience with a new lover. We use it to sign off letters and emails with warmth. We refer to it when we are thrilled with a new gadget or object – *I love my new computer... or my shoes... or my car* and so on. But infatuation, affection and pleasure are not the same as love.

Love has been associated with so many other feelings that we have muddied the waters of our understanding. Each of the emotions in these examples may contain aspects of love but they are not pure love. Our confusion with labels has diluted the meaning and, in doing so, has blocked our ability to know (and to become) its true essence. We have learnt to settle for scraps – like choosing only bread crusts when offered a magnificent feast. My concern about writing on the topic of love is how easy it is filter the concept through our current level of understanding. For the purposes of this chapter, I only ask that you suspend your existing beliefs and simply be open to comprehending something new.

Tuning into our intuition stirs the remembrance of something long forgotten – the part of us that was born whole and complete in a space of purity. So many of our actions are fundamentally orientated to reclaiming that wholeness once more; to experience again the bliss of being cradled in the arms of unconditional love. This is the home of our True Self. This is where we belong.

To even consider writing about love has me questioning my ability to do it justice. It is the purest of all states – the absolute expression of presence consciousness. To know love is the closest that we will ever come to touching something eternal and divine whilst in our human form. You have probably glimpsed flashes of its nature – in experiencing the intense connection of the merging of bodies and souls in an intimate encounter; or a moment of perfection whilst observing a star-filled sky; or the transforming moment of birth when we realise we would lay down our life for the sake of our child. We have all been touched by its grace and yet know so little of what it means to truly live from love.

Living in love is the highest stage of our evolution. This is enlightenment – the full illumination of our being whilst in human form. We cannot strive to know love. We cannot force or push it into existence. We cannot seek or chase it down. We can only recognise the nudge within that calls us home to be the loving being we were always destined to be.

Love is the ultimate synchronisation. It is what we

were born from and what we will return to. Why would we not want to reside there in between? Returning to love is a process rather than a destination. This chapter is an invitation to take the journey – to open your heart and to be the light of love.

How we withhold love

Since the first moment that we were born, we have been on a constant quest to feel loved. In our initial few weeks on earth, we cried out for the affection of our parents and carers. We had to. As we saw in Chapter 13 with the Romanian orphans, babies depend on love. Throughout our lives we will fall in and out of love many times – both with others and ourselves. We crave love and yet trying to achieve permanence takes us back to the analogy of grasping water – the tighter you hold, the more it will slip through your fingers. Connecting to love in a sustainable way has nothing to do with anyone else. Time will pass. People will move in and out of your life. Relationships will change and evolve. The only enduring love that can ever last is when we choose to live there – not to seek love but to **be** it.

We have probably all experienced the dark and empty feelings that accompany the absence of love. There is an excruciating nature to the break down of love rarely witnessed in other contexts. To lose someone you adore is a pain beyond explanation or reason. It hurts. It really hurts. That's why so many of us are still living under the premise of *once bitten, twice shy*. We would rather hold ourselves back than risk opening ourselves up to the chance of pain and suffering again. And so we dabble in the paddling pool rather than diving in. Our offerings of love come with criteria. The recipient must behave in ways that meet our expectations. They must agree to stick to the contract. They must prove themselves worthy or else our gifts will be withdrawn. This is the love we are most familiar with. A love based on adherence to conditions. As such, our experience of love is a merely a fraction of what is possible. What would happen if you tore down the barriers and defences and allowed yourself to love with an open and pure heart? This is not a fantasy – it is your True Self. This is who you are.

When I raise this idea on workshops and events, some people are concerned that being too open is dangerous. This is the myth that perpetuates the cycle of a broken heart. In both powerlessness and pursuit consciousness we are being driven to seek love by our thoughts of unworthiness. The common pattern in powerlessness is to ask for love from people who appear – at least on the surface – to have self-confidence. It tends to be a relationship based on manipulation, power or rescue. It develops into a symbiotic need for one to give away everything in order for the other to feel in control. The person who depends on another to feel worthy is attracted to the person who depends on another to feel in charge. It often has a familiar (notice the structure of this word *family*-ar – i.e. passed down through generations) quality but this is not love.

In pursuit consciousness, the quest for love still stems from a place of lack or inadequacy. Finding people to agree to love us will temporarily distract us from our feelings of unworthiness. But the gaping wound in our soul remains. As time passes, the old conditioned thoughts of not being good enough resurface. Rather than face the pain inside, we project the problems onto our loved ones. When our partnerships break down, we blame them for not being whom or what we need them to be. We hide from issues and run from honest and transparent communication. We focus on the weaknesses in others whilst missing our own blind spots. We destroy the relationships from the inside out. This is how we know we aren't acting from love. True love never wanes.

There is an enormous difference when you open your heart from a place of presence. You ask no one to fill a gap or complete you. You see every issue, niggle and problem in your relationships as an indication of the blocks and obstacles in your own heart. You may still walk away from a difficult or threatening situation but you turn your attention inwards to find the source of the problem within. You perceive every moment as an opportunity to practice love.

You will forget. You will be taken over by a negative emotion or thought but, rather than being consumed by it, you use the feeling to gently reorientate yourself back to love. Every pang of pain is the doorway to knowing more of who you really are. To know the true essence of love, we have to be present. We need to learn to see our pain and suffering not as an excuse to withdraw love but rather to open our hearts even more fully to be healed.

Before the birth of my first son, I knew nothing of true love. I had been in relationships and both experienced and enjoyed the thrill of infatuation. Some boyfriends had been caring and kind – often staying in a relationship with me despite my challenging behaviour. I was wracked with jealousy, insecurity and fear. I was often unfaithful to the relationship both emotionally and physically – seeking connection and validation with another partner when I feared I might be deserted. I continued to clutch at the hint of affection in an attempt to fill the loneliness in my heart. It was my escapism from the pain of knowing myself.

I didn't come from the most overtly affectionate of families. We rarely explicitly communicated our love to each other. With my intense sensitivity, I translated the absence of expression as a lack of love. As I reached adolescence and the longing for love grew into a deep chasm in my heart, I searched for it within my relationships. Of course, no partner could heal the gulf of unworthiness in my heart. They always fell short. I treated good men very badly when they failed to meet my unachievable demands.

In my mid-twenties, a number of experiences changed my relationship to love. The first encounter was with the birth of my son. Having been unwilling to make his entrance into the world, I arrived at the hospital two weeks past my due date with an inkling that I *might* be in labour. Approximately forty-five minutes later, Max was cradled in my arms. Without the time for mental or physical preparation, the birth experience was incredibly intense and overwhelming. My conscious mind couldn't process what was happening and as I mentally checked out, I was left with no option but to be guided by my own body. Being out of control was an enormous privilege. Without the Storyteller telling me what should or shouldn't be happening, I was temporarily freed from my own limiting thoughts and brought fully into the moment. In that presence, I was taken over by the intensity of pure, boundless love. I felt the absolute merging of my own being with my son's. There was no sense of separation. No sense that I was giving birth to him but rather that we were in perfect harmony, connecting with each other's souls. Once you have been touched by something eternal, it is impossible to ignore its truth. The energy of love had been awakened within me.

A year later and my son faced the fight of his life. I sat in the waiting room while the surgeons performed life-saving open-heart surgery. I was terrified that this bundle of preciousness would be taken away from me. I would have given my own life for his to continue and yet there I waited, knowing there was nothing I could do to alter the outcome. Once again, I was consumed by a powerful and eternal force – the energy of pure love. It asked nothing of me but to surrender to the moment. I knew that whether or not my son survived, my journey would take a different direction. I had once again been changed by love.

These two spontaneous and uncontrollable encounters had stirred the remembrance of love in my soul. I realised that I could no longer continue to live with a closed and damaged heart. As my son began to recover from his surgery, I knew I needed help to heal. I contacted a counselling service and began weekly sessions with a lady called Terry. Terry gave me a very special and unique gift that has stayed with me all of my life. Sitting with her and pouring out my heart – my fears, my mistakes, my inadequacies and my failings – she listened empathically without judgment or opinion. Terry offered me unconditional love. It didn't matter how terrible I felt about myself, she only saw me in the magnificence of my True Self. With such nurturing and positive regard, I was able to glimpse something new – the possibility of real love. As Guy Finley so profoundly says, *"the light of love doesn't judge, it illuminates."*[34]

When you consider your own life, who do you love? Think not just of your intimate relationships but everyone that you have a connection with. Can you honestly say that you love people without any expectations, demands or judgments? If I examine my own life, I observe how often I fall short of real love. Conditional love is a man-made attempt to create a sustainable feeling of security and control. We use our ability to give and withdraw love as a way of manipulating life (and relationships) to meet our standards. Does real love come with criteria or conditions? Any time we fall into the analysis of whether someone is deserving of our love, we are responding to the conditioned thoughts and beliefs of the False Identity rather than the wisdom of our True Self.

Have you noticed how we categorise love? We make distinctions between being in love and feeling love. Can you see the ridiculousness of a comment like "*I love you but I am not in love with you*"? Does true love really exist on an imaginary scale? That scale is the product of our divided mind that thinks in opposites. True love is a holistic experience – there is no beginning and no end. We can't feel the depth and richness of love when using our minds as the tool.

No other creature on the planet has been given the degree of freedom that we humans have to choose who and how we love. It is a special endowment that deserves to be honoured and respected. The truth is that we are always orientated in one of two directions – towards love or fear. When we withhold our love we are agreeing to hate, pain and suffering. Is that a conscious choice you would ever make for your own life? Fear is a destructive force that ultimately breaks your own heart. Hating anyone or anything will never achieve anything other than the theft of your own inner peace and contentment. To understand the importance of our orientation, we need only examine our own life events and experiences. Every problem can be traced back to a denial of love. Review each situation and ask yourself whether fear or love was in charge. The evidence will be undisputable.

Before we proceed, take some time to reflect on your own patterns. Where are you holding back? How do you withhold love? What has it cost you in your life so far? What would happen if you made a conscious choice to love with an open heart? How would your life be different if you were to allow pure love to awaken within you?

During a difficult and dark part of my life, I was sitting in the stillness of a meditation when a gentle and compassionate inner voice whispered:

"Where there is love, there is no fear.
Where there is love, there is no pain.
Where there is love, there is no hate.

Where there is love, there is no suffering
Love because it is all that there is"

Love - all that there is

There is something so simple and yet so profound in those words. The realisation that pain, hate and suffering cannot co-exist with love. It is the disconnection from love that causes us anguish and misery. We suffer when we aren't unified with love. The last sentence "*Love because it is all that there is*" could be easy to dismiss. How can it possibly be *all that there is*?

To make sense of that concept, we have to return to the understanding of our source. Whether you want to label it as God, the Divine, the Tao, the Universe or the Quantum Field, there was a place where all creation began. When you consider the energy that created everything living (now and ever has been) on this planet, how do you perceive it? Could you imagine it containing fear, hate or cruelty? Could anything of substance or worth be born in any other space than love? Could fear persuade a seed to grow into a tree?

Even if we can logically claim that knowing a divine source is impossible or we want to argue for the theory of evolution over any spiritual concept, our own existence still requires a beginning. Somewhere at some time, you were the energy contained within both the sperm and the egg. Most births depend on an act of copulation – often referred to as *making love*. Not all sexual encounters occur as acts of love and not all pregnancy requires sexual intercourse but the idea still holds validity. There is a very good reason why the creation of life is described as making love. Conception could accurately be described as the *making* of *love*.

We know so little of the powerful energy of love. The love we talk about in cutesy greeting cards is nothing compared to the full and forceful expression of pure love. This whole and authentic manifestation is not wishy-washy or passive – it contains a strong and active energy that has the power to heal, to guide and to change worlds. You may have heard the anecdotal stories of parents lifting automobiles to save their children. These accounts are not fictional. Such is the power of love.

While writing this book, I was deeply moved to hear about the death of Nelson Mandela whose personal story has inspired people throughout the world. Mandela lived to be one of the most influential leaders of our generation serving as president of South Africa from 1994-1999.

Mandela spent most of his adult life fighting against racial prejudice. After being convicted in the 1963 Rivonia Trial of trying to overthrow the pro-apartheid government, he was to spend the next 27 years in prison – most of it on the isolated Robben Island where he was allowed one visitor a year and one letter every six months. He spent his time in a damp concrete cell measuring just over two meters squared. He slept on a straw mat on the floor. He was verbally and physically abused by the wardens. He spent his days breaking rocks into gravel – the glare from the lime damaging his eyesight and leaving him with a permanent squint. Mandela's experience profoundly changed him. Rather than becoming bitter or angry, he became a messenger for love.

Mandela inspired a generation of activists, revolutionaries and seekers winning the Nobel Peace Prize for his efforts to challenge inequality and promote humanitarian causes. Despite sacrificing so much of his own life, Mandela left prison with a renewed faith and optimism in human nature. In the '*Long Walk to Freedom*' he wrote:

"No one is born hating another person because of the color of his skin, or his background, or his religion. People must learn to hate, and if they can learn to hate, they can be taught to love, for love comes more naturally to the human heart than its opposite".[35]

It is no coincidence that so many of life visionaries and leaders have been guided by love – Mahatma Ghandi, Mother Teresa, The Dalai Lama to name but a few. Their contribution has transformed our world. Love has been their legacy. There is no doubt that love has the power to move people and change worlds.

To turn to love is to agree to be touched by Divine grace. It is the willingness to believe and have faith in something wiser and more powerful than our human physicality. It requires that we suspend our sense of separation and desire for independence in favour of co-operating and co-creating with others for a greater good. Love speaks to our soul. When someone communicates from pure love, we cannot miss the message. It is as though the words gently reach inside our being and wrap their arms around our heart, pulling down barriers and healing wounds.

Real love exists without reason or justification. It doesn't have to be chased or forced. To understand true love is to realise that, no matter how dire the external situation, love is always available and accessible if we choose to let go and let it be. We can't make it happen, only remove the blocks that have been preventing it. With true love there is no sense of obligation. Love never tries to make you go somewhere or do something, only asks that you be here now. Love has no past and no future – to be in love is to be in the moment. That is why falling in (true) love feels so wonderful. It brings you back to the full experience of being present.

Where there is love, there can be no resistance. When we argue that *love hurts*, we are really describing our own unwillingness to stay with the moment. Any pain or suffering is an indication of resistance. It is not the love that hurts, but rather our disconnection from it. When we are willing to be present to what is happening, love will show us the way. Love will heal.

When I first worked with Chloe, she was devastated that her boyfriend had left with no explanation or reason. She was hurting and could find no way out of the pain. She felt that the only way she could move on was to talk it through with him. But he refused to take her calls or acknowledge her emails. She was suspended in limbo. Of course, it is often easier to get closure on a relationship when you know why it didn't work out. Not knowing was tormenting and consuming Chloe. I suggested that if her boyfriend were unwilling to speak to her then she would have to approach the situation from a completely different perspective.

I asked Chloe to take a few minutes to consider what had really changed in her relationship since the breakup. Initially she talked about all the things that she couldn't do without him. As she delved deeper, the pain of unrequited love began to surface. She loved him but he didn't want her. This was the root cause of her suffering. Without minimising her heartbreak, I asked her how it would feel if she just continued to love him without any expectations of what it would lead to. I invited her to love him, not because of who he was but rather because of who *she* was. This helped Chloe to understand that whilst the logistics of her relationship had changed and she wasn't able to have physical contact with her boyfriend, that didn't mean she had to turn her back on love. It was highly likely that she would continue to miss him – he had been a big part of her life. But she didn't have to suffer the biggest heartache of all– the disconnection from love. Now she had a new sense of a love that wasn't down to anyone else but herself. When we realise that our love is always our own responsibility then we are finally free. Nelson Mandela spent twenty-seven years in a prison and emerged encircled in love. We need nothing or no one to be carriers of love.

Love is eternal. It never disappears – we just unknowingly break the connection. But it is always there, contained in every moment and experience waiting for us to unify once more. Our source is love. We are born from love. We are love. Everything is love. Love is all that there is.

Opening to love

The ultimate path for any human being on this physical plane is to live a life of love. When we are being anything less than loving, we are not in the authentic expression of our True Self. There will be many hooks and triggers that invite you to turn your back. We have learnt to be cautious for the fear of being hurt. We have this mistaken perception that, in holding back, we are protecting ourselves but nothing could be further from the truth. The armour around our heart doesn't keep us safe – it locks in the pain. The greatest healing experience of our lifetime will be the day that we drop our guards and open fully to pure and unconditional love.

Loving from our heart centre is our life's work. There will be times when we fall short. We will snap at loved ones for insignificant reasons. We will be consumed by our thoughts of separation and blame others for our suffering. We will judge ourselves cruelly for our mistakes. Meanwhile, love does everything in its power to remind us of our worthiness. Falling down is part of the journey. It's how you respond to your tumbles that matters most.

There are no guarantees that making the commitment to *be* love will prevent you from getting hurt, but I can promise you that wearing your heart armour will never bring you happiness. Attempting to deprive others of your love only sacrifices your own heart. Choosing to be an open channel for love re-establishes the order of relationship with the Divine. Connect with your source. Remember who you are. Allow yourself to be used by love.

Below I have included a few exercises to help you in the process of cultivating your loving nature through compassion, listening, understanding, respect and connection. Such exercises can be seen as the training wheels for life. Each has the potential to open your heart but the actual experience of living from love will be something much deeper and more profound. Returning to love goes far beyond the conscious decision you make here – it is an ongoing and ever-evolving process. Some of these activities involve a partner or a friend but you don't need to be with anyone else in order to be a loving being. All moments of love are acts of self-love.

Love Exercises:

- ***Love thyself first***: How are you judging yourself? What would your say is your greatest fault? Take a few moments to just breathe into that awareness. Meeting this feeling will be nothing new. This is the opportunity to heal and release it. Now imagine that you are pure love. What would that feel like? How would you be as a person? Breathe deeply into the essence of being love. As you are now pure love, reconsider your fault. What is the real truth that love wants to tell you about this misconception?

- ***Just in time***: Find a number of photographs going back through your life as far as you can. You may have one for your childhood, one for your teenage years, one for your twenties and so on. Pick pictures that call out to you with a sense of significance. If you don't have photographs, you can always find images that symbolically represent that time of your life (a toy or a landmark for example). Lay the pictures out in front of you in the order that they occurred. Notice the story of your life contained in these images. Take a few minutes to acknowledge your journey – the successes, the challenges, the pain and the joy. Now invite true love to be your companion. What message does love have for you about your life this far? What advice or wisdom would it like to share for your future? Let the ideas of past and future dissolve as you breathe into the present moment. To complete the exercise, you may like to gently meditate on the idea of love being all that there is.

- ***Deep and personal questions***: Connect more deeply with friends and loved ones – find out their unfulfilled dreams and ideas. What is their greatest fear? What are they most proud of? How do they know they are loved? What would they most like to hear from you? Tell them how and why they are important. Spend some time making the conversation just about them without your comments or judgments. When we suspend our own ideas and opinions, we break through the sense of a separate self and reconnect with our true and loving nature.

- ***The presence game***: One to play with a partner or good friend. Find a place where you can sit comfortably opposite each other. Take each other's hands and make eye contact. Sit together in complete stillness and silence for ten minutes or more. What can you see in each other's eyes? Allow the merging of your beings into the moment. What can you feel in your heart? What can you feel in their heart? Let love guide the way.

- ***Create a lover list***: - Have you and your partner individually write a list of the top ten things that you most admire and respect about each other. Share your answers. If that seemed easy then do another ten. And if you managed that then try another fifty! This game can be brought into your daily life. Either you can make time each day to consciously appreciate each other or be more spontaneous and say it as and when the feeling arises. You can even do this without a partner. Make lists of all the things you love about anyone in your life (or someone you would like to be!) The words don't have to be said out loud in order for them to make a difference.

If you do it in private, it can be fun to notice not only the impact this game has on you but also how those people change too!

There are many other ways to invite in unconditional love. Bring it into your daily practice. One of the simplest and most effective approaches for developing your connection to love is to simply ask yourself "*What would love do now*?" You can use this question to gain insights into difficult situations or uncomfortable dilemmas. The answer you get may not be what you expect or even what you want, but pure love will always serve you far beyond your current level of consciousness. True synchronisation is the ability to tune into love in every experience. Remember that pure love only exists in the now. When you fall in love with the moment, the moment will bring you home to you.

STEP 4: BEING MOVED

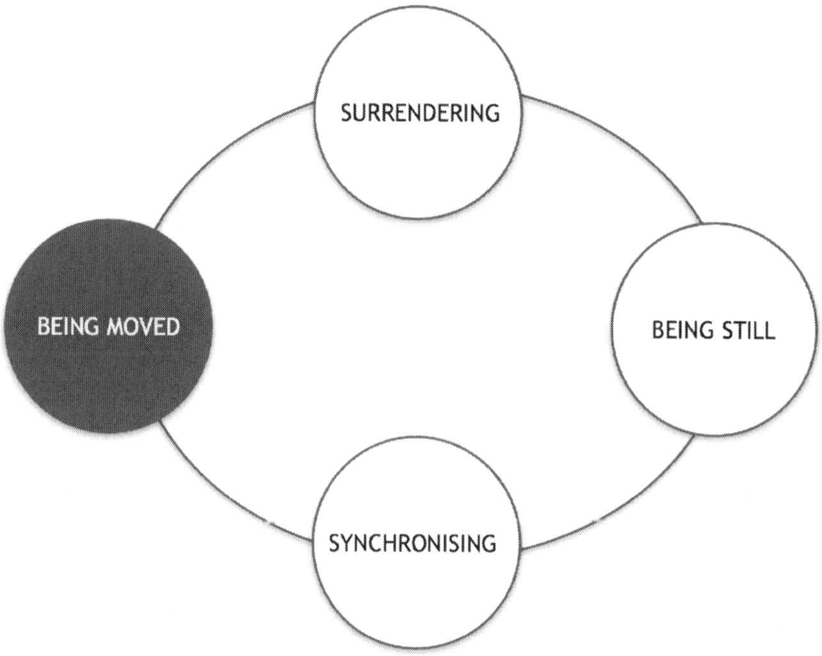

CHAPTER 16

Beyond Goals

When we contemplate making the move from pursuit to presence, one of the biggest doubts that arise is whether we will manage to get anything done again. Presence is about doing less and being more, in order to create sufficient space to witness our inner and outer relationships. Being constantly busy or rushing around just doesn't allow the scope to be in touch with our sense of self. When we slow down, we have the time to perceive and process our experiences. At last we can observe our own patterns and see when we are disconnecting, withholding love or simply making things more complicated than they need to be. Such insight not only transforms us but also brings us home to our unconditioned nature – that of pure love.

It is true that the largest part of presence is awareness – to be the awake and alert witness of our inner world of thoughts, responses and reactions. But it is through our specific actions that we create the opportunities to watch ourselves. As appealing as the proposition of escaping the world and retreating to a mountain-top may be, we are meant to be an integrated part of the global community. Learning to be in relationships and to take action, whilst also maintaining our inner connection, is essential to living in presence consciousness.

In this section, we will explore how we can be both aware and active. Presence is not a static state of being; we will ebb and flow with the natural waves of life. Understanding how action differs when we shift consciousness will help us to navigate the changing tides. As we return to the concept of action from this new vantage point, we recognise that we no longer to need to push and drive to make things happen. Instead, we allow ourselves to *be moved*.

When we are being moved, we are responding to in-the-moment guidance and intuition. We aren't projecting our ideas about the future onto our current experience. Can you understand how freeing this could be? We are much more likely to resist certain circumstances when they don't seem to be leading towards our goals and ambitions. We reject anything that is not on the master plan. The knee-jerk reaction is to fix it rather than to be with it. How can you fully experience any situation if your over-riding thought is that it shouldn't be occurring?

When we are arguing against our reality, we are missing the infinite wisdom available to us. In fact, our next action is contained in every experience when we allow ourselves to be present. Would your life be enhanced if you were being gently guided forwards step-by-step rather than trying to figure out where you should be going and what it all means? Would it be easier if you knew, with clarity, when to do something and when to stop? Would it be simpler if you were able to focus on what was right in front of you rather than trying to guess and prepare for all eventualities?

In these chapters, we will consider a number of concepts relating to action. We will return to many of the ideas outlined at the beginning of the book. For this I make no apologies. Firstly, we are revisiting the topics with a new perspective — that of presence consciousness. Secondly, all that we have covered this far belongs to a perpetual cycle with no distinctive beginning or end. Being moved also requires surrender. And so it continues to evolve.

A life without goals

You will remember from the opening chapter that the quest for more was driven by an underlying need to escape feelings of inadequacy. We had adopted a False Identity that linked our worthiness to certain criteria — *I have to be kind, respectful, powerful, smart* and so on. Only when our perception of our self measured up to these illusionary standards could we feel *good enough*. The goals we set in pursuit were attempts to close the gap and achieve that missing feeling. For example, *"I want millions in the bank because then I will feel secure and then I will know I am good enough"; "I want to win that award because then I will feel recognized for my achievements and then I will know that I am good enough"; "I want my children to exceed in their studies because then I will feel like I am being a good enough parent.*" We can have what seem to be deeply inspiring goals and yet still be driven by a need to prove our worthiness. It's not that there is anything inherently wrong with the goal, just that the premise is flawed. There is never anything you need to do in order to validate your existence. You are here right now and that is enough. Breathe into that wisdom. Say out loud "*I am enough*"!

So with that in mind, another question then emerges – If we are already enough then do we *actually* need to have goals? What are you seeking that is more than enough? More for what purpose? Yes, you can make changes and work towards certain outcomes but if you are focusing on a point in the future where life will be better than it is now, there is one aspect that will remain constant. Remember, even if you change your life, there you will be. Wouldn't it make sense to focus on simply being the *you* that you want to be in the here and now, rather than the achievement of some future-orientated, external goal?

Think about the biggest dream or goal you have for your life – what do you imagine it will give you? Challenge yourself to dig deep and find the need that you are really seeking to fulfill. If your first thoughts are that it will give you some exterior gain like money or a successful career or a bigger home, then what do you imagine *that* will give you?

Behind every goal is the search for a particular feeling that you perceive is lacking. The real truth is that your focus on the absence of that emotional state is preventing you from experiencing it now. Or, in other words, all goals are attempts to achieve a feeling that you are currently depriving yourself of. Rather than bringing you closer to what you want, it further separates you. You cannot have the feeling that you want until you have achieved your outcome.

Instead of focusing on the attainment of your goal, ask yourself instead how you are disallowing that experience. I have yet to find a single goal that isn't intrinsically linked to an emotion that people are holding themselves apart from. Here are some examples taken from client situations:

Statement	Means
I'll feel successful when my business turns over two million pounds	I can't feel successful now
I'll be happy when I meet my soulmate	I can't feel happy now
I'll feel free when I have paid off my mortgage	I can't feel free now
I'll find peace when I escape this job	I can't experience peace now

I'll stop worrying when my children are older and able to take care of themselves	I can't stop worrying now

Are you really going to keep yourself apart from feeling successful, happy, free, faithful, peaceful or any other desired state for a moment longer? Goals are always created from a place of deficiency but how can this present moment possibly lack anything. Test the theory. Wherever you are, pause and take a few deep breaths. Drop into the now. Surrender your thoughts and ideas and connect fully with your True Self. Ask yourself openly and honestly, right here and now, *is there anything missing*? Isn't it just you and this moment in perfect synchronisation? The need for goals only appears when we leave the present to explore the future. But if we recognise the perfection of the unfolding moment – and don't require it to be any different – then what would be the point of a goal? Perhaps goals have passed their sell-by date!

Beyond the misplaced need to close an illusionary gap, traditional goals are flawed in other ways. Every time we make a plan for the future, we are making a best-guess prediction about how we anticipate life will go. Even if we take steps to cover multiple eventualities, these are still based on our experiences and understanding to date. The goal that we set is constructed only on what we already know. It is therefore limited because it stems from our current level of consciousness. Do you really know how you will be in five years... in one year.... or even a month from now? Time continues to pass. You grow and develop. Within a very short space of time, the person who set the goal is not the same person working to fulfill it. What happens to your goals? If you are transforming, then your goals must be continually changing too. Aren't you in an ongoing process of evolution? Isn't growing a prerequisite to living? Fixing on a static point in the future when you imagine things will be certain way is the equivalent of denying evolution. Good luck with that!

Another issue with goals is that we rarely construct them from an aligned and grounded place. We are taken over by the False Identity telling us that we need to be a better person. Perhaps you look in the mirror and see a sagging body and decide that you really must exercise and tone up, or that you will eat only healthy foods for the rest of your life. In the moment that you make your plan, you really believe that you will be different. You are operating from a False Identity that is reminding you of your inadequacy and so your idea is supported and validated as you plan it. But with the passage of time, the problem diminishes, the false self once more fades into the background and you *forget* the intentions you once had.

Do you remember Bella in Chapter 7 who was struggling with an incongruent personality? One moment she would be filled with remorse about her antics and promising to never behave that way again. The next, she would find herself consuming alcohol and repeating the same old patterns. She was literally functioning from two different selves – the one on the night out that enjoyed drinking and having fun, and the one the following morning that regretted her actions and resolved to be different. This split in her personality made her goal unachievable. How could she be the way she wanted to be if the sense of self that chose the outcome was not present at the action stage?

With goals, it can often feel as though we are somehow sabotaging ourselves. Self-sabotage is really a way of describing how we lose out to competing False Identities. That's why returning to our True Self is so essential. I once heard a friend say that she never had to worry about what she might say whilst she was under the influence of alcohol because she was always her real self. In the unlikely event that her normal functioning was impaired, she was absolutely confident that everything would still be an authentic expression of herself. I'm not suggesting that you attempt to test this theory but it is a useful metaphor! You never have anything to fear or be concerned about when it comes from an aligned inner connection. The problem with living from a False Identity is that you can never have this consistency of truth. The false self adapts to situations like a chameleon. It drives you to pursue a goal but also keeps you afraid that it might not work out. Every fear or setback requires another plan to escape it – it is a self-perpetuating cycle where the goals just have to get bigger and more elaborate to provide an illusion of security and control.

Remember that being in control of life is a myth. If you create an all-or-nothing goal, you are setting yourself up to fail. Either you will achieve what you want or you will be unsuccessful. There are no other options. You might alter the plans but you can't escape the trap of success or failure. Even when you succeed, the ecstasy is short-lived. An inadequate sense of self can never be satisfied with any type of achievement. And what happens if you do fail? You'll feel guilty and inferior. You will hold yourself responsible or blame some other extenuating circumstance or person. This only feeds the False Identity. The True Self remains unaffected by wins and losses because it knows that they are always a product of our imagination.

If traditional goals separate us further from our True Self then what is the alternative? How can we have a sense of evolution or expansion if we don't know where we are going? How can we get anything done if we don't have a master plan? Presence requires a different approach.

The visioning quandary

In Chapter 4, I talked about how having a master plan – a vision – can cause us suffering when the reality doesn't measure up to our expectations. When we create a representation of what we want, we have established two differing realities – the one in which we are currently living and the one that we think we would rather have. The goals we set are the attempts to manifest our preferred reality but, rather than bringing happiness, far too often we find ourselves living in the gap – neither where we want to be nor satisfied with where we are. This is the basis of so much unrest and discomfort in the world.

The value in having a vision is that it gives you something to flow your energy towards. As you set and achieve goals, you have a sense of forward momentum towards the preferred reality that you believe you want. But where did the idea for your vision originate? In simplest terms, we first experience something unwanted and use that as the trigger point to determine what we would rather have instead. Let's just say that I am feeling stressed by the number of appointments in my diary, the endless interruptions and the sense that I never have any time for myself. Knowing that this is what I don't want, I create an alternative that feels better. I picture myself alone on a tropical beach, miles away from any human contact. This is my new vision. If I really dislike my current situation, then the alternative idea will be highly motivating. I may be willing to invest a large proportion of my time and energy to making it happen. The vision is compelling. I am committed to pursuing it.

But what if I hadn't experienced the challenges of appointments, interruptions or a lack of free time. Would I have had the same vision? Let's say instead that my life had seemed rather empty and lonely. When I looked at my schedule, I saw barren days stretching far ahead. I have sufficient time to do whatever I choose and yet have no one to do it with. Would I still long for an isolated tropical beach? Perhaps my vision would be to have a fulfilling career and work as part of a thriving team. Maybe I long for the interpersonal contact. Now I imagine a schedule packed with meetings and welcome interruptions from my loneliness.

From these examples, you can probably see how easy it is to become a pawn in our game of life. Our vision can ping-pong between fluctuating circumstances as the alternatives always seem better than what we already have. The preferred reality creates an inner tension and discomfort with our current reality.

When I was working with Jason, he was keen to start dating a lady who he had known for over five years. They had become good friends and seemed to be ready to progress to a more intimate relationship. Jason was concerned that he would struggle to fully commit. He was highly aware that he usually bailed at the first sign of difficulties and he liked this girl too much to jeopardise their friendship. Jason was suffering from a *grass is always greener* pattern. When he was single, he longed for the deep level of connection and passion that he knew a relationship would bring him. He enjoyed the companionship and having someone who he could share his life with. But as soon as he found himself committing to another person, he wished he could have his single life back. He missed the freedom to do what he chose whenever he wanted. He liked having his home to himself and his nights out with friends. He would literally flit between the different pictures of his life depending on his circumstances. These conflicting visions were causing him immense discomfort.

The biggest problem with visions is that they come from our unwanted experiences. We have manifested a certain set of life conditions that we subsequently object to. In our resistance, we construct a new master plan to change these experiences. But the same part of us is always doing the planning. Our divided mind is trying to envision a solution to the problems it has self-created. The energy that designs the plan is the same energy that is attempting to escape our current reality. It's a bit like trying to paint a picture with a dirty brush. The old colours will still get onto the canvas.

But we know that our unconditioned nature has a truth and a consistency that is absent in our ever-changing False Identity. This nature has no concept of time. There is no past and no future; only this present moment and what is occurring in our experience right now. It has no need to project into the future or anticipate events. The vision becomes completely irrelevant. If our True Self comes from a place of all that there is, why would it need anything to change? It is pure love and, as we have seen, what else is there?

Now we find ourselves in an interesting quandary. To live from our True Self requires that we surrender all of our expectations and remain open to all possibilities. This is the only way to be fully in the present moment. On the other hand, visions are always the product of our divided mind that thinks in opposites – *I want this and not that*. If we are deciding on a preferred reality, we have to select a vision from the wide array of options. As soon as we have landed on one choice, we are excluding other possibilities. Does this mean that having a vision is contradictory to presence consciousness?

A simple idea

My guess is the idea of completely releasing your vision probably won't sit all that comfortably with you. Humans like having a sense of direction, or at least an idea to follow. It's that need for certainty cropping up again. The absolute essence of living in the moment is to be fully present to what is, without any expectations or plans. Rather than chasing life down, we simply allow whatever will be to find its way to us.

When you consider your vision, think in terms of dreams rather than goals. As you dream at night, your mind is free to explore unlimited ideas. You can slip between worlds without knowing how you got there or how you will return. Dreams are a place of total freedom where there are no limitations and no contrived story. The best part of dreams is that when you wake, you know they were just a figment of your imagination. We never become attached to our night-time dreams because we know they were not real. You aren't devastated when you wake to find that you haven't sprouted wings and you can't fly. You know that the dream was an illusion.

If you think about the future, do so without any expectation or requirement that it should live up to your ideals. When we give up our attachment, we allow our dreams to free flow without the need to force or push things to happen. They are a tool to play with your creativity and imagination rather than a way of controlling your life. You can dream in the present moment without separating yourself from your current reality. Stay in appreciation and gratitude for all that you already have. Allow your dreams to come from a place of contentment rather than lack. Then your dreams will never try to convince you that there is anything that you *need* or that there is something you have to prove.

An even simpler idea is not to vision how you would like your life to unfold but rather to focus on the *you* that you most want to be. Take that big dream or goal that you identified in the beginning of this chapter. What kind of person would you *be* if you had achieved that goal? If, for example, you imagined having money in the bank, how would you be as a person when you saw your desired bank balance? If you believe that it would give you a sense of security and a feeling of success, see that person now as secure and successful. What do you look like? What has changed for you?

Lesson 19 - *Beyond Goals*

When we make the way we want to be the focus of our ambitions, the actions become infinitely easier to pinpoint. This process consists of three primary steps:

- Identify a goal or dream and what you think it will give you when you are successful.
- How will you be as a person having achieved your outcome? How will you be feeling?
- Now ask yourself:
  - *How am I preventing myself from feeling this way now?*
  - *What is the one thing that I can do to experience more of that desired emotion now?*

As we have said, your dream will be linked to the feelings you want to have. How are you different as you are now experiencing those feelings? Perhaps you are more peaceful, content or happier. If they aren't positive then it is a good indication that your goal was misplaced! But assuming that it does feel better, now ask yourself what you need to be that way now. In what ways are you holding yourself back? If you think security and success will make you feel happier and more peaceful, then how are you denying happiness and peace in this moment? What would you need to do differently if you outcome was happiness? What if it was peace?

Jason was struggling because he was focused on the ideas of how his life would alter in a relationship compared to being single. Both had appealing but excluding aspects so the thought of sacrificing one lifestyle for another was causing his discomfort. If I asked you to choose forever between love, passion and connection or fun, freedom and space, it would probably create a similar dilemma. Who would want to give up either of those lists? So I suggested that Jason followed the process outlined above for BOTH situations. When Jason created a picture of himself in a relationship, he saw that he felt loved. He realised that when he was single, he deprived himself of love because he had no one special to share affection with. I asked him what was the one thing he could do right now to feel more loved and he laughed and answered, "*Call my mum*"!

On the flipside, I asked him what he was depriving himself of when he was in a relationship and imagining being single. He pictured a fun loving guy and realised he was stopping himself from feeling joy. This time when I asked him what was the one thing he could do right now to feel more joyful he said he could just "*stop taking all of this so seriously*"!

When Jason focused on the person that he wanted to be and, more importantly, on being that way now, the dilemma of being in or out of relationships dissolved. He could see that developing his relationship with his friend would only enhance his life rather than detract from it. He was also much clearer that he wanted to ensure that they didn't take it too seriously and prioritised having fun-filled adventures together. His next step was to book an activity that they could both enjoy.

How we picture our lives going is always less important than the person we want to become. When we live by that concept, we can have loose dreams and ideas about what we want to happen without needing them to turn out according to our master plan. Any attachment is the basis of our suffering. It fools us into believing that what happens is more significant than the person we are becoming in the process.

We can shape our experiences through our behaviour but we can never completely control events. The achievement of any goal is only partly down to you. Something outside of your influence could alter the direction of your life in a heartbeat. If you always return to focusing on the person that you want to be living your life, you can handle any curve balls that get thrown your way. This is the essence of being a co-creative force. Be who you want to be and let life events unfold in the way that they are intended.

If we allow ourselves to exist within this cooperative process, the traditional model for taking action is limited. Rather than having to decide and do, you become more aware of both your responsibilities *and* your limitations. In presence consciousness, you understand that you function in conjunction with higher forces. You are part of a bigger team. When you understand that you don't operate isolation, a new challenge arises – how to discern when to take action and when to let go.

CHAPTER 17

Action and Non-action

In the process of being, doing and having, action is the *doing* state. When we live from pursuit consciousness we take action (*do*) in order to *have* some thing so that we can *be* a certain way. For example, you study medicine so that you gain a qualification and become a doctor. You exercise regularly so that you will have a toned body and be confident. You work hard so that you can have money and be a millionaire. The focus is primarily on the *doing* part of the cycle because we believe that will give us what we most want.

Overwhelm and burnout are the side effects of a culture that is *doing* too much. Personal effectiveness, time management and peak performance training teach you to achieve more in less time. What do we do with the free time we create? Do we kick back, relax and enjoy our leisure opportunity? Most ambitious people view the appearance of space in their schedule as an opportunity to cram more in. But what's the point of getting more done if you never have the time to enjoy it?

We are encouraged to consistently strive to do more. We should have a career; multiple hobbies and interests; a thriving and active social circle, and still get to the gym five times a week! Parents are taught that their children should be busy. They are rushed to after school clubs. Their weekends and vacations are packed with activities. When I was a child, I loved the holidays so I could go off and explore my surroundings with friends. I could choose what I wanted to do with my time. My imagination was free to roam with me. There was room to just *be* a child. Can you even remember what a day without chores, obligations or appointments is like?

In presence we focus on the *being* part of the process and our action steps arise from there. Our concerns that we will not get anything done are unfounded – after all, *being* is really the ultimate (non) action. Yes there are bound to be commitments – work to be done, people to meet, a house to run, maybe hungry children that need to be fed – but perhaps we can find a new approach that allows us more of those expansive and free days. Presence helps us to better understand the different aspects of doing: action and non-action. In other words, we can begin to more fully understand when to act and when to just stop!

The myth of getting things done

As I sit writing this chapter, it is the school holidays and my eldest son begins singing and playing his guitar upstairs. I don't have much time until my younger son returns from a day with his grandparents and I need to prepare our evening meal. This book is nearing completion and I can almost touch the feelings of fulfilment of finishing a project that has been a significant part of my life over the past few months. A little voice inside is encouraging me to speed up – "*Come on, we are nearly there, write more, write faster*" it urges. Instead, I simply stop. I gaze at the sunshine out of the window and listen to my son's voice and the musical notes as they are carried through my home. This is a perfect moment. I get to be here now. I am blessed.

Not so long ago, my reaction would have been different. What I thought I *should* be doing would have seemed infinitely more important. I may have got another thousand words written but I would have missed out on this special and unique occasion. I wouldn't have witnessed the delectable combination of sunshine, singing, guitar and inner peace in perfect harmony. These aspects will never be brought together in quite the same way again. The moment would have passed forever so I'm very glad that I chose to stay present.

I confess that I am a reformed go-getter. Instead I have become a *be-here-now-er*. Go-getters are the kind of people who are great at coming up with ideas and then taking action to bring them into fruition. There's a lot of admiration for resourceful people who get *stuff* done. I remember when I was a single parent and running two businesses that I got a great deal of praise and recognition for my achievements. In reality, I was often working sixteen hours a day and struggling to switch off, even when I slept. My mind was always working overtime – how could I improve my business, my personal life or myself? It never stopped. It wasn't a joyful experience; it was a driven one. I know not all go-getters have this problem and some are able to find a good balance between exertion and rejuvenation but I think in the realm of high achievers, the issue of constantly being on the go and the subsequent toll it takes on our mental, emotional and physical well-being is a major issue that is often swept under the carpet. If the going gets tough, we are meant to get tougher, stronger, faster and better. The biggest failure we can imagine is quitting, no matter how much it costs us to continue.

This takes us back to the idea of *making things happen*. If I imagine my life as a blank canvas and, in order to have what I want, I believe I am responsible for creating everything that shows up, I'll probably start with a great deal of enthusiasm and motivation. There may be core components that I seek out – I'll need an income so a fulfilling job or a career may be top of the list. I'll need a place to call home, whether that is somewhere I rent or buy. I may want an intimate partnership and someone to share my life with, perhaps to eventually create a family. Add to that the bells and whistles like a mode of transport, a circle of friends, a nice body, hobbies, holidays etc and now my shopping list is rather more extensive!

Perhaps you can recall what it was like to be at the beginning of the task of creating and accumulating your shopping list. Can you remember what you wanted for your life? Did you take a particular course of study to pursue a professional qualification? Do you remember what your first dates were like? Where was your first home? Did you have a first car? Who did you hang out with and what dreams and ambitions did you share?

As you reflect on your life as it is now, is it how you imagined it to be? Have you followed a particular vocational path or changed direction along route? Perhaps you have successfully and easily climbed the career ladder of your choice or, more likely, there have been disappointments, setbacks and crises along the way. Are you living where you thought you would be? Are you in an intimate relationship, happily single or still seeking? There may have been many connections that have come and go. Even great sadness or heartache along the journey, as you let go of deep or unrequited love. Do the things that mattered back then still matter now? As you have grown and matured, perhaps the youthful exuberance has given way to a more realistic perspective? Whatever your path, I am sure that change has been a familiar companion. Maybe that direct route you originally intended has instead contained many twists, turns and even a few dead ends. Life is rarely straightforward!

Sometimes those unexpected or unwanted changes can take their toll. I see so many people who have become weary of life. It might not be immediately apparent. They may be extremely optimistic and positive people. But when they hit another stumbling block – a redundancy, a break up, a failed business idea, a health scare, family arguments and issues – a wave of fatigue engulfs them. Rather than perceiving an exciting opportunity to create something new on their canvas, it is another thing to sort on the to-do list. As a spiritual teacher once said to me, '*There's an age when you can't comprehend the idea of being bone weary and another when you live it*".

The idea that we have to make things happen is a draining and exhausting pattern that we may yearn to escape from. It is the myth of getting things done that says: *If I want it – I must create it; if it gets in my way – I must fix or remove it*. This illusion can cause us endless problems. We may be too quick to take action. Like pulling the petals off a bud to find the flower, we force situations that simply aren't ready to blossom. We then have to face the disappointments of our perceived failures. This only further contributes to the feelings of weariness. We are told to handle our setbacks by getting up, dusting ourselves down and ploughing on. Who says if you fall down that you have to get straight back up? If you are on the floor then why not make the most of it. Take a load off and rest while you are down there. Everything will still be waiting for you when you get back up – if you want it to be!

When we believe we have to hack a path through life, we don't allow for natural rebalancing and realignment. There are other energies at play, much of it working behind the scenes. You don't have to make it all happen. The manifestation process is two-fold. The idea is conceived and then the result is received. You are both the channel for conception and also the receiver. If you are trying to force results, then you cannot be in receiving mode. The two parts of the process require different modes of operation. If you are weary then you are probably not in balance. Perhaps you are always on the receiving end of other people's agendas and don't have enough time to consider your own wishes. Maybe you are so busy conceiving ideas that you never get to receive the results of your efforts. If so, it may be time to bring yourself back into balance.

I have been a dedicated student of inspiration for many years. There is nothing more uplifting and invigorating than the emergence of a new idea or concept. Experiencing that rush of an idea pulsing through your body and mind can be like the most potent of drugs. Over time, I have developed my own strategy for cultivating more inspiration in my life. I've written about it, run workshops on it, lived it, breathed it and slept it. I was pretty confident that I had this whole inspiration thing down to a tee!

Having a constant stream of new ideas does have some drawbacks. Which one do you run with first? Overwhelm or procrastination are the unwelcome companions of too many options at one time. And if we can figure out what to do next, we may be lured into that pursuit trap – constantly developing and designing another new plan. We never get to experience the deep satisfaction of watching the seed of an idea grow and fully blossom. We are too busy rushing onwards to ever see the flower bloom.

Inspiration often begins as a tiny whisper – just the hint of something new arising within. In the past, my eagerness to act on the idea has sent me hurtling into the implementation phase. And boy, was I good at that! Within moments of the inkling of an idea, I was gathering resources, enlisting support and selling the concept to potential collaborators or clients. I was proud of my ability to get things done and make things happen. I think I secretly wished I had a superwoman "S" on my vest to endorse my skills.

But what if the glimmer of inspiration wasn't the cue to take action but rather the beginning of a deep experiential process. In a different context, we can recognise the pure delight of starting a new love relationship and allowing the anticipation to build before we act on the energy. Inspiration is actually incredibly similar. Instead of rushing straight into taking action, when we sit and bask in the energy it doesn't pass – it builds. That little whisper of inspiration that we thought was the big thing turns out to be nothing more than a first kiss – delightful and delicious but only the beginning of a long and passionate love affair!

I have discovered a new pleasure – that of non-action: allowing inspiration to flow without feeling the need to engage in or force the process. The ideas still come thick and fast but now I sit back, relax and allow the inspiration to breathe right through me. I welcome and appreciate the concepts but then I allow them to blend back into the landscape of my life. They merge with all of the other thoughts and ideas combining to form even more insight and understanding. And because the inspiration has fully integrated with all of me, the next idea to be birthed is a more perfect representation of who I really am. It's a never-ending cycle of incomplete completeness. It isn't driven; it's joyful!

Compulsion and procrastination

For some people, the idea of stopping feels wonderful. No more forcing or pushing for results. Just an opportunity to pause, chill out and be. The idea of resting and taking your time may seem perfectly natural and comfortable. In fact, there may be times when you think you really should do something and yet you continue to put it off for as long as possible. This is the pattern of procrastination.

For others, not doing things doesn't come easily at all. When you have time to relax, your active mind struggles to quieten down. You probably find that you can't sit still for too long before wanting to take action. Even on vacations, you are contemplating a new concept or strategy. Perhaps you have found yourself getting out of bed in the middle of the night to act on an idea or do something that you meant to do during the day. This is the pattern of compulsion.

Both these patterns have something in common. One is about not acting at a time when action would be appropriate; the other is about acting when non-action would be a better choice. I'd like to share with you some ideas about restoring the natural order so that you can know when to take action and when not to.

We all know procrastination as having something that you want or need to do but finding something – anything – else to do instead. Procrastination escalates when we label our inactivity, therefore, solidifying the problem. It goes something like this: You really want to do *x* (*x* being any dream like starting a business, writing a book, asking someone out on a date etc). For some reason you don't do *x*. You don't do *x* for a little while longer. You talk to friends and family about *x*. You still don't do anything about *x*.

A friend asks you how you are getting on with *x*. Guilt and shame kick in. You experience a burst of motivation and take some small steps to start *x*. The feeling wears off. You put *x* to one side and get on with other things. Time passes. You still don't do *x*.

Someone close to you asks why you are procrastinating. Now you have a label for it. You start to focus on why you are putting it off. You may ask for advice on your procrastination. You see a coach or mentor about your procrastination. A friend asks you how you are getting on with your procrastination. You go on a motivational course to get over your procrastination. Why can't you stop procrastinating? Now notice how *x* has disappeared off the radar and the focus is all on the procrastination. Can you even remember what *x* was?

Let's start by clearing up a few things. Firstly, if we want to understand procrastination, we have to recognise that it is a process, not a thing – it is the act of procrastinating. Not doing something is still part of the action cycle and requires energy – maybe even more energy than simply doing the task would take. The good news is that a process is not static; it has movement and flow. You may be procrastinating in this moment and be free flowing in the next. Things will always be moving and changing. But if you keep reminding yourself that you are stuck, you will get to be right! You simply won't notice the subtle energy shifts inside of you.

So what is the root cause of procrastination? We

aren't doing whatever we are meant to do because we aren't motivated to do it. Then the real question is not *why are we putting it off* but, rather, *why are we not motivated*? If you want to get motivated, then there are many resources available to support you. A course on motivation will probably get you fired up to do that thing that you have been resisting. But in presence, we ask a different question: if we are not motivated, could it be that there is a valid reason – one that we should honour rather than overpower?

There will always be some mundane tasks like household chores or completing paperwork. These can usually be handled by introducing an element of fun or lightheartedness. Such tasks can feel difficult because we resist them. It may seem as though we have no choice but you can *choose* the way you want to be whilst carrying out the action. I used to loathe doing my annual accounts for my tax return. Then I decided that I wasn't going to waste any more of my time being miserable. I stopped resisting the task and focused instead on being playful. I'd turn it into a game. I found that tax filing can be fun – who knew?

But what if we are talking about the dreams that you *know* you really want, yet somehow aren't quite motivated to do anything about? Although motivation is often described as an internal state of being or a mindset, motivation requires some kind of external stimulation. When the external stimulation isn't there (or you aren't deliberately creating it), the motivation wanes and your focus will be pulled in a different direction. So you either have to keep motivating yourself or run the risk that the motivation will never be long lasting enough to see you through a big project. In other words, you are procrastinating because you haven't got a sustainable energy system to create that thing that you think you want. Is it time for a new system?

On the surface, the structure of compulsion appears to be very different. Now the motivation is extremely high but it fails to take into account other important and significant factors, like your emotional and physical well-being. In a compulsion pattern, we are triggered by an idea of something we want or think we need to change. Once we have the representation of what could be different, we simply can't let it go. It dominates our mental processing and we filter out any exceptions or objections. Your body might tell you that you are tired or hungry but the messages won't get through. Our singular aim is to get our reality to match our representation of how we would like things to be. Nothing else matters.

Initially, a compulsion pattern can feel invigorating and energising. The need *to get something done* is highly motivating and it causes adrenaline to surge through our veins. If you remember back to chapter 7, adrenaline is useful for taking action in an emergency (the fight or flight response) but creates massive long-term damage over prolonged periods of time. If you know that you are prone to patterns of compulsion, it is definitely worth examining your activity patterns. Too much adrenaline puts our bodies under strain and leads to health problems, stress and eventual burnout. You may be able to keep going now but eventually it will catch up with you, and I can promise you that the results won't be pretty!

The voice of compulsion will tell you that stopping is not an option. It will try to convince you to squeeze another appointment or task into your already jam-packed schedule. It will say that you can only stop when you have got everything done. Just one more email before you go to bed. Just one more sales call before you finish for the day. Just finish this project and then you can have a rest day. When we attempt to pause, it will remind us of all the things that we should be doing. I call this pursuit guilt. Any time we are thinking that we should be doing more than we are, we can know that it doesn't come from the loving wisdom of presence.

If procrastination is the absence of motivation and compulsion is an excess of it, how do we restore the balance? Presence teaches us that we don't need to avoid or manipulate the world. We don't require more motivation or an enforced break. We don't even need more time management or peak performance training. The good news is that both of these patterns can be transformed through simple awareness.

Letting the path of natural activity arise

It's time for a new system – one that is built on inspiration and intuition. These are the gifts of your soul that knows less about your goals and ambitions and much more about the truth of who you really are. Inspiration isn't like motivation – it lacks force, compulsion or brutality; it comes from being in touch with your inner world rather than responding to external stimulation or demands. It will nudge you towards a particular direction rather than driving you down a one-way street.

Inspiration holds both sides of the *doing* dichotomy. It understands that non-action is as equally important as action. It will show you when to move forwards and when it is better to pause or wait. To have this guidance, we only need to pay attention to our feelings. Contained inside every emotion is the insight and awareness of our next simplest step. You need nothing outside of you to tell you what to do. Quieten your mind and tune in. Everything that you need to know is already here.

States like frustration and irritation are the emotional cues that we are forcing something when we really need to stop. In presence there is only patience and the absolute awareness of everything unfolding at a perfect time. When you try to drive something that is not ready, it is the equivalent of attempting to create a wave in the ocean. Only when the tide is ready will the water begin to move. If you attempt to push through frustration, you only create more to be frustrated with. Learning to be at peace with life's flow is discovering how to ride the waves rather than always trying to create them.

That's not to say that we shouldn't take care of the fundamentals. This is part of building and maintaining the foundations for a life of presence. It is much more challenging to stay present when worrying about how you will pay your bills, or your home is swamped with mountains of washing or clutter. Attend to the basics. Keep your life in good order. If you struggle to get the daily chores done, remember that you have a choice about how you want to be in the process. Caring for the essentials – your home, your body, your finances, your family – will provide you with the perfect grounding for deeper levels of connection, inspiration and love.

But nothing should ever be forced. If it feels heavy then it is not the right time – it may not even be the right thing. When you learn to listen to the inner guidance of your emotional state, you may just discover that some of your goals and dreams were never meant for you. There may be something more aligned that is calling you – you just haven't noticed because you were too busy trying to make things happen or actively avoiding them.

We already know that the ultimate guiding force in our lives is love. Presence feeds this highest purpose. When the contemplation of an action feels like love, this is an indication of its timely nature. Honour that feeling by just asking yourself how you could gently move forwards – *what would be the simplest next step you could take in the direction of that idea*?

ⓘ ***Lesson 20** - Simplest Next Step*

Close your eyes and centre yourself, imagining roots growing from your feet deep into the earth and a golden cord reaching upwards towards the sky. Breathe deeply into your heart. As you begin to relax, bring your attention on to your body. Notice how you are feeling. Honour any emotions or thoughts that arise.

Breathing deeply again, invite Divine guidance to come to you through inspiration and intuition. Think about a task or project that you would like to happen – perhaps something you have been dreaming of for a while or even something that you have been putting off. Notice what images or representations of your idea come to mind. What are you noticing? What do you see? What do you hear? What are you feeling?

Observe without attachment everything that arises. If you notice something unwanted, simply give thanks for that clarity. Remember to softly breathe through any emotions. What are they revealing to you?

Now go ahead and think of a time in future when this task will be completed. Again, pay attention to any images or ideas that come up. How are things different? Put yourself in the picture. How do you see yourself now that this task is complete? Notice that this is the person you are becoming. How are you feeling now?

With this awareness, what will be your simplest next step? What is the one action you could take to move you gently forward? There won't be anything heavy or intimidating about the idea that you have. If it feels overwhelming, just focus back on the person you are becoming and remind yourself that you want the *simplest* next step. It will always be the voice of loving wisdom.

You may not receive a clear action step. It may not be the right time. It may not even be the right idea for you. Take a few moments to just bask in the energy of presence, knowing that just by being here now, you are opening up the channel to Divine guidance. Inspiration doesn't fade. It grows and evolves revealing the next steps through our intuition.

Inspiration has no sense of time – nothing can ever happen a second too soon or a moment too late. When you are tuned into your guidance, the path of action will be revealed at the most perfect moment. Trust that all will be well. There is nothing you need to make happen. Let go and let it be.

Adapted from Beyond Goals by John Overdurf.[36]

Love is the language of the higher realms. Learn to discern the gentle guidance of your soul from the voice of the Storyteller and its hidden agenda. Love will never tell you that you should, ought or must do something. Love never orders or forces. Love never comes from a place of lack. All that is required is that you act with love. Initially you may not be able to see how it all fits together. It may even start from something that seemed to go wrong. Allow the full picture to emerge. If you continue to follow love then it will reveal its infinite wisdom to you – step by step, moment to moment.

We are only able to tune into these signals when we are in the here and now. The information simply isn't available to us if we are reviewing the past or trying to figure out what will happen next. Contained within every present moment is the seed of natural activity. The path of action arises through non-action. Do the simplest next step that appears right in front of you without fear or anxiety about what the future holds. Because you understand that your progression is down to your alignment with the inner guidance rather than your mental processing, you'll experience immense peace and the space to stop, rest and be. You don't have to keep coming up with the ideas and the plans. You don't have to work out how to make it happen. You just have to show up and be open to allowing the voice of wisdom to speak through you. Thoughts and opportunities that you hadn't even considered begin to arise.

Release your expectations and allow yourself to be moved through your inspiration and intuition. Act on the guidance you receive without the need to meddle or to know with any certainty how things will turn out. Soon you will observe that your own processes are being guided by something greater, something Divine. You don't need to manage or manipulate the world. Be open and willing. You will receive guidance from the higher realms. Don't demand that your goals are successful – wait to be called by something greater than you.

CHAPTER 18

Creating

Everything that exists today was born through an act of creation – every item in your home or office; every book, song, film or piece of art; every animal, plant and tree; every human being; every community and culture; every conflict and every war. This is the power of creation. To be a living thing is to be bestowed with this special gift. We have the ability to shape worlds. We can direct our energy towards adding or detracting from life. We will be a constructive or a destructive force. This is our destiny. This is our choice.

Even the idea of power can be a difficult concept for many of us to embrace. After all, we have witnessed too many dictators like Adolph Hitler, Gengis Khan and Joseph Stalin abuse their authority to cause immense destruction, death and despair for those they were meant to lead. Even in our own local communities and businesses, we see a small minority overcome and take advantage of others. Therefore, it is hardly surprising that those most committed to making the world a better place are often the same people who dismiss and reject their own inherent power. But as Marianne Williamson said "*Your playing small does not serve the world*"[37].

When we talk about our power from a place of presence, the energy is completely different to that of pursuit. This is not about forcing our will – it is not even about trying to make things happen – rather, it is our willingness to be of service to the greater good. We may not know what difference we can make. The path may not be clear. Yet we are graced with the companionship of a loving presence that calls us gently forward to add value to the world with the authentic expression of our True Self. You don't need to be a better person in order to commit to doing better things. Who you are is *all-ready* enough.

The final two chapters of this book are dedicated to harnessing the healing and innovative power of creation. Firstly, we will examine how can we best access and cultivate our creativity and then explore how we can channel it towards making our own unique contributions to the world. This is your opportunity to repay the gifts from your original creator. Some may argue that the very purpose of our physical presence is to further evolve the planet and to use our talents to enhance the world for generations to come.

Living is creating

Have you ever been touched by the authentic expression of someone's gift? Perhaps you have read a book or watched a movie and been profoundly moved by the story.

Maybe it was hearing a particular piece of music or the sound of someone's voice that brought a tear to your eye or sent shivers down your spine. You may have been captivated by an athlete's sporting acumen – their ability to run, jump, throw or dance in a way that seemed to defy human ability and limitation. When someone finds their natural flow, the results can be spectacular – we witness it when Roger Federer hits a backhand winner on the tennis court; seeing an old movie clip of Fred Astaire and Ginger Rogers dancing in perfect unison; hearing Pavarotti's unmistakable operatic voice singing *Nessun Dorma*, or when watching Usain Bolt accelerating effortlessly down the 100 meter track.

Being aligned in our flow is the closest we will come to being god-like in our human form. It is the synchronisation of our physical being with the Divine. The music, the art, the dance, the race and so on reside within us all as untapped potential. You may not have won a medal or an award but your talents are no less worthy. Directing your creative power in any positive way is the expression of your gift.

Near my son's school, there is a woman who is responsible for escorting the children across the road to and from the main building. Known as a lollipop lady because of the round stop sign on the pole she carries, she stands there morning and afternoon in all weathers simply walking with the children and their parents backwards and forwards along the same stretch of road. Most days she stops me in my car as I draw up to the crossing. Every day I bear witness to the same thing. She meets each child with a beaming smile and greeting. She is shown pictures, books, pets and siblings by the youngsters and she responds to each one with unbridled enthusiasm and praise. She even manages to get the traffic to stop whilst radiating joy and warmth. As I am approaching the place where she stands, I am hopeful that there will be children waiting just so I can return the smile and offer my thanks. That's right – I want to thank her for stopping my car because it just feels so darn good to be in her presence! I have no doubt that this lollipop lady could have chosen to be many different things in life. I love that she decided to be a road escort for children. Here she embodies the perfection of authentic expression and brings sunshine to so many children (and drivers) on a daily basis!

To be in our flow means we have aligned with something greater than our human constraints. In pursuit consciousness, we may at times glimpse our potential but to truly know it requires presence. It is much less about what we do and far more about how we are being. But whilst presence is the birthplace of states of flow, it doesn't necessarily follow that, if we are present, we will always be in our flow. You can be in the moment and be highly aware of being out of sorts. That's okay. You stay with what is occurring without trying to change or fix it, and just allow the natural realignment. The problems start when we try to go against what is happening. Remember that our suffering is caused by resistance. Resistance will only take you further out of alignment. You can't be in opposition to anything and be in your flow. The most effective way to realign is to agree to what is happening. In basic life-guarding techniques, if you find yourself in a rip tide, you should allow yourself to be carried with the surge rather than swimming against it. If you try to use your power to overcome the tide, it will exhaust you and you risk drowning. If you go with it, eventually it will lose intensity and you will be able to find a safer route back to shore. It's a helpful metaphor for understanding how to live in (and out of) flow!

To be a living creature means to be a source of creation. Living is creating. Whether or not you embrace the power, there is no escape from it. Every thought that crosses your mind is the beginning of the creative process. The chair you sit on once began as an idea that was brought into physical form through action. Your thoughts hold the same creative energy. You never need to wonder whether or not you are creating, only whether or not the things you are creating are beneficial. What do we need more of in the world – chairs, conflict, community, charity? You hold the power. Now you have to decide what you want to bring into fruition.

In fact, what we are creating depends wholly on our level of consciousness. We can only manifest from our current point of understanding. Until we can perceive – and understand – the gaps, we will just further contribute to what already exists. If we live from powerlessness consciousness, we will only be able to create more to feel powerless about. We may worry unnecessarily about future events or create drama stories. Our thoughts perpetuate more anxiety and concern.

Make no mistake, there are still many leaders today who would like you to remain powerless. People who deny their power are easy to manipulate and constrain. Some authority figures would prefer you to conform rather than have to face uncertainty, confrontation and change. Much of the news and political campaigning is designed to keep you malleable and acquiescent. When you live in fear, you are easier to keep under control. If you are apprehensive about your own safety, you aren't going to be asking questions about the future of our planet or challenging the unethical actions of organisations. This is true whether you are talking about the autocratic manager of the company you work for, or a totalitarian government seeking to be in charge of all aspects of public life. Begin to question the purpose of the stories you hear. When are you being inspired to take action and when is your personal power being diminished? Never allow the light of your creativity to be dimmed by someone else's fear-mongering.

In pursuit consciousness, we have regained our sense

of power and are now seeking to exert our influence on the world. We are directing life events rather than following the crowd. We want to speak up and be heard and acknowledged. We look to the future and the achievement of our goals, dreams and ambitions. Because the main premise of pursuit is acquisition, when we use our creative power from this consciousness, we find more things to pursue. The endless chase brings other unsavoury components like competition, desire and greed. If we are so busy focused on making sure we get more of what we want, we won't be using our creative energy towards alternative and potentially more worthwhile causes. That's not to say that we won't ever experience the desire to make a difference. Many people in pursuit consciousness genuinely want to have a positive effect on other people. Yet our actions will be blighted by our own agendas. There may be another calling beyond our own aspirations that remains masked from view. Until you let go of the chase, you won't know what awaits you. I have seen people, who have struggled for years to make something happen, suddenly changing their plans and almost instantaneously finding the fulfilment and happiness they sought for so long. What would happen if you stopped pursuing your goals? I wonder what might be asked from you instead?

Presence consciousness is the creative channel for Divine will. We are opening ourselves to all possibilities without attachment to a particular course of direction. We get to flow our creative energy towards something that inspires us without needing to know the results we will get. There is no requirement for reward and recognition when we live from presence. Witnessing your transformational power is sufficient. Your natural instinct will be to seek out places where your creative energy can be channelled and the authentic expression of your True Self will discover many different outlets. You will find that you are guided towards helping others, not to rescue them but as a co-operative and collaborating force. You know that through assisting someone else, you are sharing your creative gifts with the world. Because we know that we *need* nothing beyond what this moment offers, we are able to dedicate ourselves to being of service. We freely allow ourselves to be used by love. We say: *I'm here in this moment. Thy will be done. Now where would you have me go and what would you have me do?*

Opening the channel of creative power

Often when we talk about creativity, we are referring to our physical ability to transmit our energy into something useful. This could be through innovation, invention or artistic flair. In its broadest sense, creativity is taking something new from an idea to implementation. When we observe people coming up with amazing masterpieces or a fabulous new design for a gadget, we describe them as being creative. But those who struggle to come up with new concepts, or who aren't particularly imaginative, rebuke this identity. I can't believe the number of occasions I have heard someone say, "*I'm not creative*". Each and every time, I have found convincing evidence to prove them wrong!

Let's be clear – every human being is creative. It's not a gift that gets passed out to some while others are overlooked. The ability to create is an inherent birth right. If you have been denying this power, then it is time to adjust your thinking. Just because you have never painted a canvas, thrown a pot or written a story doesn't mean that you aren't creative. Everything that you use your hands or body to produce is creativity. Every word that you utter and every sentence that you speak is creativity. Every thought that passes through your mind is creativity. Every meaning that you surmise from your experiences – good or bad – is also an example of creativity.

So the issue is not whether or not we possess creative power but rather how productively we have been using it. Are you telling yourself negative stories about what people think of you, or are you holding meaningful conversations with the people who matter? Are you imagining everything terrible that could happen to your loved ones, or are you designing a sacred space to share with them? Are you resenting and pointing the finger of blame at colleagues, or are you actively considering how the work environment could be more conducive to harmonious relationships? This is the same creative process with very different applications and results.

Creation is the flow of Divine energy through us. How we makes use of that energy is entirely down to us. I can't imagine for one moment that we were given such a precious gift without good reason. Here we are blessed with the power of creation and yet we choose to use our superhero abilities to get into conflicts and wars, steal from the planet's natural resources and tell ourselves gloomy and destructive stories about the events we have self-created. It has to be time for a reality check!

If you have been misusing and abusing your creative power for some time it may well need some rebalancing. We need to reclaim our energy from the false identities that have exploited the privilege so that we can better use it towards making a contribution to the world. We begin this process by unlocking our own creative energy. If you haven't exercised your creative tools for a while, below are some ideas you may want to try. If you find yourself wanting to skip past this section, then pause for a moment and ask yourself why. Are you really so in tune with your creativity that such activities would be pointless, or are you in the hands of your Storyteller and believing that these exercises are unnecessary, tedious or uncomfortable? If it is the latter,

I would recommend that you challenge the story. There is a good reason why children love to paint, sculpt and play. It widens the creative connection with the Divine. Don't take my word for it; have a go. I dare you!

- *Drawing/Painting*

  When it comes to art, it really doesn't matter that your picture of a horse more closely resembles a dog or some other nondescript animal. Some of the greatest artists ever known didn't create accurate depictions. Picasso's paintings have lopsided mouths and uneven eyes and are considered great masterpieces!

  Don't get hung up on the details and trying to make things perfect. Play around with ideas, colours, textures and themes. Paint pebbles or driftwood. Draw and colour with crayons. If you get really stuck for ideas, start with a children's colouring book. I also love mandala colouring books (available in online bookstores).

- *Scrapbooking*

  Scrapbooking is a wonderful way to preserve and celebrate memories. Using a large book or journal, you can pin or stick photographs, art and crafts, drawings and text to symbolise particular events or periods in time. Scrapbooking is a huge industry. You can find a variety of instructions and ideas on the Internet and supplies are available at local craft stores.

- *Sculpture*

  When we think of sculpture, we often imagine Rodin's statue of "*The Thinker*" or Michelangelo's "*David*" – to try to replicate such fine art is enough to have anyone avoiding any further attempts at creativity! But sculpture comes in many different guises. You can make shapes and forms out of clay, polymer or plasticine. You can cover interesting objects with gypsum plaster or create mosaic patterns using broken tiles. You can even sculpt designs out of fondant icing for decorating cakes and cupcakes. The best thing about these kinds of sculptures is that because they take time to set, you can continue to play with shapes until you get something you like.

- *Cooking*

  For many, many years I denied my inner chef. I used to joke with people that I could cook anything that would fit in a toaster. Everything changed for me when I began growing my own fruit and vegetables. I started to pay much closer attention to the different colours, textures and flavours. There was something very special – almost sacred – about picking fresh ingredients and preparing a nutritious and tasty dish.

We have become so separated from our food source that it is easy to think of cooking a meal as another item to check off on the to-do list. In fact, because eating is necessary every day, it is the perfect place to practice our creativity. If you enjoy following recipes then there are plenty of ideas to be found in books or online. But you may prefer to let your imagination run wild.

Stock up on some store cupboard essentials like herbs, spices and healthy oils. Combine complimentary fresh ingredients to make delicious and visually appealing meals. Play with the colours and textures. If you don't know how to prepare certain produce, you can do a quick search online. I take pictures of my creations to inspire me with ideas in the future. Not all the meals are exactly as I would like but it is a fantastic learning curve, and I get to eat the end result – always a bonus!

- *Sewing*

  Sew, knit, crochet, weave! The options for textile arts are endless. For simple projects, perhaps you remember the craze of making pom-poms by wrapping two pieces of cardboard with wool. For more of a challenge and to add to your self-sustainability, you can learn how to make your own clothes or curtains for your home. Home based crafts are experiencing a big resurgence at the moment so there is likely to be some type of sewing or needlework class near you.

- *Writing*

  You don't need to commit to composing a best-seller to enjoy the creative process of writing. Maybe there is a book that you have always wanted to write. If not, consider capturing your life story to share with your family and generations to come. Alternatively, you may like to keep a journal or start a blog on your favourite topic or theme.

  The best way to begin a project is to simply start writing down your thoughts in a stream of consciousness. When we write, we tend to self-edit which interrupts the natural flow. When you speak, you don't stop every sentence to go back and choose a different expression, you just say the words that come to mind. The same is true in the art of free writing.

I see so many people who are stuck at the planning stage of their writing projects. That idea may never *feel* like it is ready. Begin anyway! When I write a blog post, I just sit with my hands poised above the keyboard and let the concept flow from there. Creating like this may take practice – I wrote a post every day for a year to develop the skill – but it is pays huge dividends in the whole of your life. It helps to develop a conscious presence in your life and you start to process your experiences very differently.

You may want to play with different approaches – some people write better with a paper and pen. Others find a keyboard easier to use. If you find you do struggle to translate the ideas into written words then begin by using a dictaphone or voice recorder. You can always have someone type up the audio afterwards.

- *Music*

  When I was at school, my music teacher tried in

vain to find a musical instrument I had a talent for. I had lessons on the violin, piano, clarinet and cello. It seemed as though I was a lost cause! The auditory field is my least preferred channel for creativity. I am just not able to make the same distinctions with sounds that I am able to make with visual components. When we are young, we tend to believe the bigger people know the answer. When my teacher gave up on me, I nearly gave up on music too.

When I was a teenager I was watching Phil Collins perform on TV. He was the lead singer of Genesis but because he also played the drums, the usually relegated-to-the-back drum kit was now centre stage. I was captivated by the beats. With a bit of cajoling, my parents agreed to let me take drum lessons. It became a much more appealing proposition to me when my teacher informed me that there was no kit available in the music room and so my only way of learning would be to visit the boys' school!

Although I had found reading sheet music difficult, learning to hear the distinctive sounds of a beat was something I lapped up. I'd found my inner music and it had rhythm, baby! Playing the drums was the perfect way to share my authentic song. So what is the music in you that is longing to be expressed? Maybe you have a natural talent for playing an instrument or singing. Perhaps you haven't been making enough use of it recently. But never let anyone tell you that your music isn't good enough. Take a lesson, sing along to the radio or grab some pans and a wooden spoon and start making tunes. Allow creative expression to flow through your body, mind and soul.

These are a few ideas to assist you in re-opening your channel of creativity. There are no hard and fast rules. All it requires is a willingness to release certainty and expectation in favour of novelty and innovation. This is the essence of creation – we don't try to make something happen but rather allow ourselves to be the instrument through which something new can be born. Once you are aware of your creative power, opportunities to direct your energy towards the greater good start to become more obvious and apparent.

Faith in yourself

When we compare painting a picture to making a significant contribution to the world, they may seem to be poles apart. It is easy to discount our strengths and abilities but this only further disempowers us. If you don't (yet) have any ideas for directing your creative power meaningfully, it really doesn't matter. Keep playing and flowing, and guidance will come. If you do have an inkling of an idea, you certainly don't need to know how to make it happen. The most significant aspect is your willingness to be a creative channel – to be used by the higher realms to transmute loving energy into our physical plane. That willingness is so essential because it turns you into a servant of the Divine. Rather than grasping onto your material life, you open your hands and your heart to donate yourself towards something of greater importance.

Most often, what will hamper your attempts is a lack of faith in yourself. When we entertain any ideas of unworthiness or inadequacy, we will be plagued with doubts about whether we can contribute anything of real value. That self-doubt interferes with our ability to hear the invitations and requests from the Divine. We may be moved to take action and yet stall because we think we aren't up to the task.

Nothing will ever be asked of you that you are not

capable of doing. You have been asked to use your gift of creative expression to enhance the world. This isn't about ego. You are no more or less special than anyone else on the planet. But you may well have been denying your creative power for far too long. The False Identity claiming that you are not ready is the same self that has been holding you back all these years by telling you that you need more – more stuff, more money, more time, more confidence, more authority, more help. When you end the pursuit and drop into the present moment, you reunite with your True Self that was never caught up in the chase. Follow the inspiration, connect with your creativity, act with love and the path of contribution will unfold before you.

There is nothing lacking in your life. There is no gap that has to be addressed before you can authentically express yourself through your creativity. You are whole and complete in this moment and that is all that is asked of you. Learn to trust the here and now. Learn to trust yourself. Learn to trust your creative power and you will be a constructive force in the world. To quote Johann Wolfgang Von Goethe (Poet and dramatist 1749-1832) "*As soon as you trust yourself you will know what to do*"[38]. By being an open channel to creative energy, you will be called to make a difference. Will you go?

CHAPTER 19

Contribution

Once we recognise and embrace our power, the next question that arises is "*What will I bring into creation?*" You have a choice. You can decide whether you want to be part of a movement orientated towards making the world a better place or an isolated individual who is here to consume, devour and bulldoze your way through life. Human beings who are connected to their True Self have an innate desire to use their creative energy for worthy causes. It is only under the grip of a False Identity that we would ever willingly and knowingly cause damage to fellow beings or the planet. When we are living from our True Self, we understand that all unloving acts are self-harming. We cannot cause pain without hurting ourselves the most. Our soul, guided by love, will always act with integrity in the highest and best interests of both our self and the global community. Our future depends on it. We are invited to share ourselves for the greater good. This is the path of contribution. What difference can you make? What difference will you make?

The ideas of contribution and purpose are often talked about interchangeably. Many self-improvement books purport the idea of us having a unique life purpose. This is a very appealing proposition. For starters, it has a special agent vibe that will fire us up to seek out our personal assignment, and motivate us to find the work we believe we were born to do. It can also help entrepreneurs, leaders and business executives to build their distinctive brand. When they align their actions to their purpose, they build their reputation around their core values. This is great if you want to be known for something in your niche, community or organisation. But could there be a downside to pursuing the knowledge of your life purpose?

Most life purpose theories are intrinsically linked to pursuit consciousness. They can miss the mark when it comes to creative expression in the moment. They tend to be much more about meeting the ego's needs for significance than fulfilling our True Self. We can be blind-sided into believing we are following a calling, when actually we are attempting to fill our worthiness gap through approval and legacy. We get so caught up in leaving an impression on the world that we fail to truly offer ourselves as Divine servants.

For example, let's say I believe my life purpose is supporting single mothers to set up a home-based business. Whilst I am busy focusing my attention on how to find these women to help, there may be other people in need close by that I am not noticing – the elderly man across the road who can't get out to buy his groceries, the ex-serviceman working next to me who is coping with post traumatic stress disorder, or the troubled teenage friend of my daughter struggling with a drinking problem. There is nothing wrong with life purpose per se but we must ensure that it doesn't cloud our ability to see what is real. There is a tremendous lack of community in Western culture. We don't want to be so busy trying to change the world that we miss what is happening right in front of us.

When we dedicate ourselves to contribution, we are prepared to stay with the current experience and respond to what is being asked here and now. It's not about building a business or a brand. It's not about needing to be noticed or praised. It's not about accumulating a fortune. It's a genuine concern to be fully present and to serve the moment as it is occurring. Then you are aware of the person struggling with heavy bags and you are moved to assist. You see the tearful teenager and ask if they need help. You stop to help the person push their broken-down car. You do all of this because you understand that there is nothing more precious than this moment. This is presence consciousness.

In this closing chapter, we will direct our creative energy towards contribution, not by seeking to assert our authority and make a name for ourselves, but by waking up to what is required of us right now. Of course, you may still receive global reward or recognition but it is not the intention behind your actions. Our purpose is to willingly, unconditionally and eagerly offer ourselves in service of the Divine.

Do you need a life purpose?

I talk with so many clients who are seeking ways to make meaning of their lives. They want to understand the point of their life – to know that their birth was more than a happy accident. So they search for clarity on their life purpose. There are a couple of downsides to this approach. At any time we decide that there is one thing (and one thing only) that we are meant to be doing, we limit ourselves in so many other ways. For many years, I thought that my purpose was to help organisations to be more productive so I took on a role as an office manager and then, when that wasn't fulfilling, I moved into corporate training and development. Then I decided that my purpose was to help people to transform themselves and I became a trainer of Neuro-Linguistic Programming. When that purpose was no longer satisfying, I decided that my life purpose was to assist people in designing and living inspired lives.

Clearly there is a thread that runs through each of these callings; each building on what went before. It is undoubtedly true that our sense of purpose is ever changing and evolving. The problem I encountered was that for every mission I decided upon, there was time further down the road that I outgrew it. We can think of a life purpose as being like a box. Initially it may seem huge and expansive but, as we continue to grow, what began by inspiring us can actually start to constrain us. To move on, we have to step out of the box and let go of our certainty, expectations and achievements. As we know, humans don't have a natural propensity for letting go – we are likely to cling on rather than risk the unknown, particularly when it comes to a big decision like our careers or our hard-won accomplishments. When we hold on for too long, our True Self sends us wake up calls in the form of illness, accidents or depression. We can attempt to avoid this trap by ensuring that the life purpose we assume is a big enough box for our continual development. But any box is limiting. As we evolve, we might outgrow it and, sooner or later, find we are called to a different course of direction altogether (the basis of many a mid-life crisis!)

But what if you don't even know what box to pick? I speak to so many people who have no clue about what they want to do. They understand the principle of life purpose but knowing the theory and finding the answer are two completely different things. A lack of clarity is the fastest way to stall your life. If you have "*knowing your life purpose*" as a prerequisite to moving forward, you can get stuck very quickly. A bit like Neo's consumption of the red pill in the film, The Matrix[39], once you know that you are supposed to have a life purpose, you can't get back to the blissful ignorance of not knowing. What you are doing now has to have meaning; otherwise, you feel flat, unfulfilled or disgruntled.

If you are concerned that instead of making a significant contribution, you will only succeed in boxing yourself in, what's the alternative? Rather than thinking in terms of one core purpose, we can instead start thinking in terms of gifts. Our gifts are our strengths – the authentic expression of our creative power. No one else in this world has had the same experiences as you. No one has learnt all that you have learnt. No one has developed exactly the same set of skills. That in itself makes you unique. I believe that everyone has more gifts to offer the world than they consciously know. And when we share those gifts willingly and freely, we make a significant and consistent difference to the world and get the reciprocal benefits of a life of contribution. I call this the *model of service*. It is exceptionally freeing because nothing in your life needs to change in order for you to start serving. Whether you are the CEO of a blue chip company or flipping burgers in a fast food restaurant, the model of service is available to us all.

When Becky first came for coaching, her eyes were dull and hollow, and her skin was tinged with a grey sheen. She claimed to be relatively happy but felt her life lacked purpose. She owned and ran a family business but spent most of her time feeling overwhelmed and trapped in the fine details. In principle, she had created the thing she most wanted – autonomy, freedom and independence. But rather than basking in the joy of success, she felt like something was missing. She blamed her empty feelings on being single and longed to have a significant other to share her life with but, after marrying and *"being deserted*" by her first husband, she had found it less than easy to trust anyone. After a string of unsuccessful internet dates, and never getting past the first meeting, she was ready to quit. She knew she needed something different but couldn't pinpoint what it was.

This is a familiar pattern I notice with clients when they are lacking fulfilment. It's the pursuit trap hooking us in again and telling us that there is something or someone that can fill the gap for us. We just need a new job, a new partner, a new house or a new outfit and then everything will be good again. Even if we gain a temporary sense of relief or satisfaction from our accomplishments, the reality often fails to match up to our ideals or to last beyond a fleeting pleasure. So I asked Becky if she would be prepared to try something different.

I assigned Becky with the task of finding ways to make a difference. It didn't have to be anything big or dramatic, just an intention to share more of her gifts as often as she could. She made a point of sitting down with her staff and asking them how she could assist them. She was much more open with her affection towards her close friends, greeting them with hugs and words of love and appreciation. She started to smile at people she passed on the street and if there was an opportunity to help someone out —holding a door, pushing the button at the pedestrian crossing or letting someone go in front of her in a queue – she would seize it. Gradually, she began to experience the pleasure of contribution. Her eyes began to sparkle, her skin pinked up and energy radiated from her smile. The more she allowed herself to open her heart and share her gifts, the more chances for connection arose. She started to enjoy her daily life once more. When she saw how much she had to offer, she realised that the only person who could ever truly fulfil her was herself.

So how does the model of service work? Rather than trying to pursue a life purpose, we simply ask ourselves each and every day how we can *serve* others. You take each situation and you give to the best of your ability. In this approach, there is no need for reward or recognition. The benefit to you is the feel-good vibes of knowing you are being of Divine service. You serve that grumpy customer with a smile because you feel good when you are being happy. You willingly do what your boss asks because it feels good to be an engaged employee. You play taxi to your children because it feels good to be an available and nurturing parent. You aren't seeking approval or validation – just doing the things that resonate as your True Self.

It's worth noting that there is a distinct difference

between contributing from a place of love and feeling like you are being taken advantage of. If we are operating from powerlessness consciousness, we may do things because we feel we have no choice or because we can't say no. This isn't service – it's obligation – and it breeds despair and resentment. In presence consciousness we make a deliberate and conscious decision to offer ourselves freely. The only thing you ever want to feel used by is love.

Being of service requires a different mindset, attitude and consciousness. The best kind of service is when you can use your natural gifts to make a difference. Knowing your talents supports your role as a Divine servant. So I am going to challenge you, over the next few days, to make a list of one hundred of your skills, talents and abilities. Think about all that you have learnt so far to reach this point in your life/career. Consider how you have helped others in the past. Reflect on the highlights of your life. What did you have to be good at for that to happen? How have you overcome any challenges or problems? These are the basis of your gifts list. Give yourself permission to acknowledge your strengths and then figure out how you might be able to donate them to a good cause. Once you know how much you are capable of, you will find it so much easier to identify situations to be of service in the future.

Serving with generosity

I want to focus upon an aspect of life that is often overlooked and frequently misunderstood – the concept of generosity. The idea of giving generously is usually accompanied by a set of conditioned responses. From an early age we have been subjected to others' perceptions of generosity. We may have learnt that being generous makes us a good and worthy person, or that giving too much is a sign of vulnerability or weakness. The real challenge is that we have never had an opportunity to view the topic with complete objectivity. Therefore, the chances are, we don't know what generosity really is.

Being generous can be life changing – both for the giver and the recipient. But when misjudged, it can lead to bitterness and resentment. It is essential that we understand the key difference between contribution and obligation. And for that, we need to start with the purpose of our creative power – to share our energy for a greater good.

If we take our lead from nature, we see that all creation has a purpose to serve something greater than itself. Because we inhabit physical bodies, we are also part of nature. But, as we have already seen, humans are different from the rest of the natural kingdom in that we also have consciousness (awareness of ourselves). So, like a frightened animal, we may find ourselves fleeing from a perceived danger but we also have the ability to observe ourselves mid-flight and to reflect on our actions afterwards.

We have this dual function: Part of – and therefore subject to – the laws of nature, whilst also being asked to serve the higher realms through our consciousness. In that concept of service, above and below, lies the true essence of generosity. We are here to contribute to the evolution of the world. We have a tendency to make it more complicated than that because we over-think the idea of serving.

The sun's purpose is to provide light, warmth and energy to the planet. It is essential for the existence of life here on earth and it willingly provides. It doesn't question or doubt. It doesn't fulfill its role because it thinks it should. It shares its gift simply because that is what it is here to do. How easy do we find it to give freely in the way the sun does? We allow our conditioned thinking gets in the way – *Am I being paid enough? Will I be taken advantage of? Is this what I am really meant to be doing? Is the grass greener over there?* The internal dialogue is relentless and exhausting and prevents us from being fully present to the pleasurable experience of generosity. When we aren't able to suspend our thinking and fully immerse ourselves in service, any sense of joyful contribution reverts to obligation and resentment. Let's revisit contribution through the eyes of generosity.

Can I take the task that I am being asked to do

(whether by my colleague, my partner, my parent, my child, my boss, a friend or by life itself) and let go of my thoughts or own agenda? Can I release the inner conflict manifested through the *oughts* and the *shoulds*? Can I give my full and undivided attention to this opportunity to serve? Can I stop dwelling on the appropriateness of the request? Can I share my contributions and make a difference in the world without requiring rewards or recognition? Can I respond to what is asked of me with the same willingness with which the sun warms the earth?

It's easy to dismiss these ideas as superficial. In doing so, we underestimate the immense power that comes from embracing the gift of service. When we are able to say yes to requests with a generous and open heart, we transform the quality of our life. We bring ourselves back into alignment both with nature and spirit, and fulfill our real purpose – service of the Divine.

Being generous through contribution is the ability to tap into our creative power and use it in a way that makes a difference in the lives of others; maybe that's as part of your career, a role that you take on in your family or community, or through your hobbies and interests. When we think about making a difference, many people associate it with charitable work or the helping professions but, whilst it is immediately obvious that a nurse or a therapist makes a difference, many people completely underestimate the difference they can make in the lives of others. In fact, everything we do, every action we take holds the potential to uplift or to diminish – you get to choose which side of human spirit you want to stand for.

I am a big fan of Starbucks. I regularly hang out there when I am reading, musing or meeting friends. I couldn't believe my luck when one opened just a short walk from my home. I soon became a regular. Running my own business can sometimes be a lonely path to tread. If I ever need some connection, I take a walk to Starbucks and the staff make me feel welcome. They know my drink preferences and will ask where I have been if they haven't seen me for a few days. Starbucks has become a place where I go to feel connected. But there is one member of the team who seems to struggle with service. When she takes your order, she is abrupt and curt. She never engages in a conversation and if she happens to get your order wrong, she makes it very clear that you are to blame. It isn't the most pleasant of experiences. She can make a difference for all the wrong reasons.

Of course, everyone has good and bad days – even good and bad phases of life. In the service industry, it is totally understandable that there are going to be days that you simply don't want to serve. But I have learnt over the years that service can actually bring you to a better feeling place than if you dwell on your problems. To truly serve, you have to be willing to ditch your personal agenda and when you do, you also drop your problems, at least for a little while. Having a break from contemplating a challenge and losing yourself in the moment often brings refreshing new insights when you return to it once more. As a coach, there have been times before a session when I wanted to cancel because I didn't feel up to it. Yet after the session, my own feelings are so transformed that I often wonder who should be paying whom!

Generosity through contribution is that willingness to serve others with dedication and reverence, and you can do that in whatever role you are fulfilling. I remember in my early days of networking I met a lady at an event who declared she was a "*sunshine-maker*". I was intrigued to know what career path could provide such an opportunity. I was even more impressed when she explained that she was a hairdresser. Even in the UK's unsettled weather systems, she guaranteed to make your hair shine and brighten up your day.

As you look back over your life to this point, maybe you can track how events and experiences have conspired to teach you what you most needed to learn. You don't need to change careers or ditch work altogether to be of service. I think too many of us are imagining a time in the future when our mortgage is cleared and we have sufficient savings in the bank to do something that matters. There is no need to wait. You can choose to make a contribution in whatever you are doing, wherever you are. Don't wait. Serve this moment.

When we respond to what calls us, life evolves to meet us. Chance meetings and synchronicities are the evidence of Divine agreement. A few years ago I was booked to speak at an event in Scotland. Meeting for a drink before the presentation, the organiser shared her story and I learnt how a personal tragedy had inspired her to set up a charity. As she had committed to this path, a sequence of amazing coincidences had happened. Out of the blue, she had been offered a hefty sponsorship deal. Her own business was also thriving, further evidence that this path was her current calling. Every situation provides us with the opportunity to be generous through contribution. Your willingness to serve is the only thing that is required.

Unconditional generosity is intrinsically linked to love. When we give freely without any expectations or demands, we are acting in alignment with our True Self. In Chapter 6 on Forgiveness, we explored the idea that when we feel anger or hatred towards another, we hurt ourselves the most. That is because we cut ourselves off from our source of love. We think that we feel bad because someone else has hurt us, but that is not true. We feel bad because we are thinking unloving thoughts about that person and that goes against our fundamental nature. The only reason we can ever feel bad is because we are depriving ourselves of love.

Withdrawing and withholding our love is a fear-based

response. But if we want to live fully we have to be prepared to love openly. The two go hand-in-hand. Being generous with your love is the willingness to see beyond the details and feel the love in your soul. You love because it is who you are. When you operate from a place of generous love, you make a real and significant contribution to the world. You don't need to start with big or dramatic gestures. Focus initially on being a loving presence with those you already know.

Examples:

- Cook a meal for a friend or loved one. As you are preparing the food, imagine love streaming from your heart into the various ingredients. Decorate the table with hearts or other tokens of love and affection.

- Call someone up to let him or her know what they mean to you. Avoid getting into a long and detailed explanation. "*I love you because*____________" is all you need to say. Speak from the heart.

- Tune into your own heart. Ask who in your life is in need of additional love right now – a friend, a family member, your boss or even your ex! When someone comes to mind, imagine sending them a bubble of pure love that pops above their head, raining drops of affection and kindness over them.

You'll be able to come up with many more ways to generously offer your love. You may also notice that the by-product of loving others is a tendency for it to rub off on you too. Remember that all acts of love are really self-love! Being generous isn't just about what we do. Generosity is a state of being that cradles the world gently in the arms of love.

Living on purpose

In presence consciousness, it is not so much a case of discovering your life purpose as it is about living *on purpose*. Moment to moment you bring your conscious awareness to the decisions and actions that you take. *Why am I doing this? What am I serving? How am I contributing?* Ultimately we are dedicating ourselves to the service of love. In pursuit consciousness we serve our desires; in presence consciousness we serve the Divine.

Generously offering our contributions is a win-win-win situation. We help others, we feel fulfilled and we become the intrinsic link between the physical plane and higher realms. There is no more worthy cause than being a servant of the Divine. As Guy Finley says, "*only a day spent in service of something greater than ourselves is a day well spent*".[40] Any time you are experiencing a lack of meaning or significance in your life, you only need to ask how you else you can serve. Be helpful. Be available. You will be guided to take action where it is needed most.

I'll leave you with a prayer that arose within me during a meditation on generosity:

Dear God
Teach me to work with you
Teach me to have faith in you
Teach me how to trust myself
Teach me how to be of service
Teach me how to open my heart and love without conditions or expectation
I am here
I am available
I am ready
Show me where I am needed and I will follow your lead
This is my enduring gift to the world.
Amen

FINAL THOUGHTS:

Return to Surrender

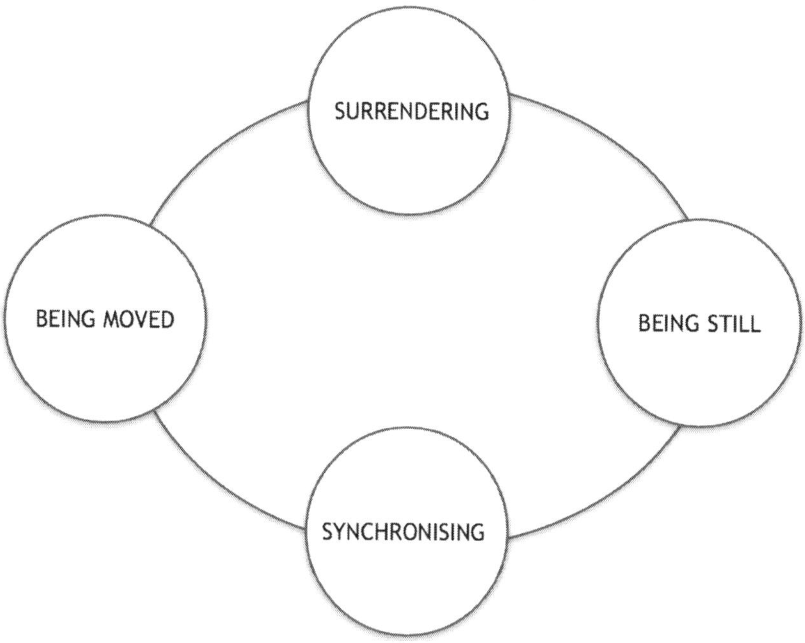

With presence consciousness, the cycle is continuous. Every action requires both an act of creation and an act of letting go. There is no place for attachment. All that stands before you and behind you are simply points in time – a series of *nows* that invite your deliberate and purposeful involvement, and that offer a deeper and more meaningful connection with life in return. Each *now* arises and then departs. We cannot hang onto a moment any more than we can catch a rainbow. And so, once more, we must learn to surrender and allow the next moment to provide a new revelation exactly as intended. This is the art of living presence.

In this book, I have shared concepts and stories to support you in making the transition *From Pursuit to Presence*. Remember that there is no one path. Even though I offer ideas, exercises and inspiration to assist with the shift, these are simply attempts to open your heart and to reconnect you with your True Self – to your wholeness, your worthiness and to your most loving self. The doorway stands before you. Will you enter?

The only thing worth pursuing in life is your connection to the Divine. Even then, it is not about striving or *effort-ing*. Surrender your thoughts about what *should* be happening in favour of being wide open to the pure possibility and potential contained in every moment. When you stop resisting life's events, your inner world transforms into a place of inner peace, calm and contentment. Will there be challenges or difficulties? Undoubtedly. As surely as there will be periods of joy, inspiration, adventure and delight. Each will bring you something different. Times to celebrate. Times to learn. Times to grieve. Times to rejoice. Nothing is ever wrong. Trust it is as it is meant to be.

Let go of the need to make your life better. Your desire to shape your experiences to conform to your plans only prevents the natural and organic creation of something more beautiful. Never doubt the perfection of the unfolding because of your own short-sightedness. It is only from the higher realms that the entire view can be seen. Do what is asked of you without complaint or fear. Don't force or push because you think you know best. The next simplest step will always be the right one to take.

Are you willing to trust the present moment? Will you release your need for control and the desire to know what will happen in the future? Will you ditch the unnecessary drama and dismiss the unhelpful Storyteller? Will you let go of anything that doesn't serve you, or prevents you from living fully and entirely in the now? Will you allow and honour your emotions, your body, your wellbeing, and the requests of your soul? Will you dedicate yourself to the greater good and become the much-needed servant of the Divine? Will you be the messenger of love that the world needs most right now?

This is the simplest path through life. It may not always be easy. It requires that you stay awake. There will be distractions, demands, diversions and digressions. You will be swayed from the path. But through your awareness and attention, you will be brought back around. Stop, be still and breathe. No one is judging your progress. There is no race to an imaginary finish line. There is nothing left to chase. The moment you are seeking is already here. This is presence. Welcome to your life.

I love you, Tiffany.

About the Author

Tiffany Kay is a transformation and transitions coach who helps people to make life (and business) simple. All of the demands and pressures have become overwhelming, making it practically impossible to live in and enjoy the present moment – which is a shame because that is where all the good stuff happens!

Tiffany works with her clients to discover where things are more complicated than they need to be and to create space for more of what makes them happy. She loves to help others to ditch the rat race and find the natural joy and contentment that comes from living in the now.

Tiffany has written two books. Her first book '*JoyScope ~ Daily Inspiration to Nourish Your Heart & Soul*' was published in 2012 and this second book, '*From Pursuit to*

Presence' was completed in 2014. In addition to her private coaching practice, she mentors and supports other coaches through her 'Spiritual Solopreneur' programme – helping them to make a difference and grow their business. She lives in Warrington, England with her husband and their four children.

For details of other products, programmes and workshops, please visit the website **www.tiffanykay.com**. Tiffany is open to any conversation and dialogue about the topics contained within this book. You can contact her at **mail@tiffanykay.com**

Qualifications

- Certified HNLP coach
- Master Practitioner & Trainer in Neuro-Linguistic Programming
- Master Practitioner & Trainer in Humanistic Linguistic Psychology
- Master Hypnotherapist and Trainer in Ericksonian Hypnosis
- B.A.(hons) in Interdisciplinary Human Studies (Psychology major)
- Certificate in Counselling
- Accredited to use Myers Briggs Type Indicator and DISC personal profiling system

References

[1] Beyond the Personality: The Beginner Guide to Enlightenment by the Implicate Technology Centre (1987), Page 7

[2] Tao Te Ching by Lao-Tzu (Taken from Living the Wisdom of the Tao: The complete Tao Te Ching and Affirmations by Dr Wayne W. Dyer (Hay House 2008),

[3] The Life Visioning Kit: A Step by Step Process for Realising Your Higher Potential by Michael Bernard Beckwith (Sounds True 2009)

[4] Dying to be Me: My Journey from Cancer to Near Death to True Healing by Anita Moorjani (Hay House 2012)

[5] With thanks to Andy Grant. If you would like to find out more about Andy's story, you can visit his website at **www.AndyGrantMotivation.com**

[6] Taken from Pema Chodron's blog: "*Talking to Ourselves*" Shambhala Mountain Center 8.19.03 (www.shambhala.org/teachers/pema/talking.php)

[7] Guy Finley presents a series of lectures that are recorded and shared on his online wisdom school at www.guyfinleynow.org

[8] The Magical Number Seven, Plus or minus Two: Some Limits on Our Capacity for Processing Information by George A. Miller (Psychological Review 1956)

[9] This quotation appears to have come from an unknown Author who wrote this in the mid to late 1970's for Carleton Cards, a Canadian card company. Back in the day, Carleton employed "contractors", were paid a pittance to write a ditty for a greeting card. The author sold it away for under a dollar, copyright included!

[10] At the time of writing, a men's and women's version of this watch is available to purchase at **www.robertholden.org**

[11] Walt Disney Productions presents Alice in Wonderland (based on Lewis Carroll's Alice's Adventures in Wonderland). Released 1951.

[12] A group of stimulant drugs with the street name '*speed*' - that people take to keep them awake and alert so they can do more for longer eg dancing.

[13] The Old Testament: Psalms 46:10

[14] For more information about John Overdurf, visit **www.johnoverdurfing.com**
Recommended resource for additional information: https://stores.modularmarket.com/johnoverdurf/product/72/Managing-and-Thriving-in-Uncertainty

[15] The Unfolding Now: Realise your True Nature Through the Practice of Presence by A.H. Almaas (Shambhala 2008)

[16] Watch the full interview with Gabby and Mel : "Living and Learning with Cancer" at Share the Love TV (**www.sharethelove.tv**)

[17] Originated in 1964 by George J. Goodheart, Applied Kinesiology is s a system that evaluates structural, chemical, and mental aspects of health by using a method referred to as manual muscle testing (MMT) alongside conventional diagnostic methods. The essential premise of applied kinesiology, is that every organ dysfunction is accompanied by a weakness in a specific corresponding muscle in what is termed the "viscerosomatic" relationship. For more information visit **http://www.appliedkinesiology.com/**. If you would like to see the process in action, there are a number of videos available on You Tube by searching for muscle testing.

[18] Data collected from World Bank (**http://www.worldbank.org/**)

[19] Castaway starring Tom Hanks and presented by 20th Century Fox. Released 2000.

[20] Perlez, Jane. "Romanian 'Orphans': Prisoners of Their Cribs." New York Times (1996)

[21] BBC News: What happened to Romania's orphans?" BBC News Front Page. 3rd May 2009

[22] A Theory of Human Motivation by Abraham Maslow (Psychological Review 1943)

[23] Diana, Prince of Wales (the first wife of Charles, Prince of Wales and eldest child of Queen Elizabeth II) was killed in Paris on 31 August 1997. She died as a result the injuries sustained in a car crash in the Pont de l'Alma road tunnel. Despite an 18-month Judical investigation that reported the crash was caused by the driver, Henri Paul who lost control

of the car at high speed whilst under the influence of alcohol, many - include the father of Diana's boyfriend, Mohammed Al-Fayed have claimed that the accident was the result of a conspiracy.

[24] Tuesdays with Morrie: An Old Man, a Young Man and life's greatest lesson by Mitch Albem (Sphere 2003)

[25] My stroke of Insight: A Brain Scientist's Personal Journey by Jill Bolte Taylor (Hodder 2009)

[26] Sengzhao (Seng-Chao) was a Buddhist monk who lived during China's "Period of Disunity" between the stability of the Han and Tang dynasties. His *Zhaolun* (*Treatises of* [Seng]*zhao*) is perhaps the most significant text for the study of early *Mādhyamika* ("middle-ist") or *Sanlun* ("Three-Treatise") Buddhism in China. (384-414)

[27] Ancient Huna.com (Tad James Co, 2005-2011)

[28] "The Secret to Finding Miracles Where you Least Expect them" by Martha Beck (Oprah Magazine December 2010)

[29] Quantum Change: When Epiphanies and Sudden Insights Transform Ordinary Lives by William R Miller & Janet C'de Baca (Guilford Press 2001)

[30] The Tao of Physics: An Exploration of the Parallels between Modern Physics and Eastern Mysticism by Fritjof Capra (Shambala 2010)

[31] Arthur Schopenhauer, German Philosopher (1788-1860)

[32] Albert Einstein, Theoretical Physicist (1879-1955)

[33] The Life Visioning Kit: A Step by Step Process for Realising Your Higher Potential by Michael Bernard Beckwith (Sounds True 2009)

[34] Guy Finley presents a series of lectures that are recorded and shared on his online wisdom school at **www.guyfinleynow.org**

[35] Long Walk to Freedom by Nelson Mandela (Abacus 2013)

[36] For more information about John Overdurf, visit **www.johnoverdurfing.com**
Recommended resource for additional information:
https://stores.modularmarket.com/johnoverdurf/product/72/Managing-and-Thriving-in-Uncertainty

[37] Return to Love by Marianne Williamson (Harper Collins 1992)

[38] Johann Wolfgang Von Goethe, Poet and Dramatist (1749-1832)

[39] The Matrix presented by Warner Brothers (1999)

[40] Guy Finley presents a series of lectures that are recorded and shared on his online wisdom school at **www.guyfinleynow.org**

11410532R00242

Printed in Great Britain
by Amazon.co.uk, Ltd.,
Marston Gate.